Douglas Quadling and Julian Gilbey

Cambridge International AS and A Level Mathematics:
Mechanics 1

Coursebook

Revised Edition

CAMBRIDGE
UNIVERSITY PRESS

CAMBRIDGE
UNIVERSITY PRESS

University Printing House, Cambridge CB2 8BS, United Kingdom

One Liberty Plaza, 20th Floor, New York, NY 10006, USA

477 Williamstown Road, Port Melbourne, VIC 3207, Australia

4843/24, 2nd Floor, Ansari Road, Daryaganj, Delhi – 110002, India

79 Anson Road, #06–04/06, Singapore 079906

Cambridge University Press is part of the University of Cambridge.

It furthers the University's mission by disseminating knowledge in the pursuit of education, learning and research at the highest international levels of excellence.

Information on this title: education.cambridge.org

First published 2002
Second edition 2016
20 19 18 17 16 15 14 13 12 11 10 9 8 7 6 5 4

Printed in Spain by GraphyCems

A catalogue record for this publication is available from the British Library

ISBN 978-1-316-60030-6 Paperback

Contents

Contents

v

Introduction

Cambridge International Examinations AS and A Level Mathematics has been written especially for the Cambridge International Examinations syllabus. There is one book corresponding to each syllabus unit, except that units P2 and P3 are contained in a single book. This book covers the first Mechanics unit, M1.

The syllabus content is arranged by chapters which are ordered so as to provide a viable teaching course. Occasionally a section or an example deals with a topic which goes beyond the requirements of the syllabus; these are marked with a vertical coloured bar.

The treatment of force as a vector quantity introduces some simple vector notation, consistent with that in Chapter 13 of unit P1. Students may find this useful in writing out their solutions, although it is not a requirement of the examination.

Some paragraphs within the text appear in *this type style*. These paragraphs are usually outside the main stream of the mathematical argument, but may help to give insight, or suggest extra work or different approaches.

Numerical work is presented in a form intended to discourage premature approximation. In ongoing calculations inexact numbers appear in decimal form like 3.456..., signifying that the number is held in a calculator to more places than are given. Numbers are not rounded at this stage; the full display could be, for example, 3.456 123 or 3.456 789. Final answers are then stated with some indication that they are approximate, for example '1.23 correct to 3 significant figures'.

The approximate value of g is taken as $10\,\mathrm{m\,s^{-2}}$.

There are plenty of exercises, and each chapter ends with a Miscellaneous exercise which includes some questions of examination standard. There are two Revision exercises, and two Practice exam-style papers.

Some exercises have a few questions towards the end which are longer or more demanding than those likely to be set in the examination. Teachers may wish to assign these questions to selected students to enhance the challenge and interest of the course.

Cambridge University Press would like to thank Cambridge International Examinations, for permission to use past examination questions.

The author thanks Cambridge International Examinations and Cambridge University Press, in particular Diana Gillooly, for their help in producing this book. However, the responsibility for the text, and for any errors, remains with the author.

Douglas Quadling, 2002

Introduction to the revised edition

This revised edition has been prepared to bring the textbook in line with the current version of the Cambridge International Examinations specification. As much as possible of the original edition has been left unchanged to assist teachers familiar with the original edition; this includes section numbers, question numbers and so on. A few small paragraphs have been added: section 1.1 has an explanation of the crucial difference between speed and distance on the one hand and velocity and displacement on the other; section 1.7 has definitions of average velocity and average speed; section 5.3 describes some limitations of the friction model, and section 10.5 offers Lami's theorem as an alternative method for solving equilibrium problems.

The major change in this edition is the replacement of all of the older OCR examination questions in the Miscellaneous exercises by more recent Cambridge International Examinations questions. This will be of benefit to students preparing for the current style of examination questions. In order to maintain the numbering of the other questions, the newer questions have been slotted in to the exercises. While this has inevitably meant some loss of order within the Miscellaneous exercises, this was felt to be more than compensated by the preservation of the original numbering. In a few of the exercises, an insufficient number of past paper questions were available to replace the existing questions; in these cases, the exercises have either been shortened or new questions written to replace the old ones. Further past papers can, of course, be requested from Cambridge International Examinations. All questions and answers taken from Cambridge International Examinations past papers have been clearly referenced. All other questions and answers have been written by the authors of this book.

The editor of this edition thanks Cambridge International Examinations and Cambridge University Press, in particular Cathryn Freear and Andrew Briggs, for their great help in preparing this revised edition.

Julian Gilbey

London, 2016

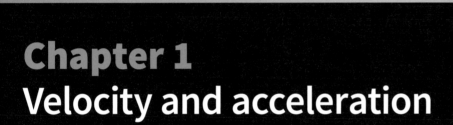

Chapter 1
Velocity and acceleration

This chapter introduces kinematics, which is about the connections between displacement, velocity and acceleration. When you have completed it, you should

- know the terms 'displacement', 'velocity', 'acceleration' and 'deceleration' for motion in a straight line
- be familiar with displacement–time and velocity–time graphs
- be able to express speeds in different systems of units
- know formulae for constant velocity and constant acceleration
- be able to solve problems on motion with constant velocity and constant acceleration, including problems involving several such stages
- understand what is meant by the terms 'average speed' and 'average velocity'.

1.1 Motion with constant velocity

A Roman legion marched out of the city of Alexandria along a straight road, with a velocity of 100 paces per minute due east. Where was the legion 90 minutes later?

Notice the word **velocity**, rather than speed. This is because you are told not only how fast the legion marched, but also in which direction. Velocity is speed in a particular direction.

Two cars travelling in opposite directions on a north–south motorway may have the same speed of 90 kilometres per hour, but they have different velocities. One has a velocity of 90 k.p.h. north, the other a velocity of 90 k.p.h. south.

The abbreviation k.p.h. is used here for 'kilometres per hour' because this is the form often used on car speedometers. A scientist would use the abbreviation $\mathrm{km\,h^{-1}}$, *and this is the form that will normally be used in this book.*

The answer to the question in the first paragraph is, of course, that the legion was 9000 paces (9 Roman miles) east of Alexandria. The legion made a **displacement** of 9000 paces east. Displacement is distance in a particular direction.

This calculation, involving the multiplication $100 \times 90 = 9000$, is a special case of a general rule.

> **An object moving with constant velocity u units in a particular direction for a time t units makes a displacement s units in that direction, where $s = ut$.**

The word 'units' is used three times in this statement, and it has a different sense each time. For the Roman legion the units are paces per minute, minutes and paces respectively. You can use any suitable units for velocity, time and displacement provided that they are consistent.

The equation $s = ut$ can be rearranged into the forms $u = \dfrac{s}{t}$ or $t = \dfrac{s}{u}$. You decide which form to use according to which quantities you know and which you want to find.

EXAMPLE 1.1.1

An airliner flies from Cairo to Harare, a displacement of 5340 kilometres south, at a speed of 800 k.p.h. How long does the flight last?

You know that $s = 5340$ and $u = 800$, and want to find t. So use

$$t = \frac{s}{u} = \frac{5340}{800} = 6.675.$$

For the units to be consistent, the unit of time must be hours. The flight lasts 6.675 hours, or 6 hours and $40\frac{1}{2}$ minutes.

This is not a sensible way of giving the answer. In a real flight the aircraft will travel more slowly while climbing and descending. It is also unlikely to travel in a straight line, and the figure of 800 k.p.h. for the speed looks like a convenient approximation. The solution is based on a **mathematical model**, in which such complications are ignored so that the data can be put into a simple mathematical equation. But when you have finished using the model, you should then take account of the approximations and give a less precise answer, such as 'about 7 hours'.

The units almost always used in mechanics are metres (m) for displacement, seconds (s) for time and metres per second (written as $m\,s^{-1}$) for velocity. These are called **SI units** (SI stands for Système Internationale), and scientists all over the world have agreed to use them.

EXAMPLE 1.1.2

Express a speed of 144 k.p.h. in $m\,s^{-1}$.

If you travel 144 kilometres in an hour at a constant speed, you go $\dfrac{144}{60 \times 60}$ kilometres in each second, which is $\frac{1}{25}$ of a kilometre in each second.

A kilometre is 1000 metres, so you go $\frac{1}{25}$ of 1000 metres in a second.

Thus a speed of 144 k.p.h. is $40\,m\,s^{-1}$.

You can extend this result to give a general rule: to convert any speed in k.p.h. to $m\,s^{-1}$, you multiply by $\frac{40}{144}$, which is $\frac{5}{18}$.

Note that in this section you have met two pairs of quantities which are related in the same way to each other:

velocity is speed in a certain direction
displacement is distance in a certain direction.

Quantities that are directionless are known as **scalar quantities**: speed and distance are two examples. Quantities that have a direction are known as **vector quantities**: velocity and displacement are two examples. You will meet several different types of quantities during the mechanics course. For each one, it is important to ask yourself whether it is a scalar or vector quantity. It would be incorrect to say that something has a velocity of $30\,km\,h^{-1}$ without giving a direction, and it would also be wrong to say that it had a speed of $30\,km\,h^{-1}$ due south.

1.2 Graphs for constant velocity

You do not always have to use equations to describe mathematical models. Another method is to use graphs. There are two kinds of graph which are often useful in kinematics.

The first kind is a **displacement–time graph**, as shown in Fig. 1.1. The coordinates of any point on the graph are (t,s), where s is the displacement of the moving object after a time t (both in appropriate units). Notice that $s = 0$ when $t = 0$, so the graph passes through the origin. If the velocity is constant, then $\frac{s}{t} = u$, and the gradient of the line joining (t,s) to the origin has the constant value u. So the graph is a straight line with gradient u.

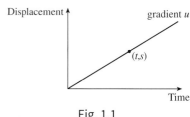

Fig. 1.1

For an object moving along a straight line with constant velocity u, the displacement–time graph is a straight line with gradient u.

The second kind of graph is a **velocity–time graph** (see Fig. 1.2). The coordinates of any point on this graph are (t,v), where v is the velocity of the moving object at time t. If the velocity has a constant value u, then the graph has equation $v = u$, and it is a straight line parallel to the time-axis.

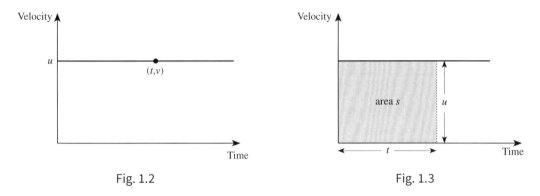

Fig. 1.2   Fig. 1.3

How is displacement shown on the velocity–time graph? Fig. 1.3 answers this question for motion with constant velocity u. The coordinates of any point on the graph are (t,u), and you know that $s = ut$. This product is the area of the shaded rectangle in the figure, which has width t and height u.

> For an object moving along a straight line with constant velocity, the displacement from the start up to any time t is represented by the area of the region under the velocity–time graph for values of the time from 0 to t.

Exercise 1A

1 How long will an athlete take to run 1500 metres at $7.5\,\mathrm{m\,s^{-1}}$?

2 A train maintains a constant velocity of $60\,\mathrm{m\,s^{-1}}$ due south for 20 minutes. What is its displacement in that time? Give the distance in kilometres.

3 How long will it take for a cruise liner to sail a distance of 530 nautical miles at a speed of 25 knots? (A knot is a speed of 1 nautical mile per hour.)

4 Some Antarctic explorers walking towards the South Pole expect to average 1.8 kilometres per hour. What is their expected displacement in a day in which they walk for 14 hours?

5 Here is an extract from the diary of Samuel Pepys for 4 June 1666, written in London.

'We find the Duke at St James's, whither he is lately gone to lodge. So walking through the Parke we saw hundreds of people listening to hear the guns.'

These guns were at the battle of the English fleet against the Dutch off the Kent coast, a distance of between 110 and 120 km away. The speed of sound in air is $344\,\mathrm{m\,s^{-1}}$. How long did it take the sound of the gunfire to reach London?

6 Light travels at a speed of $3.00 \times 10^{8}\,\mathrm{m\,s^{-1}}$. Light from the star Sirius takes 8.65 years to reach the Earth. What is the distance of Sirius from the Earth in kilometres?

4

7 The speed limit on a motorway is 120 km per hour. What is this in SI units?

8 The straightest railway line in the world runs across the Nullarbor Plain in southern Australia, a distance of 500 kilometres. A train takes $12\frac{1}{2}$ hours to cover the distance.

Model the journey by drawing

a a velocity–time graph,   **b** a displacement–time graph.

Label your graphs to show the numbers 500 and $12\frac{1}{2}$ and to indicate the units used.

Suggest some ways in which your models may not match the actual journey.

9 An aircraft flies due east at 800 km per hour from Kingston to Antigua, a displacement of about 1600 km. Model the flight by drawing

a a displacement–time graph,   **b** a velocity–time graph.

Label your graphs to show the numbers 800 and 1600 and to indicate the units used. Can you suggest ways in which your models could be improved to describe the actual flight more accurately?

1.3 Acceleration

A vehicle at rest cannot suddenly start to move with constant velocity. There has to be a period when the velocity increases. The rate at which the velocity increases is called the **acceleration**.

In the simplest case the velocity increases at a constant rate. For example, suppose that a train accelerates from 0 to 144 k.p.h. in 100 seconds at a constant rate. You know from Example 1.1.2 that 144 k.p.h. is 40 m s^{-1}, so the speed is increasing by 0.4 m s^{-1} in each second.

The SI unit of acceleration is 'm s^{-1} per second', or (m s^{-1}) s^{-1}; this is always simplified to m s^{-2} and read as 'metres per second squared'. Thus in the example above the train has a constant acceleration of $\frac{40}{100}$ m s^{-2}, which is 0.4 m s^{-2}.

Consider the period of acceleration. After t seconds the train will have reached a speed of $0.4t$ m s^{-1}. So the velocity–time graph has equation $v = 0.4t$. This is a straight line segment with gradient 0.4, joining (0,0) to (100,40). It is shown in Fig. 1.4.

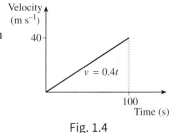

Fig. 1.4

This is a special case of a general rule.

> **The velocity–time graph for an object moving with constant acceleration a is a straight line segment with gradient a.**

Now suppose that at a later time the train has to stop at a signal. The brakes are applied, and the train is brought to rest in 50 seconds. If the velocity drops at a constant rate, this is $\frac{40}{50}$ m s^{-2}, or 0.8 m s^{-2}. The word for this is **deceleration** (some people use **retardation**).

Fig. 1.5 shows the velocity–time graph for the braking train. If time is measured from the instant when the brakes are applied, the graph has equation $v = 40 - 0.8t$.

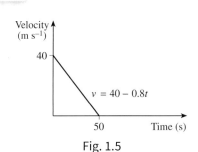

Fig. 1.5

There are two new points to notice about this graph. First, it doesn't pass through the origin, since at time $t = 0$ the train has a velocity of $40\,\mathrm{m\,s^{-1}}$. The velocity when $t = 0$ is called the **initial velocity**.

Secondly, the graph has negative gradient, because the velocity is decreasing. This means that the acceleration is negative. You can either say that the acceleration is $-0.8\,\mathrm{m\,s^{-2}}$, or that the deceleration is $0.8\,\mathrm{m\,s^{-2}}$.

The displacement is still given by the area of the region between the velocity–time graph and the t-axis, even though the velocity is not constant. In Fig. 1.4 this region is a triangle with base 100 and height 40, so the area is $\frac{1}{2} \times 100 \times 40 = 2000$. This means that the train covers a distance of $2000\,\mathrm{m}$, or $2\,\mathrm{km}$, while gaining speed.

In Fig. 1.5 the region is again a triangle, with base 50 and height 40, so the train comes to a standstill in $1000\,\mathrm{m}$, or $1\,\mathrm{km}$.

A justification that the displacement is given by the area will be found in Section 11.3.

1.4 Equations for constant acceleration

You will often have to do calculations like those in the last section. It is worth having algebraic formulae to solve problems about objects moving with constant acceleration.

Fig. 1.6 shows a velocity–time graph which could apply to any problem of this type. The initial velocity is u, and the velocity at time t is denoted by v. If the acceleration has the constant value a, then between time 0 and time t the velocity increases by at. It follows that, after time t,

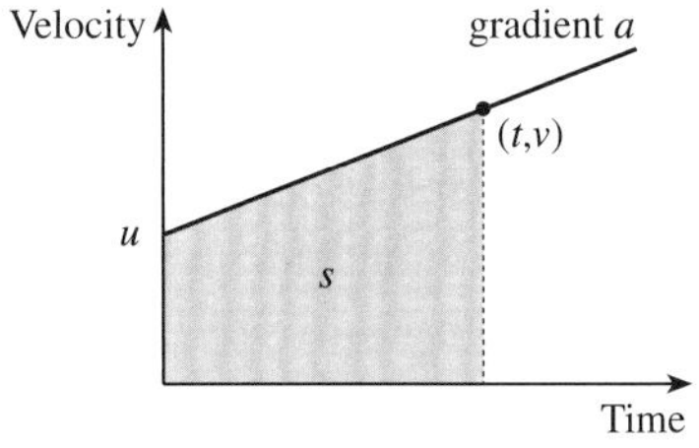

$$v = u + at.$$

Remember that in this equation u and a are constants, but t and v can vary. In fact, this equation is just like $y = mx + c$ (or, for a closer comparison, $y = c + mx$). The acceleration a is the gradient, like m, and the initial velocity u is the intercept, like c. So $v = u + at$ is just the equation of the velocity–time graph.

There is, though, one important difference. This equation only applies so long as the constant acceleration lasts, so the graph is just part of the line.

There are no units in the equation $v = u + at$. You can use it with any units you like, provided that they are consistent.

To find a formula for the displacement, you need to find the area of the shaded region under the graph between $(0,u)$ and (t,v) in Fig. 1.6. You can work this out in either of two ways, illustrated in Figs. 1.7 and 1.8.

Fig. 1.6

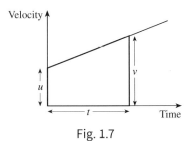

Fig. 1.7

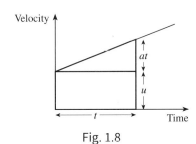

Fig. 1.8

In Fig. 1.7 the region is shown as a trapezium, with parallel vertical sides of length u and v, and width t. The formula for the area of a trapezium gives

$$s = \tfrac{1}{2}(u+v)t.$$

Fig. 1.8 shows the region split into a rectangle, whose area is ut, and a triangle with base t and height at, whose area is $\tfrac{1}{2} \times t \times at$. These combine to give the formula

$$s = ut + \tfrac{1}{2}at^2.$$

EXAMPLE 1.4.1

A racing car enters the final straight travelling at $35\,\mathrm{m\,s^{-1}}$, and covers the $600\,\mathrm{m}$ to the finishing line in $12\,\mathrm{s}$. Assuming constant acceleration, find the car's speed as it crosses the finishing line.

Measuring the displacement from the start of the final straight, and using SI units, you know that $u = 35$. You are told that when $t = 12$, $s = 600$, and you want to know v at that time. So use the formula connecting u, t, s and v.

Substituting in the formula $s = \tfrac{1}{2}(u+v)t$,

$$600 = \tfrac{1}{2}(35+v) \times 12.$$

This gives $35 + v = \dfrac{600 \times 2}{12} = 100$, so $v = 65$.

Assuming constant acceleration, the car crosses the finishing line at $65\,\mathrm{m\,s^{-1}}$.

EXAMPLE 1.4.2

A cyclist reaches the top of a slope with a speed of $1.5\,\mathrm{m\,s^{-1}}$, and accelerates at $2\,\mathrm{m\,s^{-2}}$. The slope is $22\,\mathrm{m}$ long. How long does she take to reach the bottom of the slope, and how fast is she moving then?

You are given that $u = 1.5$ and $a = 2$, and want to find t when $s = 22$. The formula which connects these four quantities is $s = ut + \tfrac{1}{2}at^2$, so displacement and time are connected by the equation

$$s = 1.5t + t^2.$$

When $s = 22$, t satisfies the quadratic equation $t^2 + 1.5t - 22 = 0$. Solving this by the quadratic formula (see P1 Section 4.4), $t = \dfrac{-1.5 \pm \sqrt{1.5^2 - 4 \times 1 \times (-22)}}{2}$,

giving $t = -5.5$ or 4. In this model t must be positive, so $t = 4$. The cyclist takes 4 seconds to reach the bottom of the slope.

To find how fast she is then moving, you have to calculate v when $t = 4$. Since you now know u, a, t and s, you can use either of the formulae involving v.

The algebra is simpler using $v = u + at$, which gives

$$v = 1.5 + 2 \times 4 = 9.5.$$

The cyclist's speed at the bottom of the slope is $9.5\,\mathrm{m\,s^{-1}}$.

Exercise 1B

1 A police car accelerates from $15\,\mathrm{m\,s^{-1}}$ to $35\,\mathrm{m\,s^{-1}}$ in 5 seconds. The acceleration is constant. Illustrate this with a velocity–time graph. Use the equation $v = u + at$ to calculate the acceleration. Find also the distance travelled by the car in that time.

2 A marathon competitor running at $5\,\mathrm{m\,s^{-1}}$ puts on a sprint when she is 100 metres from the finish, and covers this distance in 16 seconds. Assuming that her acceleration is constant, use the equation $s = \frac{1}{2}(u+v)t$ to find how fast she is running as she crosses the finishing line.

3 A train travelling at $20\,\mathrm{m\,s^{-1}}$ starts to accelerate with constant acceleration. It covers the next kilometre in 25 seconds. Use the equation $s = ut + \frac{1}{2}at^2$ to calculate the acceleration. Find also how fast the train is moving at the end of this time. Illustrate the motion of the train with a velocity–time graph.

   How long does the train take to cover the first half kilometre?

4 A long-jumper takes a run of 30 metres to accelerate to a speed of $10\,\mathrm{m\,s^{-1}}$ from a standing start. Find the time he takes to reach this speed, and hence calculate his acceleration. Illustrate his run-up with a velocity–time graph.

5 Starting from rest, an aircraft accelerates to its take-off speed of $60\,\mathrm{m\,s^{-1}}$ in a distance of 900 metres. Assuming constant acceleration, find how long the take-off run lasts. Hence calculate the acceleration.

6 A train is travelling at $80\,\mathrm{m\,s^{-1}}$ when the driver applies the brakes, producing a deceleration of $2\,\mathrm{m\,s^{-2}}$ for 30 seconds. How fast is the train then travelling, and how far does it travel while the brakes are on?

7 A balloon at a height of 300 m is descending at $10\,\mathrm{m\,s^{-1}}$ and decelerating at a rate of $0.4\,\mathrm{m\,s^{-2}}$. How long will it take for the balloon to stop descending, and what will its height be then?

1.5 More equations for constant acceleration

All the three formulae in Section 1.4 involve four of the five quantities u, a, t, v and s. The first leaves out s, the second a and the third v. It is also useful to have formulae which leave out t and u, and you can find these by combining the formulae you already know.

To find a formula which omits t, rearrange the formula $v = u + at$ to give $at = v - u$, so $t = \dfrac{v - u}{a}$. If you now substitute this in $s = \frac{1}{2}(u+v)t$, you get

$$s = \tfrac{1}{2}(u+v) \times \frac{v-u}{a},$$

which is $2as = (u+v)(v-u)$. The right side of this is $(v+u)(v-u) = v^2 - u^2$, so that finally $2as = v^2 - u^2$, or

$$v^2 = u^2 + 2as.$$

The fifth formula, which omits u, is less useful than the others. Turn the formula $v = u + at$ round to get $u = v - at$. Then, substituting this in $s = ut + \frac{1}{2}at^2$, you get $s = (v - at)t + \frac{1}{2}at^2$, which simplifies to

$$s = vt - \frac{1}{2}at^2.$$

> **For an object moving with constant acceleration a and initial velocity u, the following equations connect the displacement s and the velocity v after a time t.**
>
> $$v = u + at \qquad s = ut + \frac{1}{2}at^2 \qquad v^2 = u^2 + 2as$$
> $$s = \frac{1}{2}(u + v)t \qquad s = vt - \frac{1}{2}at^2$$

You should learn these formulae, because you will use them frequently throughout this mechanics course.

EXAMPLE 1.5.1

The barrel of a shotgun is 0.9 m long, and the shot emerges from the muzzle with a speed of 240 m s^{-1}. Find the acceleration of the shot in the barrel, and the length of time the shot is in the barrel after firing.

In practice the constant acceleration model is likely to be only an approximation, but it will give some idea of the quantities involved.

The shot is initially at rest, so $u = 0$. You are given that $v = 240$ when $s = 0.9$, and you want to find the acceleration, so use $v^2 = u^2 + 2as$.

$$240^2 = 0^2 + 2 \times a \times 0.9.$$

This gives $a = \dfrac{240^2}{2 \times 0.9} = 32\,000$.

You can now use any of the other formulae to find the time. The simplest is probably $v = u + at$, which gives $240 = 0 + 32\,000t$, so $t = 0.0075$.

Taking account of the approximations in the model and the data, you can say that the acceleration of the shot is about 30 000 m s^{-2}, and that the shot is in the barrel for a little less than one-hundredth of a second.

EXAMPLE 1.5.2

The driver of a car travelling at 96 k.p.h. in mist suddenly sees a stationary bus 100 metres ahead. With the brakes full on, the car can decelerate at 4 m s^{-2} in the prevailing road conditions. Can the driver stop in time?

You know from Example 1.1.2 that 96 k.p.h. is $96 \times \frac{5}{18}$ m s^{-1}, or $\frac{80}{3}$ m s^{-1}. This suggests writing $u = \frac{80}{3}$ and $a = -4$ in the formula $v^2 = u^2 + 2as$ to find v when $s = 100$. Notice that a is negative because the car is decelerating.

EXAMPLE 1.6.1

A sprinter in a 100-metre race pushes off the starting block with a speed of $6\,\mathrm{m\,s^{-1}}$, and accelerates at a constant rate. He attains his maximum speed of $10\,\mathrm{m\,s^{-1}}$ after 40 metres, and then continues at that speed for the rest of the race. What is his time for the whole race?

> For the accelerating stage you know that $u = 6$, $v = 10$ and $s = 40$. The equation $s = \frac{1}{2}(u + v)t$ gives $40 = 8t$, so $t = 5$.
>
> As the remaining 60 metres are run at a constant speed of $10\,\mathrm{m\,s^{-1}}$, you can measure s and t from the time when the sprinter reaches his maximum speed, and use the formula $s = ut$ to find that $t = \dfrac{s}{u} = \dfrac{60}{10} = 6$.
>
> So the sprinter takes 5 seconds to accelerate and then a further 6 seconds at maximum speed, a total of 11 seconds.
>
> Fig. 1.9 shows the velocity–time graph for the run. You could use this to find the time, but the calculation is essentially no different.

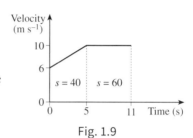

Fig. 1.9

EXAMPLE 1.6.2

Two stops on a tramline are 960 metres apart. A tram starts from one stop, accelerates at a constant rate to its maximum speed of $15\,\mathrm{m\,s^{-1}}$, maintains this speed for some time and then decelerates at a constant rate to come to rest at the other stop. The total time between the stops is 84 seconds.

a For how many seconds does the tram travel at its maximum speed?

b If the tram accelerates at $0.5\,\mathrm{m\,s^{-2}}$, at what rate does it decelerate?

> You can draw a single velocity–time graph (Fig. 1.10) for the whole journey. This is made up of three line segments: the first with positive gradient, the second parallel to the t-axis, and the third with negative gradient.

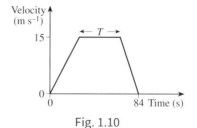

Fig. 1.10

> **a** The region between the velocity–time graph and the t-axis has the shape of a trapezium. The area of this trapezium represents the distance between the two stops.
>
> If the tram travels at its maximum speed for T seconds, this trapezium has parallel sides 84 and T, height 15 and area 960. So
>
> $$960 = \tfrac{1}{2}(84 + T) \times 15,$$
>
> which gives $84 + T = \dfrac{2 \times 960}{15}$, and $T = 44$.

b To reach a speed of $15\,\mathrm{m\,s^{-1}}$ from rest with an acceleration of $0.5\,\mathrm{m\,s^{-2}}$ takes $\dfrac{15}{0.5}$ seconds, which is 30 seconds. So the tram takes 30 seconds accelerating and 44 seconds at maximum speed, and this leaves 10 seconds in which to come to rest. The deceleration is therefore $\dfrac{15}{10}\,\mathrm{m\,s^{-2}}$, which is $1.5\,\mathrm{m\,s^{-2}}$.

The tram travels at its maximum speed for 44 seconds, and then decelerates at a rate of $1.5\,\mathrm{m\,s^{-2}}$.

EXAMPLE 1.6.3

A truck is travelling at a constant speed of $96\,$k.p.h. The driver of a car, also going at $96\,$k.p.h., decides to overtake it. The car accelerates up to $120\,$k.p.h., then immediately starts to decelerate until its speed has again dropped to $96\,$k.p.h. The whole manoeuvre takes half a minute. If the gap between the car and the truck was originally 35 metres, the truck is 10 metres long and the car is 4 metres long, what will be the gap between the truck and the car afterwards?

You are not told the acceleration and deceleration, or when the car reaches its greatest speed, so if you try to use algebra there will be several unknowns. It is much simpler to use velocity–time graphs.

Fig. 1.11 shows the velocity–time graphs for both the truck and the car over the half minute. The distance travelled by the truck is represented by the area of the region between the horizontal line segment AB and the time-axis, and the distance travelled by the car is represented by the area between the two-part graph AMB and the time-axis. So the difference in the distances travelled is represented by the area of the triangle AMB.

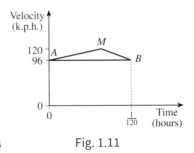

Fig. 1.11

To do the calculation you must use a consistent system of units, and kilometre–hour units is the obvious choice. Since half a minute is $\frac{1}{120}$ hours, the difference in the distances is $\frac{1}{2} \times \frac{1}{120} \times (120 - 96)\,\mathrm{km}$, which is $\frac{1}{10}\,\mathrm{km}$, or 100 metres.

Fig. 1.12 shows the relative positions of the car and the truck before and afterwards. The front of the car was originally $35 + 10$, or 45 metres behind the front of the truck, so it ends up $(100 - 45)$ metres, or 55 metres in front. The gap afterwards is therefore $(55 - 4)$ metres, or 51 metres.

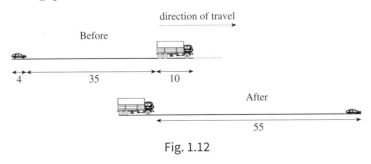

Fig. 1.12

1.7 Average velocity and average speed

You can if you like omit this section on a first reading, and come back to it later.

Sometimes we may not be interested in the instantaneous velocity or speed of an object, but only how it behaves on average. We can therefore define two quantities:

$$\text{average velocity} = \frac{\text{change in displacement}}{\text{change in time}}$$

$$\text{average speed} = \frac{\text{distance travelled}}{\text{time taken}}$$

The slightly different definitions are due to displacement being a vector quantity and distance being a scalar quantity. Since displacement is a vector, so is average velocity; since distance is a scalar, so is average speed.

As an example to illustrate the difference between the two, consider an object travelling at $1\,\mathrm{m\,s^{-1}}$ once around a square of side length $5\,\mathrm{m}$. Its average velocity will be zero: it is at the same point at the start and end, so the change in displacement is zero. However, it is travelling at a speed of $1\,\mathrm{m\,s^{-1}}$, so the total distance travelled is $20\,\mathrm{m}$ and the time taken is $20\,\mathrm{s}$, giving an average speed of $1\,\mathrm{m\,s^{-1}}$.

So the average speed and average velocity tell you two different things. It is important to carefully distinguish between these two quantities.

In the case of an object moving with constant acceleration, the formula $s = \frac{1}{2}(u+v)t$ can be rearranged as

$$\frac{s}{t} = \frac{1}{2}(u+v)$$

The fraction on the left, the displacement divided by the time, is the average velocity. So what this equation states is that, for an object moving with constant acceleration, the average velocity is equal to the mean of the initial and final velocities.

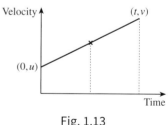

Fig. 1.13

Notice also that, in Fig. 1.13, the mid-point of the line segment which represents the motion has coordinates $\left(\frac{1}{2}t,\ \frac{1}{2}(u+v)\right)$. So $\frac{1}{2}(u+v)$ is also the velocity of the object when half the time has passed.

For an object moving with constant acceleration over a period of time, these three quantities are equal:

- the average velocity,

- the mean of the initial and final velocities,

- the velocity when half the time has passed.

But Fig. 1.13 shows that, if the acceleration is positive, the area under the graph for the first half of the period is less than the area for the second half. So when half the time has passed, less than half the distance has been covered.

The idea of average velocity is sometimes useful in solving problems.

EXAMPLE 1.7.1

A passenger notices that a train covers 4 km in 3 minutes, and 2 km in the next minute. Assuming that the acceleration is constant, find how fast the train is travelling at the end of the fourth minute.

Method 1 In the first 3 minutes the average velocity is $\frac{4}{3}$ km min^{-1}, so this is the velocity of the train after $1\frac{1}{2}$ minutes. In the last minute the average velocity is 2 km min^{-1}, so this is the velocity after $3\frac{1}{2}$ minutes. It follows that in $\left(3\frac{1}{2} - 1\frac{1}{2}\right)$ minutes the velocity increases by $\left(2 - \frac{4}{3}\right)$ km min^{-1}. So the velocity increases by $\frac{2}{3}$ km min^{-1} in 2 minutes. This is an acceleration of $\frac{1}{3}$ km min^{-2}.

The velocity after $3\frac{1}{2}$ minutes is 2 km min^{-1} and in a further $\frac{1}{2}$ minute it increases by $\frac{1}{2} \times \frac{1}{3}$ km min^{-1}, which is $\frac{1}{6}$ km min^{-1}.

So after 4 minutes the velocity is $2\frac{1}{6}$ km min^{-1}.

Method 2 Suppose that the velocity after 4 minutes is v km min^{-1}, and that the acceleration is a km min^{-2}. The train travels 6 km in the whole 4 minutes, and 2 km in the last minute. Using the equation $s = vt - \frac{1}{2}at^2$ for each of these periods,

$$6 = v \times 4 - \frac{1}{2}a \times 16 \qquad \text{and} \qquad 2 = v \times 1 - \frac{1}{2}a \times 1,$$

giving $\quad 6 = 4v - 8a \qquad\qquad$ and $\qquad 2 = v - \frac{1}{2}a.$

Eliminating a from these equations,

$$16 \times 2 - 6 = 16\left(v - \frac{1}{2}a\right) - (4v - 8a), \qquad \text{which gives} \qquad 26 = 12v.$$

Therefore $v = \frac{26}{12} = 2\frac{1}{6}$.

The train is travelling at $2\frac{1}{6}$ km min^{-1}, which is 130 km per hour, at the end of the fourth minute.

Exercise 1D

1 A cyclist travels from A to B, a distance of 240 metres. He passes A at 12 m s^{-1}, maintains this speed for as long as he can, and then brakes so that he comes to a stop at B. If the maximum deceleration he can achieve when braking is 3 m s^{-2}, what is the least time in which he can get from A to B?

2

Aytown   Beeburg   City

•·······················•·····················•

      9 km   7 km

The figure shows a map of the railway line from Aytown to City. The timetable is based on the assumption that the top speed of a train on this line is 60 km per hour; that it takes 3 minutes to reach this speed from rest, and 1 minute to bring the train to a stop, both at a constant rate; and that at an intermediate station 1 minute must be allowed to set down and pick up passengers. How long must the timetable allow for the whole journey

   a   for trains which don't stop at Beeburg,

   b   for trains which do stop at Beeburg?

3   Two villages are 900 metres apart. A car leaves the first village travelling at $15\,\mathrm{m\,s^{-1}}$ and accelerates at $\frac{1}{2}\,\mathrm{m\,s^{-2}}$ for 30 seconds. How fast is it then travelling, and what distance has it covered in this time?

The driver now sees the next village ahead, and decelerates so as to enter it at $15\,\mathrm{m\,s^{-1}}$. What constant deceleration is needed to achieve this? How much time does the driver save by accelerating and decelerating, rather than covering the whole distance at $15\,\mathrm{m\,s^{-1}}$?

4   A car rounds a bend at $10\,\mathrm{m\,s^{-1}}$, and then accelerates at $\frac{1}{2}\,\mathrm{m\,s^{-2}}$ along a straight stretch of road. There is a junction 400 m from the bend. When the car is 100 m from the junction, the driver brakes and brings the car to rest at the junction with constant deceleration. Draw a (t,v) graph to illustrate the motion of the car. Find how fast the car is moving when the brakes are applied, and the deceleration needed for the car to stop at the junction.

5   A car comes to a stop from a speed of $30\,\mathrm{m\,s^{-1}}$ in a distance of 804 m. The driver brakes so as to produce a deceleration of $\frac{1}{2}\,\mathrm{m\,s^{-2}}$ to begin with, and then brakes harder to produce a deceleration of $\frac{3}{2}\,\mathrm{m\,s^{-2}}$. Find the speed of the car at the instant when the deceleration is increased, and the total time the car takes to stop.

6   A motorbike and a car are waiting side by side at traffic lights. When the lights turn to green, the motorbike accelerates at $2\frac{1}{2}\,\mathrm{m\,s^{-2}}$ up to a top speed of $20\,\mathrm{m\,s^{-1}}$, and the car accelerates at $1\frac{1}{2}\,\mathrm{m\,s^{-2}}$ up to a top speed of $30\,\mathrm{m\,s^{-1}}$. Both then continue to move at constant speed. Draw (t,v) graphs for each vehicle, using the same axes, and sketch the (t,s) graphs.

   a   After what time will the motorbike and the car again be side by side?

   b   What is the greatest distance that the motorbike is in front of the car?

7   A roller-skater increases speed from $4\,\mathrm{m\,s^{-1}}$ to $10\,\mathrm{m\,s^{-1}}$ in 10 seconds at a constant rate.

   a   What is her average velocity over this period?

   b   For what proportion of the time is she moving at less than her average velocity?

   c   For what proportion of the distance is she moving at less than her average velocity?

8   A cyclist is free-wheeling down a long straight hill. The times between passing successive kilometre posts are 100 seconds and 80 seconds. Assuming his acceleration is constant, find this acceleration.

9   A train is slowing down with constant deceleration. It passes a signal at A, and after successive intervals of 40 seconds it passes points B and C, where $AB = 1800\,\mathrm{m}$ and $BC = 1400\,\mathrm{m}$.

   a   How fast is the train moving when it passes A?

   b   How far from A does it come to a stop?

10 A particle is moving along a straight line with constant acceleration. In an interval of T seconds it moves D metres; in the next interval of $3T$ seconds it moves $9D$ metres.

How far does it move in a further interval of T seconds?

Miscellaneous exercise 1

1 A train leaves a station, starting from rest, with a constant acceleration of $a\,\mathrm{m\,s^{-2}}$. It reaches a signal 100 seconds later at a speed of $40\,\mathrm{m\,s^{-1}}$. Find

  a the value of a,

  b the distance between the station and the signal.

2 A woman skis down a slope with constant acceleration. She starts from rest and is travelling at $25\,\mathrm{m\,s^{-1}}$ when she reaches the bottom of the slope. The slope is $125\,\mathrm{m}$ long. Find

  a her acceleration down the slope,

  b the time taken to reach the bottom of the slope.

3 A particle moves along a straight line ABC with constant acceleration. $AB = 50\,\mathrm{cm}$ and $BC = 150\,\mathrm{cm}$. After passing through A, the particle travels for 2 seconds before passing through B, and for a further 3 seconds before passing through C. Find the acceleration of the particle and the speed with which it reaches C.

4 A car is travelling at $V\,\mathrm{m\,s^{-1}}$ along a straight road and passes point A at $t = 0$. When the car is at point A the driver sees a pedestrian crossing the road at a point B ahead and decelerates at $1\,\mathrm{m\,s^{-2}}$ for 6 seconds. The car then travels at a constant speed and reaches B after a further 6 seconds. The distance AB is $180\,\mathrm{m}$.

  a Sketch a velocity–time graph for the car's journey.

  b Determine the value of V.

5 A car is travelling along a road. It passes point A at a constant speed of $V\,\mathrm{m\,s^{-1}}$, and drives for T seconds at this speed. It then accelerates at a constant rate for 6 seconds until it reaches a speed of $2V\,\mathrm{m\,s^{-1}}$. Maintaining this speed, it arrives at point B after a further $2T$ seconds. The total distance travelled between A and B was $528\,\mathrm{m}$ and the average speed was $20\,\mathrm{m\,s^{-1}}$. Find V and T.

6 A train starts from rest at a station A and travels in a straight line to station B, where it comes to rest. The train moves with constant acceleration $0.025\,\mathrm{m\,s^{-2}}$ for the first $600\,\mathrm{s}$, with constant speed for the next $2600\,\mathrm{s}$, and finally with constant deceleration $0.0375\,\mathrm{m\,s^{-2}}$.

  i Find the total time taken for the train to travel from A to B.

  ii Sketch the velocity–time graph for the journey and find the distance AB.

  iii The speed of the train t seconds after leaving A is $7.5\,\mathrm{m\,s^{-1}}$. State the possible values of t.

(Cambridge International AS and A level Mathematics 9709/41
Paper 4 Q5 June 2011)

7 Two runners, Ayesha and Fatima, are completing a long-distance race. They are both running at $5\,\mathrm{m\,s^{-1}}$, with Ayesha $10\,\mathrm{m}$ behind Fatima. When Fatima is $50\,\mathrm{m}$ from the finish line, Ayesha accelerates but Fatima doesn't. What is the least acceleration Ayesha must produce to overtake Fatima?

If instead Fatima accelerates at $0.1\,\mathrm{m\,s^{-2}}$ up to the finish line, what is the least acceleration Ayesha must produce?

8 A woman stands on the bank of a frozen lake with a dog by her side. She slides a bone across the ice at a speed of $3\,\mathrm{m\,s^{-1}}$. The bone slows down with deceleration $0.4\,\mathrm{m\,s^{-2}}$, and the dog chases it with acceleration $0.6\,\mathrm{m\,s^{-2}}$. How far out from the bank does the dog catch up with the bone?

9 A man is running for a bus at $3\,\mathrm{m\,s^{-1}}$. When he is $100\,\mathrm{m}$ from the bus stop, the bus passes him going at $8\,\mathrm{m\,s^{-1}}$. If the deceleration of the bus is constant, at what constant rate should the man accelerate so as to arrive at the bus stop at the same instant as the bus?

10 A train travels from A to B, a distance of $20\,000\,\mathrm{m}$, taking $1000\,\mathrm{s}$. The journey has three stages. In the first stage the train starts from rest at A and accelerates uniformly until its speed is $V\,\mathrm{m\,s^{-1}}$. In the second stage the train travels at constant speed $V\,\mathrm{m\,s^{-1}}$ for $600\,\mathrm{s}$. During the third stage of the journey the train decelerates uniformly, coming to rest at B.

i Sketch the velocity–time graph for the train's journey.

ii Find the value of V.

iii Given that the acceleration of the train during the first stage of the journey is $0.15\,\mathrm{m\,s^{-2}}$, find the distance travelled by the train during the third stage of the journey.

(Cambridge International AS and A level Mathematics 9709/04
Paper 4 Q6 November 2008)

11 If a ball is placed on a straight sloping track and then released from rest, the distances that it moves in successive equal intervals of time are found to be in the ratio $1:3:5:7:\ldots$. Show that this is consistent with the theory that the ball rolls down the track with constant acceleration.

Chapter 2
Force and motion

This chapter introduces the idea of force, and shows how forces affect the motion of an object. When you have completed it, you should

- understand Newton's first law of motion
- know some different types of force
- know and be able to apply Newton's second law to simple examples of objects moving in a straight line
- understand the idea of equilibrium.

2.1 Newton's first law

Chapter 1 showed how you can use mathematics to describe how objects move. The English scientist Isaac Newton (1643–1727) went on from there to try to answer the question 'How can mathematics be used to explain why objects move in the way they do?' In his book *Principia*, he put his findings in the form of three laws, called **Newton's laws of motion**. It is a remarkable fact that the whole of mechanics results from applying these three laws in different situations.

In 1977 the United States launched the *Voyager* space probe to send back pictures of the outer planets of the solar system and their moons. By clever timing and programming it was possible for *Voyager* to pass close to Jupiter, Saturn, Uranus and Neptune in turn. Then it headed out into space, getting further and further from the Sun. By now the effect of the Sun's attraction is almost negligible, and the probe continues to travel into outer space with constant velocity.

This is an instance of what is called 'Newton's first law', although in fact this law was already known to Galileo, who died in the year that Newton was born.

> Newton's first law **Every object remains in a state of rest or of uniform motion in a straight line unless forces act on it to change that state.**

It is difficult to demonstrate this law on or near the Earth's surface because you can't eliminate all the forces. Many inventors have tried to make a permanent motion machine, but none has succeeded.

But you can make some approximations. When you are riding a bicycle on a level path and start to free-wheel, you can keep up an almost constant velocity for some time. But eventually you will slow down, partly because of air resistance. This is shown in Fig. 2.1, where the resistance is indicated by an arrow.

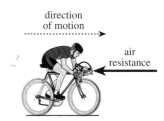

Fig. 2.1

Another example is when a stone is sent sliding across the frozen surface of a lake. However smooth the ice appears, the stone eventually slows down because of friction between the two surfaces (see Fig. 2.2).

What Newton's first law states is that, if an object is seen to speed up (accelerate) or slow down (decelerate), there must be some agent causing the change. Newton called this agent a **force**. Air resistance and friction are two types of force.

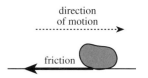

Fig. 2.2

2.2 Force and acceleration

Newton's first law is a purely qualitative statement, that force is the agent which produces a change in the velocity of an object. It says nothing about the size of the force, or the amount of acceleration or deceleration that it produces. That is the subject of Newton's second law.

Suppose that the car you are driving runs out of petrol within sight of a filling station. You may persuade your passenger to get out and push. The effect of this is shown in Fig. 2.3. The car is stationary at first, and the result of the push is to give the car a velocity, so that the car accelerates. The figure uses arrows to show both the force and the acceleration, which are in the same direction. It is sensible to use one kind of arrow for force, and a different kind of arrow for acceleration.

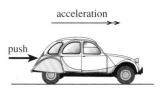

Fig. 2.3

It is intuitively obvious that the harder the push, the greater the acceleration of the car. You would expect that two people pushing with equal force would produce twice the acceleration that one person would achieve alone. This is summarised in the second of Newton's laws of motion, in which he stated that

change of motion is proportional to the applied force, and in the same direction.

However, by 'change of motion' Newton meant more than simply acceleration. It takes much more force to push a limousine than a Mini with the same acceleration, because a limousine is much heavier. So the full statement of the law must also take into account the heaviness of the object being accelerated. This is measured by a quantity called **mass**.

In SI the unit of mass is the **kilogram**, usually abbreviated to kg. You will be familiar with this from buying vegetables or posting parcels. For heavy objects it is sometimes more convenient to give the mass in tonnes, where 1 tonne = 1000 kg. For light objects the mass can be given in grams, where $1 \text{ gram} = \frac{1}{1000} \text{ kg}$. For example, the mass of a small car is about a tonne, and the mass of a drawing pin is about a gram.

The full statement of Newton's second law is that the force acting on an object is proportional to the product of its mass and the acceleration produced. Denoting the force by F, the mass of the object by m, and the acceleration by a, the law can be written as an equation

$$F = cma,$$

where c is a constant.

How do you deal with the constant c? The answer is to use a very neat trick, and to choose the unit of force so that c has the value 1. You can do this because, although you know that in SI the units of mass and acceleration are kg and m s^{-2} respectively, nothing has yet been said about the unit of force.

So define the unit of force, the **newton**, as the force needed to give a mass of 1kg an acceleration of 1 m s^{-2}. Then, substituting in the equation $F = cma$, you get

$$1 = c \times 1 \times 1, \quad \text{giving} \quad c = 1.$$

The abbreviation for newton is N. A newton is approximately the force you need to hold a medium-sized apple. Pulling on a towline, a fit person might be able to exert a pull of about 200 N.

You can now summarise Newton's second law as a simple equation.

Newton's second law   **When a force of F newtons acts on an object of mass m kg, it produces an acceleration, a m s^{-2}, given by $F = ma$.**

EXAMPLE 2.2.1

A car of mass 1200 kg is pushed with a force of 150 N. Calculate the acceleration of the car, and find how long it will take to reach a speed of $1\frac{1}{2}$ m s^{-1} from rest.

Substituting $F = 150$ and $m = 1200$ in the equation $F = ma$ gives $150 = 1200a$, so $a = \frac{15}{120} = \frac{1}{8}$.

To find the time, use the equation $v = u + at$ with $u = 0$ and $a = \frac{1}{8}$. This gives $v = \frac{1}{8}t$. When $v = 1\frac{1}{2}$, $t = \frac{\frac{3}{2}}{\frac{1}{8}} = 12$.

The acceleration of the car is $\frac{1}{8}\,\mathrm{m\,s^{-2}}$, and the car takes 12 seconds to reach a speed of $1\frac{1}{2}\,\mathrm{m\,s^{-1}}$ from rest.

EXAMPLE 2.2.2

In the sport of curling, a stone of mass 18 kg is placed on ice and given a push. If this produces a speed of $2\,\mathrm{m\,s^{-1}}$, and the stone goes 30 metres before coming to rest, calculate the deceleration, and find the frictional force between the stone and the ice.

You know that $u = 2$ and that $v = 0$ when $s = 30$. So use the equation $v^2 = u^2 + 2as$ to get $0 = 2^2 + 2 \times a \times 30$, which gives $a = -\frac{4}{60} = -\frac{1}{15}$. The negative value of a indicates that it is a deceleration.

In Fig. 2.4 the friction is shown as R newtons opposite to the direction of motion. So the equation $F = ma$ takes the form

$$-R = 18 \times \left(-\frac{1}{15}\right),$$

which gives $R = 1.2$.

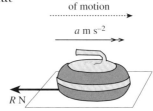

Fig. 2.4

The deceleration is $\frac{1}{15}\,\mathrm{m\,s^{-2}}$, and the frictional force is 1.2 newtons.

2.3 Some other types of force

There would be other ways of getting the car in Section 2.2 to the filling station. You might stop a passing car and get a tow. The force accelerating the car is then provided through the towing rope. A force like this is called a **tension**. It is represented by the force T newtons in Fig. 2.5.

Another possibility would be to walk to the filling station and buy a can of petrol. The car could then be driven to the filling station. Although the motive force has its origin in the engine, the force which actually moves the car forward is provided by the grip between the tyres and the road. It is therefore shown by the force $D\,\mathrm{N}$ at road level in Fig. 2.6. This is called the **driving force**.

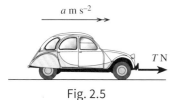

Fig. 2.5

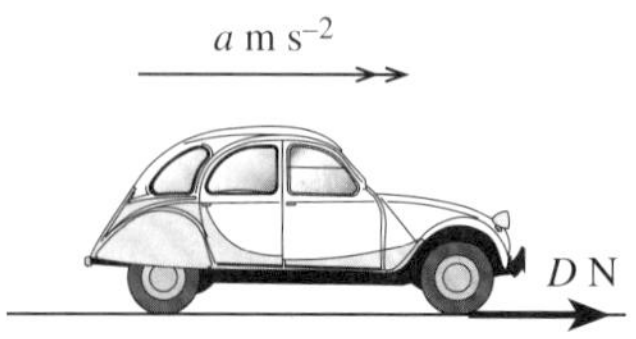

Fig. 2.6

EXAMPLE 2.3.1

The World's Strongest Man has a cable attached to a harness round his shoulders. The cable is horizontal, and the other end is attached to a 20 tonne truck. The man starts to pull so that the tension in the cable is 800 N. How long will it take for the truck to move 1 metre from rest?

In SI units, the mass of the truck is 20 000 kg. If the acceleration is $a\,\text{m s}^{-2}$, the equation $F = ma$ gives

$$800 = 20\,000 \times a, \quad \text{so} \quad a = 0.04.$$

You now want to find the time, t seconds, given that $u = 0$ and $a = 0.04$.

The equation $s = ut + \frac{1}{2}at^2$ gives $s = 0.02t^2$. So when $s = 1$,

$$t = \sqrt{\frac{1}{0.02}} = \sqrt{50} = 7.07\ldots.$$

The truck will take just over 7 seconds to move 1 metre from rest.

Exercise 2A

1   The engine of a car of mass 800 kg which is travelling along a straight horizontal road, is producing a driving force of 1200 N. Assuming that there are no forces resisting the motion, calculate the acceleration of the car.

2   A van is pulling a broken-down car of mass 1200 kg along a straight horizontal road. The only force acting on the car which affects the motion of the car is the tension in the horizontal towbar. Calculate the acceleration of the car when the tension is 750 N.

3   For the first stage of its motion on the runway, before take-off, an aircraft of mass 2200 kg has a constant acceleration of $4.2\,\text{m s}^{-2}$. Calculate the magnitude of the force necessary to provide this acceleration.

4   A water-skier is being towed by a motor-boat. Given that her acceleration of $0.8\,\text{m s}^{-2}$ is provided by a force of 52 N, calculate her mass.

5   A wooden block of mass m kg is at rest on a table, 1.6 metres from an edge. The block is pulled directly towards the edge by a horizontal string. The tension in the string has magnitude $0.2m$ N. Calculate the time taken for the block to reach the edge of the table.

6   Two children are sliding a box to each other on a frozen lake. The box, of mass 0.4 kg, leaves one child with speed $5\,\text{m s}^{-1}$ and reaches the other, who is 8 m away, after 2.5 s. Calculate the deceleration of the box, and find the frictional force resisting the motion of the box.

7   A particle P of mass m kg is moving in a straight line with constant deceleration. It passes point A with speed $6\,\text{m s}^{-1}$ and point B with speed $3.6\,\text{m s}^{-1}$. Given that the distance between A and B is 12 m, calculate, in terms of m, the magnitude of the force resisting the motion of P.

23

8 A man pushes a car with a force of 127.5 N along a straight horizontal road. He manages to increase the speed of the car from $1\,\mathrm{m\,s^{-1}}$ to $2.8\,\mathrm{m\,s^{-1}}$ in 12 s. Find the mass of the car.

9 A runaway sledge of mass 10 kg travelling at $15\,\mathrm{m\,s^{-1}}$ reaches a horizontal snow field. It travels in a straight line before it comes to rest. Given that the force of friction slowing the sledge down has magnitude 60 N, calculate how far the sledge travels in the snow field.

10 A hockey player hits a stationary ball of mass 0.2 kg. The contact time between the stick and the ball is 0.15 s and the force exerted on the ball by the stick is 60 N. Find the speed with which the ball leaves the stick.

11 A boy slides a box of mass 2 kg across a wooden floor. The initial speed of the box is $8\,\mathrm{m\,s^{-1}}$ and it comes to rest in 5 m. Calculate the deceleration of the box and find the frictional force between the box and the floor.

12 A boat of mass 3000 kg, travelling at a speed of $u\,\mathrm{m\,s^{-1}}$, is brought to rest in 20 s by water resistance of 370 N. Find the value of u.

13 A car of mass of 1000 kg runs out of petrol and comes to rest just 30 m from a garage. The car is pushed, with a force of 120 N, along the horizontal road towards the garage. Calculate the acceleration of the car and find the time it takes to reach the garage.

14 A bullet of mass 0.12 kg is travelling horizontally at $150\,\mathrm{m\,s^{-1}}$ when it enters a fixed block of wood. Assuming that the bullet's motion remains horizontal and that the force resisting motion has constant magnitude 10 000 N, calculate how far the bullet penetrates the block.

15 A jet plane of mass 30 tonnes touches down with a speed of $55\,\mathrm{m\,s^{-1}}$ and comes to rest after moving for 560 m in a straight line on the runway. Assuming that the only forces stopping the plane are provided by the reverse thrust of its two engines, and that these forces are equal and directed opposite to the direction of motion, calculate the magnitude of the thrust in each engine.

2.4 Forces acting together

Often there is more than one force acting on an object. For example, think again about the car being pushed to the filling station. It takes quite a large force to accelerate the car up to walking speed, as in Example 2.2.1. But after that you just want to keep it moving with constant velocity.

Newton's first law suggests that no force is needed to do this, but in practice a small push is still required. When the car is moving there is some resistance, which would slow it down if it were left to run by itself. So the pusher has to exert enough force to balance the resistance.

This is shown in Fig. 2.7. The push is denoted by F newtons, and the resistance by R newtons. Since there is no acceleration, $F = R$, which can be written as

$$F - R = 0.$$

The quantity $F - R$ is sometimes called the 'net force' on the car in the forward direction. You can use the idea of net force to write Newton's laws in a more general form.

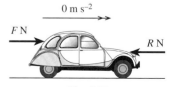

Fig. 2.7

If several forces act on an object parallel to a given direction, then the net force **is the sum of the forces in that direction minus the sum of the forces in the opposite direction.**

If the net force is zero, the forces on the object are said to be in equilibrium. **The object then remains at rest, or moves with constant velocity. (Newton's first law)**

The net force is equal to the product of the mass of the object and its acceleration in the given direction. (Newton's second law)

You will meet the word 'equilibrium' in two slightly different senses in mechanics. If an object is not moving, so that the net force on it is zero, then the object itself is said to be 'in equilibrium'. But if the net force is zero and the object is moving, then the definition says that the forces are in equilibrium, but you would not usually say that the object is in equilibrium.

EXAMPLE 2.4.1

A heavy box of mass 32 kg has a handle on one side. Two children try to move it across the floor. One pulls horizontally on the handle with a force of 20 N, the other pushes from the other side of the box with a force of 25 N, but the box does not move. Find the frictional force resisting the motion.

Fig. 2.8 shows the forces on the box in diagrammatic form. (Don't try to draw the children.) If the frictional force is R newtons, the net force on the box is $(20 + 25 - R)$ newtons.

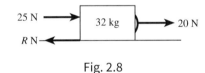

Fig. 2.8

Since the box remains at rest,

$$20 + 25 - R = 0,$$

so $R = 45$.

The frictional force is 45 newtons.

Notice that one item of data, that the mass is 32 kg, is never used in solving this example. The frictional force is the same whatever the mass of the box, so long as the box remains stationary.

EXAMPLE 2.4.2

Two builders push a rubbish skip of mass 300 kg across the ground. They both push horizontally, one with a force of 200 N, the other with 240 N. Motion is resisted by a frictional force of 380 N. Find the acceleration of the skip.

Fig. 2.9 shows the forces on the skip producing an acceleration of $a\,\text{m}\,\text{s}^{-2}$.

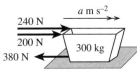

Fig. 2.9

Applying Newton's second law,

$$200 + 240 - 380 = 300a,$$

which gives

$$60 = 300a, \qquad \text{so} \qquad a = 0.2.$$

The acceleration of the skip is $0.2\,\text{m s}^{-2}$.

EXAMPLE 2.4.3

A wagon of mass $250\,\text{kg}$ is pulled by a horizontal cable along a straight level track against a resisting force of $150\,\text{N}$. The wagon starts from rest. After 10 seconds it has covered a distance of $60\,\text{m}$. Find the tension in the cable.

If the tension in the cable is T newtons, and the acceleration of the wagon is $a\,\text{m s}^{-2}$ (see Fig. 2.10), Newton's second law gives

$$T - 150 = 250a.$$

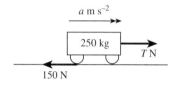

Fig. 2.10

You can't find T from this equation until you know a. To calculate this, use the equation $s = ut + \frac{1}{2}at^2$ with $u = 0$, which is $s = \frac{1}{2}at^2$. You are given that $s = 60$ when $t = 10$, so

$$60 = \frac{1}{2}a \times 100, \qquad \text{which gives} \qquad a = 1.2.$$

Substituting 1.2 for a in the first equation,

$$T - 150 = 250 \times 1.2, \qquad \text{so} \qquad T = 150 + 300 = 450.$$

The tension in the cable is 450 newtons.

You will notice that in Fig. 2.10 the resisting force has been drawn at ground level. In fact, it is probably a mixture of air resistance and a frictional force, but in this example you don't need to know how it is split between the two.

EXAMPLE 2.4.4

A small boat of mass $90\,\text{kg}$ is moved across a horizontal beach at a steady speed of $2\,\text{m s}^{-1}$. One of the crew pulls with a force of P newtons, the other pushes with a force of $(P + 15)$ newtons. The frictional force resisting the motion is 105 newtons. Find P.

The forces are shown in Fig. 2.11. There is no need to show the velocity in the figure, since it doesn't come into the equation.

As the boat is moving with constant velocity, you know from Newton's first law that the net force is zero, so

$P + (P + 15) - 105 = 0.$

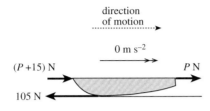

Fig. 2.11

This gives $2P = 90$, so $P = 45$.

In solving this example you don't use the mass of the boat. In practice, this might well affect the size of the frictional force, but since that force is part of the data you have all the information you need to apply Newton's first law.

2.5 The particle model

In this chapter Newton's laws have been applied to objects as various as stones, cars, boats, boxes, skips and space vehicles. These are very different in size, but what they have in common is that the forces acting on them may cause a change in velocity, but do not make them rotate. In such cases, the object is being modelled as a **particle**.

In ordinary language a particle is something very small, but this need not be the case when the word 'particle' is used in a modelling sense. In all the examples it would have been sufficient to picture the situation by a figure such as Fig. 2.12, without trying to draw something that looks like the particular object.

You could even describe an object such as the Earth as a particle, so long as you are only interested in its motion through space rather than what makes it spin on its axis.

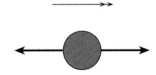

Fig. 2.12

Exercise 2B

1 Three men are trying to move a skip. Two of the men are pushing horizontally with forces of magnitude 120 N and 150 N and one man is pulling with a horizontal force of magnitude X N. The frictional force resisting the motion is 385 N. Given that the skip does not move, find the value of X.

2 A boy is pushing one side of a box, of mass m kg, with a force of 25 N. His sister is pushing from the opposite side of the box with a force of 13 N. The box does not move. Given that the frictional force resisting the motion has magnitude $3m$ N, calculate the value of m. The boy now pushes with an increased force of 35 N. Assuming that the frictional force remains as before, show that the box accelerates at $2.5 \, \text{m s}^{-2}$.

3 A motorcyclist moves with an acceleration of $5\,\mathrm{m\,s^{-2}}$ along a horizontal road against a total resistance of $120\,\mathrm{N}$. The total mass of the rider and the motorcycle is $400\,\mathrm{kg}$. Find the driving force provided by the engine.

4 A car of mass $1200\,\mathrm{kg}$ is moving with a constant speed of $20\,\mathrm{m\,s^{-1}}$ in a horizontal straight line, against a resisting force of $300\,\mathrm{N}$. What driving force is being provided to sustain this motion? The driver speeds up uniformly over the next $30\,\mathrm{s}$ to reach a speed of $30\,\mathrm{m\,s^{-1}}$. Assuming that the resisting force remains at $300\,\mathrm{N}$, calculate the extra driving force produced.

5 A student is dragging a luggage trunk of mass $85\,\mathrm{kg}$ along a corridor with an acceleration of $0.18\,\mathrm{m\,s^{-2}}$. The horizontal force the student exerts is $180\,\mathrm{N}$. Find the frictional force between the floor and the trunk.

6 A boy is pushing, horizontally, a box of old newspapers of mass $8\,\mathrm{kg}$ along a straight path, against a frictional force of $16\,\mathrm{N}$. Calculate the force with which the boy is pushing when he is moving

   a with constant speed,   **b** with a constant acceleration of $1.2\,\mathrm{m\,s^{-2}}$.

7 A particle of mass $5\,\mathrm{kg}$ is pulled, with constant speed, along a rough surface by a horizontal force of magnitude $45\,\mathrm{N}$. Calculate the magnitude of the frictional force. Assuming that this force remains constant, calculate the acceleration of the particle when the magnitude of the horizontal force is increased to $55\,\mathrm{N}$.

8 A water-skier of mass $80\,\mathrm{kg}$ is towed over a straight 100-metre run of water. The tension in the horizontal towline is constant and of magnitude $300\,\mathrm{N}$. The resistance to motion of the skier has magnitude $140\,\mathrm{N}$. Given that the skier takes 6.8 seconds to complete the run, calculate her speed at the start of the run.

9 A railway engine of mass $5000\,\mathrm{kg}$ is moving at $0.25\,\mathrm{m\,s^{-1}}$ when it strikes the buffers in a siding. Given that the engine is brought to rest in $0.4\,\mathrm{s}$, find the force, assumed constant, exerted on the engine by the buffers.

10 A barge of mass $2 \times 10^5\,\mathrm{kg}$ is being towed, with a force of $2.5 \times 10^4\,\mathrm{N}$, in a straight line with an acceleration of $0.06\,\mathrm{m\,s^{-2}}$. Calculate the magnitude of the resisting force provided by the water.

11 A particle of mass $2.5\,\mathrm{kg}$ is pulled along a horizontal surface by a string parallel to the surface with an acceleration of $2.7\,\mathrm{m\,s^{-2}}$. Given that the frictional force resisting motion has magnitude $4\,\mathrm{N}$, calculate the tension in the string. At the instant that the particle is moving with speed $3\,\mathrm{m\,s^{-1}}$, the string breaks. Calculate how much further the particle moves before coming to rest.

12 At a particular instant a river boat, which is driven by a force of magnitude $5400\,\mathrm{N}$, is accelerating at $1.6\,\mathrm{m\,s^{-2}}$ against a resistance of $1200\,\mathrm{N}$. Calculate the mass of the boat.

13 A porter is pushing a heavy crate of mass $M\,\mathrm{kg}$ along a horizontal floor with a horizontal force of $180\,\mathrm{N}$. The resistance to motion has magnitude $3M$ newtons. Given that the acceleration of the crate is $0.45\,\mathrm{m\,s^{-2}}$, find the value of M.

14 A motor-boat of mass 8 tonnes is travelling along a straight course with a constant speed of $28\,\mathrm{km\,h^{-1}}$. The constant force driving the boat forward has magnitude 780 N. Find the force resisting motion, assumed constant. The engine is now shut off. Calculate, to the nearest second, the time it takes the motor-boat to stop, assuming that the resistance remains the same as before.

15 One horse pulls, with a force of $X\,\mathrm{N}$, a cart of mass 800 kg along a horizontal road at constant speed. Three horses, each pulling with a force of $X\,\mathrm{N}$, give the cart an acceleration of $0.8\,\mathrm{m\,s^{-2}}$. Find the time it would take two horses to increase the speed of the cart from $2\,\mathrm{m\,s^{-1}}$ to $5\,\mathrm{m\,s^{-1}}$, given that each horse pulls with a force of $X\,\mathrm{N}$, and that the resistance to motion has the same constant value at all times.

Miscellaneous exercise 2

1 A tram of mass 10 tonnes is moving along straight horizontal tracks. Its engine produces a driving force of 12 kN while the resistance to motion is 1 kN. Find the acceleration of the tram,

2 A toy car of mass m kg is pulled along a horizontal playground by a horizontal string. The tension in the string has magnitude $4.5m\,\mathrm{N}$ and the frictional force resisting the motion has magnitude $4m\,\mathrm{N}$. How long does it take for the car to move 30 m from rest?

3 At a particular instant the engine of a motor-boat of mass 2300 kg is producing a driving force of magnitude 6000 N and the boat is accelerating at $2\,\mathrm{m\,s^{-1}}$. Find the magnitude of the force opposing the motion of the boat.

4 A child is pulling a toy animal of mass 1.8 kg, with constant speed $0.6\,\mathrm{m\,s^{-1}}$, along a horizontal path by means of a horizontal string. She then increases the pulling force by 0.36 N. Calculate the time taken for the toy to move 16 m, from the instant that the pulling force is increased, given that the resistance to motion remains constant throughout the whole motion.

5 Three men, each providing a horizontal force of 250 N, cannot move a skip of mass 280 kg. Find the magnitude of the frictional force opposing the motion. When a fourth man pushes with a horizontal of force 300 N, the skip moves with acceleration of $0.4\,\mathrm{m\,s^{-2}}$. Find the force resisting the motion in this case.

6 A laundry basket, which is initially at rest on a horizontal surface, is pulled along the surface with a horizontal force of magnitude 6 N for 8 seconds. At the end of the period the speed of the basket is $2.4\,\mathrm{m\,s^{-1}}$. Assuming that the surface may be modelled as frictionless, find the mass of the basket.

7 A twin-engined aircraft of mass 12 000 kg is flying level at a steady speed of $75\,\mathrm{m\,s^{-1}}$, against air resistance of magnitude 9000 N. Calculate the thrust provided by each engine.

8 A large box, of total mass 45 kg, is being transported on the floor of a van. The box will begin to slip if a force of more than 90 N is applied to it. When the van is travelling at $12\,\mathrm{m\,s^{-1}}$ the driver brakes uniformly until the van comes to rest in a distance of 35 m. Does the box slip?

9 The total mass of a cyclist and his bicycle is 100 kg. He is travelling along a straight horizontal road with speed 15 m s^{-1} when he stops pedalling and free-wheels until coming to rest in 1 minute. Calculate the deceleration of the cyclist and find the force resisting motion (assuming this to be constant).

10 When a missile launcher of mass 2000 kg fires a missile horizontally, the launcher recoils horizontally with an initial speed of 3 m s^{-1}. Find the minimum force, assumed constant, that needs to be applied to the launcher to bring it to rest within 2 m.

11 On a particular journey the resistance to motion of a car of mass 1000 kg is proportional to its speed. The car is travelling at a constant speed of 15 m s^{-1} with a driving force of 870 N. The driving force is instantaneously increased to 1200 N.

   a Find the instantaneous acceleration produced.

   b Find the resistance to motion and the acceleration when the car is moving at 20 m s^{-1}.

12 A van of mass 800 kg, moving in a straight line along a horizontal road, is brought to rest in 5 seconds from a speed of 12 m s^{-1}. Given that there is a constant resisting force of magnitude 200 N, find the braking force, assumed constant.

13 A particle of mass 2 kg is acted upon by a horizontal force of magnitude 10 N for 8 seconds, in which time it moves from rest until it is travelling with speed v m s^{-1}. Show that $v = 40$. The particle continues to move with this speed for the next 10 seconds. It is then brought to rest by the application of a constant resisting force of magnitude X newtons. The total distance travelled is 800 m. Find the time for which the particle is decelerating, and the value of X.

Chapter 3
Vertical motion

This chapter continues the topic of force and motion, and applies Newton's laws to objects moving in a vertical line. When you have completed it, you should

- know that, if there is no air resistance, objects fall with constant acceleration g
- know the meaning of weight, and be able to distinguish weight from mass
- know that an object of mass m has weight mg
- be able to write equations for motion and equilibrium in a vertical direction
- understand the normal contact force
- understand the function of scales and balances for measuring mass.

3.1 Acceleration due to gravity

Newton wrote, 'If I have seen further than other men it is because I stood on the shoulders of giants.' Most important of these giants was Galileo (1564–1642).

By combining experimental observation with mathematical argument Galileo showed that, when an object is dropped, it falls with constant acceleration. This now seems a very simple idea, but at the time it was so novel that Galileo only published it near the end of his life.

Other experiments compared the motion of spheres of different masses. When these were dropped from a height, they took the same time to fall; and if swung on a string like a pendulum they kept time with each other. From this it follows that all objects fall with the same constant acceleration. This assumes that air resistance is neglected.

> **All objects, when dropped, fall towards the Earth in a vertical line with the same constant acceleration, provided that there is no air resistance.**

This acceleration is called the **acceleration due to gravity**, and it is always denoted by the letter g. Another name for it is the **acceleration of free fall**.

But the value of g is not quite the same at all points on the Earth's surface. This is because the Earth is not a perfect sphere, and because it spins on its axis. The acceleration is about $9.78 \, \text{m s}^{-2}$ at points on the equator and $9.83 \, \text{m s}^{-2}$ at the poles. It also varies a little with height; at the top of Mount Everest it is about $\frac{1}{4}\%$ less than at sea level. But everywhere on Earth its value is $9.8 \, \text{m s}^{-2}$, correct to 2 significant figures.

If you only want a good estimate to an answer, it is often sufficient to use the simpler value $10 \, \text{m s}^{-2}$ for g. This is the value used in this book. However, you need to understand that if answers based on this value are given to 2 or 3 significant figures, some of the figures will probably not be correct.

But solving mechanics problems usually involves setting up a mathematical model to represent a real situation, and this already introduces some simplification. So in most cases you need not worry that approximating for g will make your solutions too inaccurate.

3.2 Weight

If an object has an acceleration, then Newton's second law (Section 2.2) states that there is a force which causes it.

For an object falling with acceleration g, that force must act vertically downwards. It is a force of attraction on the object from the Earth, called the **force of gravity**. For a particular object it is called the 'weight' of the object.

> **The weight of an object on or near the surface of the Earth is the force of gravity with which the Earth attracts it.**

Fig. 3.1 is a force–acceleration diagram for a falling object. It shows an object of mass m kg, with an acceleration of $10\,\text{ms}^{-2}$. Let the weight of the object be W newtons. Then, by Newton's second law,

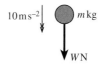

Fig. 3.1

$$W = m \times 10, \text{ or } 10m.$$

In SI units, the weight of an object of mass m kilograms is approximately $10m$ newtons.

EXAMPLE 3.2.1

Determine the weight of

a a table of mass 42 kg,

b a car of mass 1 tonne,

c a sack of mass 15 lb.

    a Taking g as $10\,\text{ms}^{-2}$, the weight is approximately $42 \times 10\,\text{N} = 420\,\text{N}$.

    b 1 tonne = 1000 kg. So the weight is approximately $1000 \times 10\,\text{N} = 10\,000\,\text{N}$. You can, if you like, write this as 10 kilonewtons; a kilonewton (kN) is 1000 newtons.

    c 1 kg is approximately 2.2 lb, so 15 lb is approximately $\dfrac{15}{2.2}\,\text{kg} = 6.8\ldots\text{kg}$.

       The weight is therefore approximately $6.8 \times 10\,\text{N} = 68\,\text{N}$.

Units such as the tonne and the kilonewton are called 'supplementary' SI units, to distinguish them from 'basic' SI units such as the kilogram and the newton.

EXAMPLE 3.2.2

An injured sailor is being winched up to a rescue helicopter. The mass of the sailor is 55 kg. Find the tension in the cable when the sailor is being raised

a at a steady speed of $4\,\text{ms}^{-1}$,

b with an acceleration of $0.8\,\text{ms}^{-2}$.

Fig. 3.2

The two forces acting on the sailor (see Fig 3.2) are his weight and the tension T N in the cable. The weight is approximately $55 \times 10\,\text{N}$, or $550\,\text{N}$.

a As the sailor is moving at a steady speed his acceleration is zero, so the forces are in equilibrium. That is, $T - 550 = 0$, or $T = 550$.

The tension in the cable is approximately 550 newtons.

b The acceleration is now $0.8\,\mathrm{m\,s^{-2}}$, so by Newton's second law,

$T - 550 = 55 \times 0.8$, which gives $T = 594$.

If you are working algebraically, then you don't need to substitute a numerical value for g. Fig. 3.3 is a modified version of Fig. 3.1. It shows an object of mass m, falling with acceleration g. Let the weight of the object be W. (Notice that no units have been stated. You can use any units you like, provided that they are consistent.) Then, by Newton's second law,

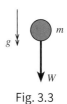

Fig. 3.3

$W = m \times g$, or just mg.

The weight of an object of mass m is mg.

EXAMPLE 3.2.3

A pulley system is used to lift a heavy crate. There are six vertical sections of rope, each having tension T, and the crate has an upward acceleration a. Find the mass of the crate, expressing your answer in terms of T, a and g.

Denote the mass of the crate by m. The forces and the acceleration are shown in Fig. 3.4. The net force upwards on the container is $6T - W$, where $W = mg$.

So, by Newton's second law,

$6T - mg = ma$.

In this example it is supposed that T, a and g are known, and the mass m is unknown. So write

$6T = mg + ma = m(g + a)$,

which gives $m = \dfrac{6T}{g + a}$.

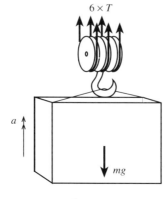

Fig. 3.4

EXAMPLE 3.2.4

Machinery of total mass 280 kg is being lowered to the bottom of a mine by means of two ropes attached to a cage of mass 20 kg. For the first 3 seconds of the descent, the tension in each rope is 900 N. Then for a further 16 seconds, the tension in each rope is 1500 N. For the final 8 seconds, the tension in each rope is 1725 N. Find the depth of the mine.

The mass of the combined machinery and cage is 300 kg, so its weight is 300×10 N, which is 3000 N. The forces are shown in Fig. 3.5.

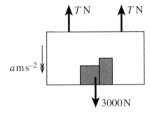

Fig. 3.5

The descent is in three stages and you can find the acceleration of the cage during each stage by using Newton's second law.

Stage 1

With $T = 900$, $3000 - 2 \times 900 = 300a$, giving $a = 4$.

Stage 2

With $T = 1500$, $3000 - 2 \times 1500 = 300a$, giving $a = 0$.

Stage 3

With $T = 1725$, $3000 - 2 \times 1725 = 300a$, giving $a = -1.5$.

The descent is represented by the velocity–time graph shown in Fig. 3.6.

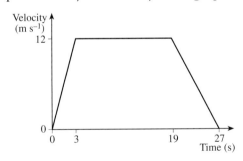

Fig. 3.6

During Stage 1 the acceleration is $4 \,\mathrm{m\,s^{-2}}$, which means that the speed reached after 3 seconds is $12 \,\mathrm{m\,s^{-1}}$. You can now find the distance travelled by calculating the area of the region under the graph.

This region has a trapezium shape, with parallel sides of 27 and 16, and height 12. So the area is $\frac{1}{2}(27 + 16) \times 12 = 258$.

The depth of the mine is about 258 m.

Exercise 3A

1 Find the weight of

   a a baby of mass 3 kg,

   b a coin of mass 10 grams,

   c a tree of mass 800 kg.

2 A piece of luggage weighs 170 N. Find its mass.

3 A crane is lifting a load of mass 350 kg. The tension in the cable as the load is lifted is 4200 N. Calculate the acceleration of the load.

4 A lift bringing miners to the surface of a mine shaft is moving with an acceleration of $1.2 \, \text{m s}^{-2}$. The total mass of the cage and the miners is 1600 kg. Find the tension in the lift cable.

5 The total mass of a hot-air balloon, occupants and ballast is 1300 kg. What is the upthrust on the balloon when it is travelling vertically upwards with constant velocity? The occupants now release 50 kg of ballast. Assuming no air resistance, find the immediate acceleration of the balloon. (The upthrust is the upward buoyancy force, which does not change when the ballast is thrown out.)

6 A steel ball of mass 1.8 kg is dropping vertically through water with an acceleration of $5.6 \, \text{m s}^{-2}$. Find the magnitude of the force resisting the motion of the ball.

7 In a simulation of a spacecraft's lift-off an astronaut of mass 85 kg experiences a constant force of 7000 N from the seat. Calculate the acceleration of the astronaut in the simulation.

8 A boy of mass 45 kg is stranded on a beach as the tide comes in. A rescuer of mass 75 kg is lowered down, by rope, from the top of the cliff. The boy and rescuer are raised together, initially with a constant acceleration of $0.6 \, \text{m s}^{-2}$. Find the tension in the rope for this stage of the ascent.

As they near the top of the cliff, the tension in the rope is 1020 N and they are moving with a constant deceleration. Calculate the magnitude of this deceleration.

9 The maximum load that a lift of mass 600 kg can hold is 450 kg. Find the tension in the cable when the lift is holding a maximum load and the lift is moving

   a upwards with an acceleration of $0.2 \, \text{m s}^{-2}$,

   b at a constant speed of $3 \, \text{m s}^{-1}$,

   c downwards with an acceleration of $0.2 \, \text{m s}^{-2}$,

   d downwards with a deceleration of $0.2 \, \text{m s}^{-2}$.

10 The tension in the vertical cable of a crane is 1250 N when it is raising a girder with constant speed. Calculate the tension in the cable when it is raising the girder with an acceleration of $0.2 \, \text{m s}^{-2}$, assuming no air resistance.

11 A balloon of total mass 840 kg is rising vertically with constant speed. As a result of releasing some ballast, the balloon immediately accelerates at $0.5 \, \text{m s}^{-2}$. Calculate the mass of ballast released.

12 The resisting force, R N, experienced by a parachutist travelling with speed v m s^{-1} may be modelled as $R = 135v$. It may be assumed that the parachutist moves vertically downwards at all times. At the instant that she is moving with a speed of 8 m s^{-1} she has a deceleration of 2 m s^{-2}. Find her mass. The speed of the parachutist continues to drop until it reaches a constant value (the terminal speed); find this speed.

13 A stone of mass 0.1 kg drops vertically into a lake, with an entry speed of 15 m s^{-1}, and sinks a distance of 18 metres in 2 seconds. Find the resisting force, assumed constant, acting on the stone.

14 A bucket of mass 4 kg is being lowered down a well at constant speed. Find the tension in the lowering rope. When filled with water, the bucket is raised with a constant acceleration of 0.8 m s^{-2} for part of the ascent. The tension in the rope in this stage is 216 N. Calculate the mass of water in the bucket.

15 A load of mass M is raised with constant acceleration, from rest, by a rope. The load reaches a speed of v in a distance of s. The tension in the rope is T. Find an expression for s in terms of M, T, v and g.

16 A container of total mass 200 kg is being loaded on to a cargo ship by using a pulley system, similar to that used in Example 3.2.3, but with only two vertical sections of rope. In this operation the container is lifted vertically off the ground to a height of h metres. For the first 3 seconds of the ascent the tension in each cable is 1200 N. For the next second it travels at constant speed. For the final 6 seconds, before it comes to rest, the tension in each rope is T N. Find the values of h and T.

17 A load of weight 7 kN is being raised from rest with constant acceleration by a cable. After the load has been raised 20 metres, the cable suddenly becomes slack. The load continues upwards for a distance of 4 metres before coming to instantaneous rest. Assuming no air resistance, find the tension in the cable before it became slack.

3.3 Normal contact force

A radio is placed on a table (Fig. 3.7). Why doesn't it fall through?

The obvious answer is 'because the table is there'. But mechanics requires an explanation in terms of forces. Since the radio doesn't move, the net force on it must be zero.

You already know one force acting on the radio, its weight. So if the net force is zero, there must be a second force, with the same magnitude as the weight but acting upwards. This force comes from the contact between the radio and the table. It is called the 'normal contact force'. This is shown in Fig. 3.8.

The word 'normal' is used in the same sense as for a graph, where the normal is the line at right angles to the tangent. The direction of the contact force is at right angles to the region over which the table and the radio are in contact.

Fig. 3.7

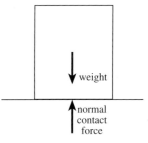

Fig. 3.8

When an object is in contact with a surface, there is a force on the object at right angles to the region of contact. This is called the normal contact force.

37

The normal contact force is sometimes called the **normal reaction**.

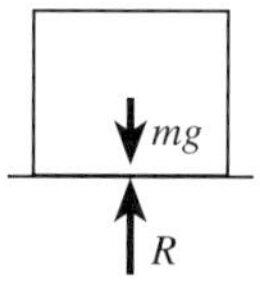

When an object of mass m rests on a horizontal surface, as in Fig. 3.9, the two forces on it are its weight mg and the normal contact force R, which acts vertically upwards. These forces are in equilibrium, so $R = mg$.

Fig. 3.9

It would be nicer to call the normal contact force N rather than R. But force is often measured in newtons, and it would be awkward to write N N. However, if you are doing an algebraic problem which doesn't involve units, there is no reason why you shouldn't use N for the force.

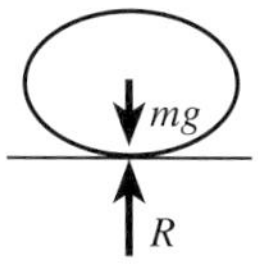

For a rounded object like a pebble or a ball there may be only one point of contact with the surface, rather than a region. The surface is then a tangent plane to the object, and the contact force is at right angles to this plane. This is illustrated in Fig. 3.10.

Fig. 3.10

EXAMPLE 3.3.1

A book of mass 0.5 kg is placed flat on a horizontal shelf, as in Fig. 3.11. Find the magnitude of the normal contact force.

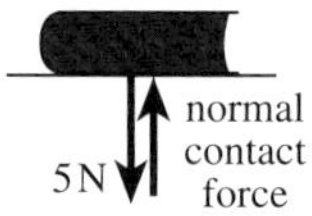

Fig. 3.11

The weight of the book is $0.5 \times 10\,\text{N}$, which is $5\,\text{N}$. The only other force on the book is the normal contact force, so this is also $5\,\text{N}$.

EXAMPLE 3.3.2

A container sits on the dockside waiting to be loaded on to a container ship. The mass of the container is 6000 kg. A cable from a crane is attached to the container. At first, the cable is slack; the tension is then gradually increased until the container rises off the ground. Draw a graph to show the relationship between the normal contact force and the tension in the cable.

There are three forces acting on the container: its weight, the normal contact force from the ground and the tension in the cable. (See Fig. 3.12.)

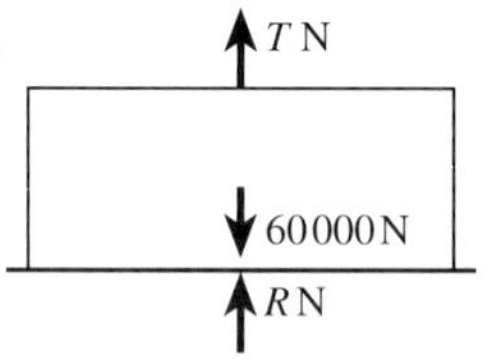

The weight of the container is 60000 N. Denote the normal contact force by R newtons, and the tension by T newtons. Since the three forces are in equilibrium the net force is zero, so

$$R + T - 60000 = 0.$$

This equation is represented by the graph in Fig. 3.13. Note that it is drawn only for $T \geq 0$ and $R \geq 0$, because neither the tension nor the contact force can be negative.

At first, while the cable is slack, $T = 0$ and $R = 60000$. As the cable tightens, T increases and R correspondingly decreases. Eventually, when T reaches the value 60000, $R = 0$ and the container is on the point of being lifted from the dockside.

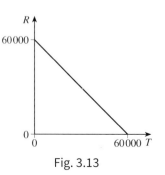

Fig. 3.12

Fig. 3.13

3.4 Mass and weight

Some of the words used in science and mathematics are taken from everyday language, but they are given a more precise meaning. One such word is 'weight'.

Here are some remarks which you might hear or read in a newspaper.

'This bag of potatoes has a weight of 3 kilograms.'

'The weight of an elephant is about 6 tonnes.'

'My rucksack weighs 16 kg.'

'The boxer weighed in at 159 pounds.'

These are all statements for which, in mechanics, the correct usage would be to replace 'weight' by 'mass', and 'weighs' by 'has mass'.

In the case of the potatoes, you might be interested in both the mass and the weight. Mass is important from the point of view of feeding the family; but if you have to carry the bag home, it is the weight of about 30 newtons that will concern you, since this has to be supported by your arm muscles.

With the elephant, it is mass which matters if it charges your safari jeep; but if it walks across a bridge, it is the weight which might cause the bridge to collapse.

The mass of the rucksack remains constant, but its weight (about 160 newtons) decreases very slightly as you climb a mountain, because the value of g decreases with height.

For the boxer, the weight is irrelevant. It is his mass which determines how he can stand up to a punch, or how much he can damage his opponent.

A particular difficulty arises when you use measuring instruments, such as bathroom scales or a spring balance. People who use bathroom scales do so because they are worried about their mass. But mass is difficult to measure directly; it is much easier to measure force. So what the scales actually measure is the force with which they support your body, and this is equal to your weight. So if the scales indicate that your mass is 80 kg, what they are really measuring is a force of $80 \times 10 \, \text{N} = 800 \, \text{N}$.

You can demonstrate this by trying out an experiment like the one in the next example.

EXAMPLE 3.4.1

A mechanics student lives on the tenth floor of a tall building. She has just bought new bathroom scales, and decides to try them out by standing on them as she goes up in the lift. Initially the scales read 50 kg. After the doors have closed the reading briefly goes up to 60 kg, but then returns to 50 kg. As the lift nears the tenth floor, the reading drops to 35 kg. Explain.

Before the lift starts moving, the scales show 50 kg. This is the mass of the student. What the scales are really doing is measuring the normal contact force from the scales on her shoes. This is equal to her weight, which is 500 N.

As the lift starts to ascend, the scales show 60 kg. This does not mean that the student's mass has changed, but that the normal contact force is now 600 N.

It is the acceleration of the lift which has caused the change. The forces on the student are her weight and the normal contact force, as in Fig. 3.14.

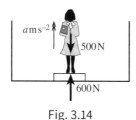

Fig. 3.14

Apply Newton's second law to the upward motion.

$$600 - 500 = 50a, \quad \text{which gives} \quad a = 2.$$

For a brief time at the start, the lift accelerates at $2\,\text{m\,s}^{-2}$.

Then the reading on the scales returns to $50\,\text{kg}$. So the normal contact force is $500\,\text{N}$, the same as her weight. The forces are in equilibrium. Since the lift is moving, it must be going at a constant speed.

Towards the end of the ascent, as the lift slows down, the scales show $35\,\text{kg}$. The normal contact force is now $350\,\text{N}$, as shown in Fig. 3.15.

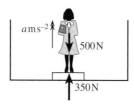

Fig. 3.15

Newton's second law now gives

$$350 - 500 = 50a, \quad \text{so} \quad a = -3.$$

For the final phase of the ascent, the lift is accelerating at $-3\,\text{m\,s}^{-2}$. That is, it is decelerating at $3\,\text{m\,s}^{-2}$.

EXAMPLE 3.4.2

A heavy mass $m\,\text{kg}$ is suspended from the roof of a lift by a wire. The wire is cut, and a spring balance is inserted between the two free ends. When the lift is accelerating upwards at $a\,\text{m\,s}^{-2}$, the reading on the balance is $y\,\text{kg}$. Find the equation connecting a and y.

The apparatus is shown in Fig. 3.16.

The usual function of a spring balance is to measure the mass of an object when the upper end is held stationary. This means that, when the balance reads $y\,\text{kg}$, the tension in the wire supporting the mass is $yg\,\text{N}$.

So, when the lift is accelerating, the forces on the mass are its weight, $mg\,\text{N}$, and the tension in the wire, $yg\,\text{N}$.

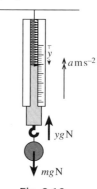

Fig. 3.16

By Newton's second law,

$$yg - mg = ma.$$

This can be rearranged as $a = \dfrac{g}{m}y - g$.

This apparatus can be used as an instrument for measuring acceleration. It is called an 'accelerometer'. You read the value of y from the spring balance, and then use the equation to calculate a.

Exercise 3B

1 A book rests on a table. The magnitude of the normal contact force on the book from the table is 28 N. What is the mass of the book?

2 A truck of mass 4 tonnes is at rest on a platform. What is the magnitude of the normal contact force on the truck from the platform when the platform is

a stationary,

b descending with an acceleration of $0.5\,\mathrm{m\,s^{-2}}$?

3 An oil drum of mass 250 kg rests on the ground. A vertical cable is attached to the drum and the tension is gradually increased. At one stage the tension in the cable has magnitude 1800 N. What is the magnitude of the normal contact force between the drum and the ground at this instant? What happens when the tension reaches 2500 N?

4 A girl of mass 38 kg is standing in a lift. Find the magnitude of the normal contact force on the girl's feet from the lift floor when the lift is

a stationary,

b moving upwards with an acceleration of $1.8\,\mathrm{m\,s^{-2}}$,

c moving upwards with a constant speed of $4\,\mathrm{m\,s^{-1}}$.

5 A fork-lift truck is raising a container of car batteries with an acceleration of $1.5\,\mathrm{m\,s^{-2}}$. The normal contact force on the container from the horizontal forks is 1610 N. Calculate the mass of the load.

6 A jet aircraft of mass 7 tonnes stands at rest on a part of the deck of an aircraft carrier that can be lowered to allow the jet to be housed in the hold of the carrier. Find the magnitude of the normal contact force on the wheels of the aircraft from the lowering part of the deck as it is lowered with an acceleration of $0.4\,\mathrm{m\,s^{-2}}$.

7 The pilot of a hot-air balloon has mass 85 kg. As the balloon leaves the ground, the normal contact force on the pilot from the floor of the balloon immediately increases to 901 N and remains at this value for the first stage of the ascent. Calculate the acceleration of the balloon in this stage of its motion.

41

8   When a man stands on bathroom scales placed on the floor of a stationary lift the reading is 90 kg. While the lift is moving upwards he finds that the reading is 86 kg. Account for this change and describe the motion of the lift at this time.

9   A lift starting from rest moves downwards with constant acceleration. It covers a distance s in time t, where $s = \frac{1}{6}gt^2$. A box of mass m is on the floor of the lift. Find, in terms of m and g, an expression for the normal contact force on the box from the lift floor.

10   A spring balance is attached to the roof of a lift which is moving downwards. When an object of mass 8 kg is suspended from the balance the reading on the balance is 8.4 kg. Show that the lift is slowing down and find the magnitude of the deceleration.

11   A man of mass M kg and his son of mass m kg are standing in a lift. When the lift is accelerating upwards with magnitude $1\,\mathrm{m\,s^{-2}}$ the magnitude of the normal contact force exerted on the man by the lift floor is 880 N. When the lift is moving with constant speed the combined magnitude of the normal contact forces exerted on the man and the boy by the lift floor is 1000 N. Find the values of M and m.

12   A spring balance hangs from the roof of a lift. A case of mass m kg is hung from the spring balance by a string. While the lift is accelerating upwards with magnitude $a\,\mathrm{m\,s^{-2}}$, the reading on the balance is 12.5 kg; when the lift is moving downwards with an acceleration of $a\,\mathrm{m\,s^{-2}}$, the reading is 9 kg. Find the values of m and a.

Miscellaneous exercise 3

1   A food relief parcel of mass 80 kg is being lowered vertically to the ground, by means of a cable, from a helicopter. Assuming there is no air resistance, calculate the tension in the cable when the parcel is being lowered with acceleration $0.5\,\mathrm{m\,s^{-2}}$.

2   A particle is projected vertically upwards from a point O with initial speed $12.5\,\mathrm{m\,s^{-1}}$. At the same instant another particle is released from rest at a point 10 m vertically above O. Find the height above O at which the particles meet.

(Cambridge International AS and A level Mathematics 9709/04
Paper 4 Q2 November 2007)

3   As a load moves downwards at a constant speed of $2\,\mathrm{m\,s^{-1}}$ the tension in the cable supporting it is 6000 N. Calculate the tension in the cable when the load is moving downwards with an acceleration of $2\,\mathrm{m\,s^{-2}}$.

4   A balloon of total mass 680 kg is descending with a constant acceleration of $0.4\,\mathrm{m\,s^{-2}}$. Find the upthrust acting on the balloon. When the balloon is moving at $1.5\,\mathrm{m\,s^{-1}}$, enough ballast is released for the balloon to fall with a deceleration of $0.2\,\mathrm{m\,s^{-2}}$. Calculate

   a   how much ballast was released,

   b   the time for which the balloon continues to fall before it begins to rise.

5 A stone of mass m is released from rest on the surface of a tank of water of depth d. During the motion, the water exerts a constant resisting force of magnitude R. The stone takes t seconds to reach the bottom of the tank. Show that $R = m\left(g - \dfrac{2d}{t^2} \right)$.

6 A box of weight W rests on a platform. When the platform is moving upwards with acceleration a, the normal contact force from the platform on the box has magnitude kW. When the platform is moving downwards with acceleration $2a$, the box remains in contact with it. Find the normal contact force in terms of k and W, and deduce that $k < \frac{3}{2}$.

7 An acrobat of mass m slides down a vertical rope of height h. For the first three-quarters of her descent she grips the rope with her hands and legs so as to produce a frictional force equal to five-ninths of her weight. She then tightens her grip so that she comes to rest at the bottom of the rope. Sketch a (t, v) graph to illustrate her descent, and find the frictional force she must produce in the last quarter. If the rope is 60 metres high, calculate

   a her greatest speed,   b the time she takes to descend.

8 A construction worker drops a screwdriver of mass $0.15\,\text{kg}$ into a tank of water 1 metre deep. It enters the water with a speed of $8\,\text{m s}^{-1}$, and when it hits the base of the tank it is moving at $9\,\text{m s}^{-1}$.

   a What forces, apart from its weight, act on the screwdriver in the water?

   b Assuming that, in the water, the screwdriver falls with constant acceleration $a\,\text{m s}^{-2}$, calculate a. Hence find the total force opposing the motion of the screwdriver in the water.

9 An object is released from rest at a height of $125\,\text{m}$ above horizontal ground and falls freely under gravity, hitting a moving target P. The target P is moving on the ground in a straight line, with constant acceleration $0.8\,\text{m s}^{-2}$. At the instant the object is released P passes through a point O with speed $5\,\text{m s}^{-1}$. Find the distance from O to the point where P is hit by the object.

(Cambridge International AS and A level Mathematics 9709/41
Paper 4 Q1 November 2012)

Chapter 4
Resolving forces

This chapter deals with the combined effect of all the forces on an object, including forces which are neither horizontal nor vertical. When you have completed it, you should

■ understand the idea of resolving in a chosen direction
■ know how to find the resolved part of a force in a given direction
■ be able to solve problems by resolving in various directions.

4.1 Resolving horizontally and vertically

Suppose that a cyclist starts from rest and accelerates at $0.4\,\mathrm{m\,s^{-2}}$. The combined mass of the cyclist and machine is $75\,\mathrm{kg}$.

Since the cyclist and the bicycle have the same acceleration, they can be treated as a single object. What are the forces acting on it?

Clearly there is a force driving it forward, which is produced by the grip of the rear wheel on the road. Denote this by D newtons. There may also be some air resistance, R newtons, though at low speeds this will be small compared with the driving force; in a simplified model you might decide to neglect it.

Also there is the combined weight of bicycle and rider, which is 750 newtons. This is opposed by the normal contact forces from the road on the front and rear wheels, P newtons and Q newtons respectively.

Fig. 4.1 shows all these forces, and the acceleration, in a single diagram.

Whenever you have to solve a problem about forces and acceleration, you should begin by drawing a diagram showing all the forces and the acceleration.

Two equations for the forces can be written down. One uses Newton's second law of motion in a horizontal direction, the other states that the vertical forces are in equilibrium. These equations are $D - R = 75 \times 0.4$ and $P + Q - 750 = 0$.

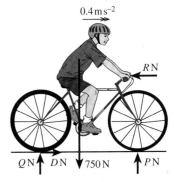

Fig. 4.1

Forming equations like this is called **resolving**. The first equation is 'resolving horizontally', and the second is 'resolving vertically'. A convenient shorthand for this is to write $\mathcal{R}(\rightarrow)$ and $\mathcal{R}(\uparrow)$. So you could set out the equations for the cyclist like this:

$$\mathcal{R}(\rightarrow) \qquad D - R = 75 \times 0.4,$$
$$\mathcal{R}(\uparrow) \qquad P + Q - 750 = 0.$$

When you write a resolving equation, you should always indicate, either in words or by using the $\mathcal{R}(\ )$ shorthand, which direction you are considering.

You can write the equilibrium equation $\mathcal{R}(\uparrow)$ either as $P + Q - 750 = 0$ or as $P + Q = 750$, whichever you prefer. The convention is that the arrow indicates the direction of the forces on the left side of the equation. But if you are using Newton's second law, it is best to put all the forces on the left and the 'ma' term by itself on the right.

4.2 Forces at an angle

So far all the forces considered have been either horizontal or vertical, but in many situations some forces act at an angle.

Suppose you are on a boating holiday with a friend. As you bring the boat towards a dock, you turn off the engine and your friend jumps on to the dock and steers the boat with a rope. Fig. 4.2 shows an aerial view of the situation. Suppose that the tension from the rope is T newtons, and that the rope is horizontal.

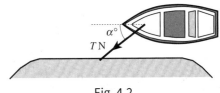

Fig. 4.2

For obvious reasons the rope can't be directed straight forward from the boat. Also, since the tension has to provide the forward movement of the

45

boat, the rope can't be at right angles to the centre line of the boat (the broken line in Fig. 4.2). So the direction will make some acute angle, $\alpha°$, with the centre line of the boat. The question then is, how much effect does the tension have in a forward direction?

The answer must be that it depends on both T and α. If α could be 0, then the forward effect would be the full T newtons. If α were 90, the forward effect would be zero. For values of α between 0 and 90, the forward effect must be rT newtons, where r is some number between 1 and 0 depending on α.

You can find the connection between r and α by doing experiments. (Some ideas for possible experiments are given at the end of Section 4.4 and in Section 7.1.) It turns out that r is equal to $\cos\alpha°$.

You can see that this fits the requirements of the paragraph before last. When $\alpha = 0$, the forward effect is $(\cos 0°) \times T$ newtons, which is $1 \times T$ newtons, or just T newtons. When $\alpha = 90$, the forward effect is $(\cos 90°) \times T$ newtons, which is zero. Between 0 and 90, the value of $\cos\alpha°$ is between 1 and 0.

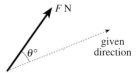

Fig. 4.3

You can make this into a general rule, illustrated in Fig. 4.3.

> If a force of F newtons makes an angle of $\theta°$ with a given direction, then the effect of the force in that direction is $F \times \cos\theta°$. This is called the resolved part of the force in the given direction.

It is now possible to write down equations for the motion of the boat. Suppose that the boat is brought in parallel to the side of the dock at a steady speed. There is a resistance from the water of R newtons to the forward motion of the boat, and a force of S newtons preventing the boat from moving sideways. Fig. 4.4 shows all three horizontal forces on the boat. You can then resolve parallel and perpendicular to the line of the boat.

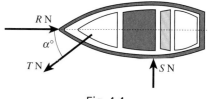

Fig. 4.4

$\mathcal{R}(\parallel$ to the line of the boat$)$ $\qquad$ $T\cos\alpha° - R = 0.$

The rope makes an angle $(90 - \alpha)°$ with the sideways direction, so

$\mathcal{R}(\perp$ to the line of the boat$)$ $\qquad$ $T\cos(90 - \alpha)° - S = 0.$

Notice that there are also vertical forces on the boat: its weight and the buoyancy force from the water. It is easier to show these in a separate diagram (Fig. 4.5), to avoid having to draw a three-dimensional picture.

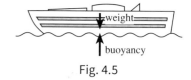

Fig. 4.5

EXAMPLE 4.2.1

A box of mass 15 kg is dragged along the floor at a constant speed of $1.2\,\mathrm{m\,s^{-1}}$ by means of a rope at 30° to the horizontal. The tension from the rope is 50 N. Calculate the frictional force resisting the motion and the normal contact force from the floor.

Fig. 4.6 shows the four forces acting on the box. The frictional force is F N, and the normal contact force is R N. The weight of the box is 150 N. The tension makes angles of 30° with the horizontal and 60° with the vertical. You needn't show the speed in the diagram, but because the box is moving with constant speed it helps to show the acceleration of $0\,\mathrm{m\,s^{-2}}$ in the direction of motion.

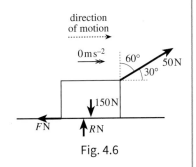

Fig. 4.6

$$\mathcal{R}(\rightarrow) \qquad 50\cos 30° - F = 15 \times 0.$$
$$\mathcal{R}(\uparrow) \qquad R + 50\cos 60° - 150 = 0.$$

These equations give $F = 50\cos 30° = 43.3\dots$ and $R = 150 - 50\cos 60° = 125$.

The frictional force is about 43 N, and the normal contact force is 125 N. Notice that the normal contact force is less than the weight of the box, because the tension in the rope is helping to support the weight.

EXAMPLE 4.2.2

A child pushes a toy car of mass 2 kg across the floor with a force of 5 newtons at an angle of 35° to the horizontal. Neglecting resistance forces, find the acceleration of the car.

Fig. 4.7 shows the forces and the acceleration of $a\,\mathrm{m\,s^{-2}}$.

$$\mathcal{R}(\rightarrow) \qquad 5\cos 35° = 2a.$$

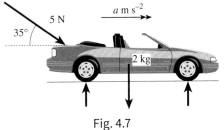

This gives $a = \dfrac{5\cos 35°}{2} = 2.04\dots$.

The car accelerates at just over $2\,\mathrm{m\,s^{-2}}$.

Fig. 4.7

EXAMPLE 4.2.3

A small child is strapped into the seat of a swing which is supported by two ropes. To start her off, her father pulls the swing back with a horizontal force, so that the ropes make an angle of 20° with the vertical. The child and swing together have mass 18 kg. Calculate the tension in each rope, and the force exerted by her father before he lets go.

Denote the tension in each rope by T N, and the force from the father by F N.

These forces, with the weight of 180 N, are shown in Fig. 4.8.

Fig. 4.8

47

The forces are in equilibrium.

$$\mathcal{R}(\rightarrow) \qquad F = 2T\cos 70°.$$
$$\mathcal{R}(\uparrow) \qquad 2T\cos 20° = 180.$$

The second equation gives

$$T = \frac{180}{2\cos 20°} = 95.7\ldots.$$

Substituting this in the first equation gives $F = 65.5\ldots.$

Each rope acts on the swing with a tension of about 96 N. The father must pull the swing with a horizontal force of about 66 N.

EXAMPLE 4.2.4

A game played on the deck of a ship uses wooden discs of mass 2 kg. These have a small depression in the top surface into which a broom handle can be inserted. Two parallel lines 6 metres apart are painted on the deck. Players begin with their discs on the back line and, by pushing on the broom handle, accelerate them towards the front line. When a disc crosses the front line the handle is pulled out and the disc slides across the deck until friction brings it to rest. When the broom handle is pushed with a force of 20 newtons at 60° to the horizontal, the frictional force is 4 newtons. After the handle is removed, the friction drops to 2 newtons. Find how far the disc travels beyond the front line.

The two stages of the motion are illustrated in Fig. 4.9 and Fig. 4.10. Let the acceleration in the first stage be a m s^{-2}, and the deceleration in the second stage b m s^{-2}.

Stage 1

$$\mathcal{R}(\rightarrow) \quad 20\cos 60° - 4 = 2a,$$
$$\text{so} \quad a = \frac{10-4}{2} = 3.$$

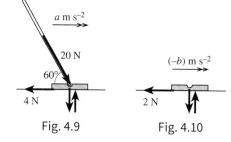

Fig. 4.9   Fig. 4.10

Stage 2

$$\mathcal{R}(\rightarrow) \qquad -2 = 2 \times (-b), \qquad \text{so} \qquad b = 1.$$

Fig. 4.11 is a velocity–time graph for the two stages. The two line segments have gradients of 3 and −1, and the area of the triangle on the left is 6 because it represents the distance between the two lines which the disc covers in Stage 1.

You can deduce from the gradients that the bases of the two triangles are in the ratio 1 to 3, and the areas of the two triangles are in the same ratio. So the area of the triangle on the right is $3 \times 6 = 18$.

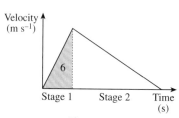

Fig. 4.11

This means that in Stage 2 the disc travels 18 metres.

Exercise 4A

1 For each of the diagrams shown below find the resolved parts of each of the forces in the directions Ox and Oy.

a 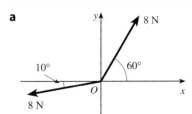   b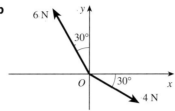

c 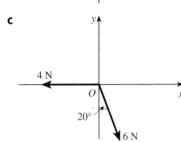   d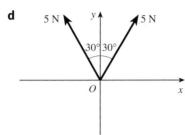

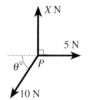

2 The diagram shows three coplanar forces acting on a particle P, which is in equilibrium. By resolving in the direction of the $5\,N$ force, calculate the value of θ; by resolving in the direction of the $X\,N$ force, calculate the value of X.

3 A toy of mass $1.8\,kg$ is pulled along a horizontal surface by a string inclined at $30°$ to the horizontal. Given that the tension in the string is $6\,N$ and that there are no forces resisting motion, calculate the acceleration of the particle.

4 A laundry basket of mass $5\,kg$ is being pulled, with constant speed, along a corridor by a rope inclined at $20°$ to the horizontal. Given that the frictional force has magnitude $33\,N$, find the tension in the rope.

5 A van of mass $750\,kg$ is being towed along a horizontal road with constant acceleration $0.8\,m\,s^{-2}$ by a breakdown vehicle. The connecting towbar is inclined at $40°$ to the horizontal. Given that the tension in the towbar has magnitude $1000\,N$, calculate the magnitude of the force resisting the motion of the car.

6 A car of mass $850\,kg$ is being pushed along a level road with a force of magnitude $T\,N$, directed upwards at $25°$ to the horizontal, and also pulled by a horizontal force of $283\,N$. There is a constant force of $600\,N$ opposing the motion. The car is moving at constant speed. Find the value of T, and the total normal contact force from the road.

7 A particle P of mass $4m\,kg$ is at rest on a horizontal table. A force of magnitude $50m\,N$, acting upwards at an acute angle $\theta°$ to the horizontal, is applied to the particle. Given that $\tan\theta° = \frac{3}{4}$ and that there is a resistance to motion of magnitude $20m\,N$, find the acceleration with which P moves. Find, in terms of m, the magnitude of the normal contact force of the table on P.

8 A shopper pushes a supermarket trolley in a straight line towards her car with a force of magnitude $20\,N$, directed downwards at an angle of $15°$ to the horizontal. Given that the acceleration of the trolley is $2.4\,m\,s^{-2}$, calculate its mass. Find also the magnitude of the normal contact force exerted on the trolley by the ground.

9 A lamp is supported in equilibrium by two chains fixed to two points A and B at the same level. The lengths of the chains are 0.3 m and 0.4 m and the distance between A and B is 0.5 m. Given that the tension in the longer chain is 36 N, show by resolving horizontally that the tension in the shorter chain is 48 N. By resolving vertically, find the mass of the lamp.

10 The diagram shows three horizontal forces acting on a mass of 4 kg. Given that the mass moves in the direction of the dotted line, show that $\theta = 30$ and find the magnitude of the acceleration.

11 A paraglider of mass 90 kg is pulled by a rope attached to a speedboat. With the rope making an angle of 20° to the horizontal the paraglider is moving in a straight line parallel to the surface of the water with an acceleration of 1.2 m s^{-2}. The tension in the rope is 250 N. Calculate the magnitude of the vertical lift force acting on the glider, and the magnitude of the air resistance.

12 A child's toy of mass 5 kg is pulled along level ground by a string inclined at 30° to the horizontal. Denoting the tension in the string by T N, find, in terms of T, an expression for the normal contact force between the toy and the floor, and deduce that T cannot exceed 100.

13 A block of wood of mass 5 kg rests on a table. A force of magnitude 35 N, acting upwards at an angle of $\theta°$ to the horizontal, is applied to the block but does not move it. Given that the normal contact force between the block and the table has magnitude 30 N, calculate

 a the value of θ,

 b the frictional force acting on the block.

14 A container of mass 35 kg is pushed along a horizontal yard by a force of 130 N acting downwards at an angle of 30° to the horizontal, against a frictional force of 60 N.

 Calculate the acceleration of the container, and the magnitude of the normal contact force between the container and the floor.

15 A boy travelling in a railway carriage decides to try to calculate the acceleration of the train. He suspends a parcel of mass 2 kg from the roof of the carriage with a string and measures the angle that the string makes with the vertical. When the train is travelling with a constant acceleration of a m s^{-2} the angle is 8°. Find the value of a.

16 A concrete slab of mass m kg is being raised vertically, at a constant speed, by two cables. One of the cables is inclined at 10° to the vertical and has a tension of 2800 N; the other cable has a tension of 2400 N. Calculate the angle at which this cable is inclined to the vertical, and also find the value of m, assuming there is no air resistance.

17 A barge of mass 4 tonnes is pulled in a straight line by two tugboats with an acceleration of 0.6 m s^{-2}. The tension in one towrope is 1800 N and the tension in the other is 1650 N. Given that the angles the ropes make with the direction of motion are 20° and $x°$ respectively, find the value of x and the resistance to motion of the barge.

18 A man is pulling a chest of mass 40 kg along a horizontal floor with a force of 140 N inclined at 30° to the horizontal. His daughter is pushing with a force of 50 N directed downwards at 10° to the horizontal. The chest is moving with constant speed. Calculate the magnitude, F N, of the frictional force, and the magnitude, R N, of the normal contact force from the ground on the chest. Show that the ratio $F : R$ lies between 0.50 and 0.51.

4.3 Some useful trigonometry

If you write equations of resolving in two perpendicular directions, and a force F makes an angle of $\theta°$ with one of the directions, then it makes an angle of $(90 - \theta°)$ with the other (see Fig. 4.12). The force then has a resolved part of $F\cos\theta°$ in one direction, and $F\cos(90 - \theta°)$ in the other.

You can write this second resolved part in another way. In P1 Section 10.4 it is shown that $\cos(90 - \theta°) = \sin\theta°$. So the resolved parts of F in the two directions can be written as $F\cos\theta°$ and $F\sin\theta°$.

Sometimes the second angle is $(90 + \theta°)$, as in Fig. 4.13, rather than $(90 - \theta°)$. In that case you can use $\cos(90 + \theta°) = -\sin\theta°$, so that the resolved part in the second direction is $-F\sin\theta°$.

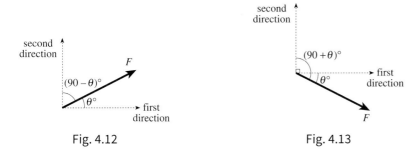

Fig. 4.12   Fig. 4.13

Another result that is sometimes useful is that $\dfrac{\sin\theta°}{\cos\theta°} = \tan\theta°$ (P1 Section 10.2). For example, in Example 4.2.3 the first equation could have been written as

$$F = 2T\sin 20°,$$

and you can notice from the second equation that

$$2T = \frac{180}{\cos 20°}.$$

Substituting for $2T$ in the first equation gives

$$F = \left(\frac{180}{\cos 20°}\right)\sin 20° = 180 \times \left(\frac{\sin 20°}{\cos 20°}\right) = 180\tan 20°.$$

From this you can find $F = 65.5...$ directly, without first having to calculate T.

4.4 Resolving in other directions

You can write equations of resolving in any direction you like, not just horizontally and vertically. One type of problem in which this is often useful is when an object is placed on a track which is inclined at an angle to the horizontal.

EXAMPLE 4.4.1

A crate of mass 30 kg is at rest on a ramp which slopes at an angle of 18° to the horizontal. It is prevented from sliding down the ramp by friction. Find the frictional force and the normal contact force.

Let the friction be F N and the normal contact force R N (see Fig. 4.14). Notice that the normal contact force is not vertical, but perpendicular to the plane of the ramp. The weight is 300 N.

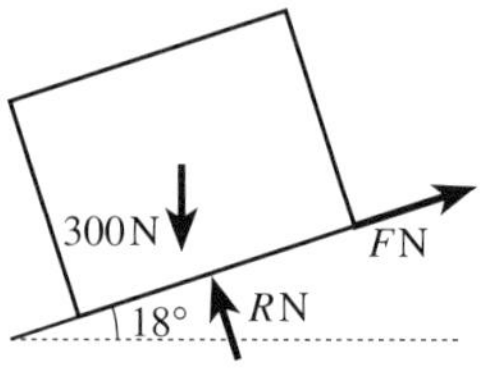

Fig. 4.14

The simplest directions to choose for resolving are parallel to the ramp, and perpendicular to the ramp. To do this, you are going to need to calculate the angles marked $x°$ and $y°$ in Fig. 4.15. It is easy to see that $x = 90 - 18 = 72$, and $y = 90 - x = 90 - 72 = 18$.

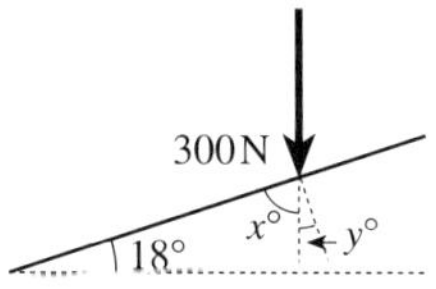

Fig. 4.15

$$\mathcal{R}(\parallel \text{to ramp}) \qquad F - 300\cos x° = 0.$$

$$\mathcal{R}(\perp \text{to ramp}) \qquad R - 300\cos y° = 0.$$

So $F = 300\cos 72° = 92.7$ and $R = 300\cos 18° = 285.3$, to 1 decimal place.

The frictional force is about 93 N and the normal contact force is about 285 N.

EXAMPLE 4.4.2

Re-work Example 4.2.3 if the child's father pulls on the swing at right angles to the ropes, rather than horizontally.

The diagram of forces now has the form of Fig. 4.16. Notice that, although the situation being modelled is quite different from that in the previous example, the three forces are related in just the same way in Fig. 4.14 and Fig. 4.16. This suggests resolving in the directions corresponding to those in Example 4.4.1; that is, perpendicular and parallel to the ropes.

Fig. 4.16

$$\mathcal{R}(\perp \text{to ropes}) \qquad F = 180\cos 70° = 61.6,$$

to 3 significant figures.

$$\mathcal{R}(\parallel \text{to ropes}) \qquad 2T = 180\cos 20°,$$

so $T = 90\cos 20° = 84.6$, to 3 significant figures.

The father must pull on the swing with a force of about 62 N. Each rope acts on the swing with a tension of about 85 N.

EXAMPLE 4.4.3

A rail track is laid on the floor of a quarry, sloping down at 11° to the horizontal from the side of the cliff. A truck is filled with stone, and when full may have mass up to 600 kg. It is prevented from running downhill by a cable from the truck to the top of the cliff, as shown in Fig. 4.17. For safety reasons the tension of the cable should not exceed 1600 N.

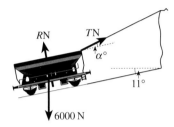

Fig. 4.17

Find

a the greatest angle that the cable should be allowed to make with the track,

b the smallest value of the total normal contact force on the truck.

  a The maximum weight of a full truck is 6000 N. If the cable makes an angle $\alpha°$ with the track, and the tension from the cable is T N, then

$$\mathcal{R}\left(\parallel \text{to track}\right) \qquad T\cos\alpha° = 6000\cos79°.$$

So $\cos\alpha° = \dfrac{6000\cos79°}{T}$. The requirement $T \leq 1600$ means that

$$\cos\alpha° \geq \frac{6000\cos79°}{1600} = 0.715\ldots, \text{ so } \alpha \leq 44.3\ldots.$$

The cable should make an angle no greater than 44° with the track.

  b If the total normal contact force on all the wheels is R N,

$$\mathcal{R}\left(\perp \text{to track}\right) \qquad R + T\cos(90-\alpha)° = 6000\cos11°.$$

Since $\cos(90-\alpha)° = \sin\alpha°$,

$R = 6000\cos11° - T\sin\alpha° = 5889.7\ldots - T\sin\alpha°.$

The greatest acceptable value of T is 1600, and the greatest value of $\sin\alpha°$ is $\sin44.3\ldots° = 0.698\ldots$. So the least possible value of R is

$$5889.7\ldots - 1600\sin44.3\ldots° = 4772, \text{ to the nearest integer.}$$

The total normal contact force will never be less than 4770 N.

The final example takes the form of an experiment which you could carry out to test the theory that the resolved part of a force F at an angle $\theta°$ is $F\cos\theta°$. It could conveniently be performed in a gymnasium equipped with horizontal wall bars. You need a straight length of model railway track fixed on to a long plank. You also need a small wagon, which should be loaded to make it as heavy as possible; this reduces the relative effect of resistance forces. You need to fix brackets at one end of the plank which can be hooked over the wall bars, so that the height of that end of the plank can be varied.

EXPERIMENT 4.4.4

A track of length d has one end on the floor and the other end at a height h above the floor. A wagon of mass m is placed at the upper end of the track, and runs freely down to the bottom. Show that the time T to reach the bottom of the track satisfies the equation $\dfrac{1}{T^2} = \left(\dfrac{g}{2d^2}\right)h.$

Fig. 4.18 shows the wagon at some point of its run down the track, which is at an angle $\theta°$ to the horizontal. The weight of the wagon is mg, and its acceleration is a.

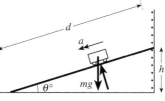

Fig. 4.18

$$\mathcal{R}\,(\text{down the track}) \qquad mg\cos(90-\theta)° = ma.$$

Since $\cos(90-\theta)° = \sin\theta°$, this gives $a = g\sin\theta°$. Also $\sin\theta° = \dfrac{h}{d}$, so $a = \dfrac{gh}{d}$.

The time taken for the wagon to travel down the track can be found by using the constant acceleration equation $s = ut + \frac{1}{2}at^2$, with $u = 0$ and $a = \dfrac{gh}{d}$, so that $s = \left(\dfrac{gh}{2d}\right)t^2$. You know that $s = d$ when $t = T$, so $d = \left(\dfrac{gh}{2d}\right)T^2$.

This can be rearranged to give the required result,

$$\frac{1}{T^2} = \left(\frac{g}{2d^2}\right)h.$$

The reason for putting the equation into the form given is that it shows the connection between the two variables, h and T, in the experiment. By using different wall bars, h can be varied, and the value of T recorded for different values of h. The other quantities in the equation, g and d, remain constant.

You can then plot your results in a form like Fig. 4.19. If the theory is correct, the plotted points should lie approximately on a straight line through the origin.

As an additional spin-off, you can measure from your graph the gradient of the straight line, which should equal $\dfrac{g}{2d^2}$. Since you know the length of the track, you can use the value of the gradient to estimate a value for g.

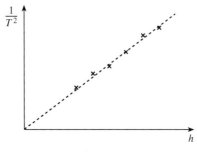

Fig. 4.19

Exercise 4B

1 For each of the forces defined below give their resolved parts in the Ox and Oy directions respectively, in terms of F and θ.

a 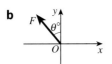 b 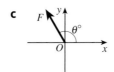 c 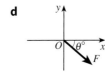 d

2 A block of wood of mass 4 kg is released from rest on a plane inclined at 30° to the horizontal. Assuming that the surface can be modelled as smooth (no friction), calculate the acceleration of the block, and its speed after it has moved 3 m.

3 A car of mass 850 kg is travelling, with acceleration 0.3 m s⁻², up a straight road inclined at 12° to the horizontal. There is a force resisting motion of 250 N. Calculate the magnitude of the driving force.

4 A cyclist of mass 60 kg free-wheels down a hill inclined at 6° to the horizontal. Assuming no resisting forces, calculate her acceleration down the hill, and show that her speed increases from 4 m s⁻¹ to 16 m s⁻¹ in about 117 m.

5 A sack of mass 8 kg is pulled up a ramp inclined at 20° to the horizontal by a force of magnitude 45 N acting parallel to a line of greatest slope of the ramp. The acceleration of the sack is 1.4 m s⁻². Find the frictional force.

6 A particle is in equilibrium under the action of the three forces shown in the diagram. By resolving in the direction of the force of magnitude Y N, show that $Y = 5$. Calculate the value of X.

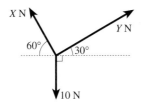

7 Calculate the magnitude of the horizontal force needed to maintain a crate of mass 6 kg in equilibrium, when it is resting on a frictionless plane inclined at 20° to the horizontal. Calculate also the magnitude of the normal contact force acting on the crate.

8 A skier of mass 78 kg is pulled at constant speed up a slope, of inclination 12°, by a force of magnitude 210 N acting upwards at an angle of 20° to the slope (see diagram). Find the magnitudes of the frictional force and the normal contact force acting on the skier.

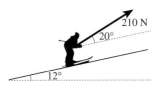

9 A particle of weight 10 N is placed on a smooth plane inclined at 35° to the horizontal. Find the magnitude of the force required to keep the particle in equilibrium if it acts

    a parallel to the plane,

    b horizontally,

    c upwards at an angle of 25° to a line of greatest slope of the plane.

Without making any calculations state, with a reason, which of the three cases has the greatest normal contact force.

10 The lid of a desk is hinged along one edge so that it can be tilted at various angles to the horizontal. A book of mass 1.8 kg is placed on the lid. The lid is tilted to an angle of 15°, as shown in the diagram. Find the frictional force, given that the book does not move.

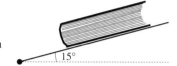

As the desk lid is tilted further, the book begins to move when the lid is inclined at $\theta°$ to the horizontal. Given that the maximum magnitude that the frictional force can attain is 8.45 N, find the maximum value of θ for which equilibrium remains unbroken.

The book is held at rest and the lid is tilted until it is inclined at 40° to the horizontal. The book is then released. Find the acceleration of the book down the desk lid, assuming the maximum frictional force still acts.

11 A metal sphere of weight 500 N is suspended from a fixed point O by a chain. The sphere is pulled to one side by a horizontal force of magnitude 250 N and the sphere is held in equilibrium with the chain inclined at an angle $\theta°$ to the vertical. Find, in either order, the tension in the string and the value of θ.

12 A picture of mass 12 kg is supported in equilibrium by two strings, inclined at 20° and 70° to the horizontal. Calculate the tension in each string.

13 A box of mass 12 kg is dragged, with a constant acceleration of 1.75 m s⁻², up a path inclined at 30° to the horizontal. The force pulling the box has magnitude $2X$ N and acts at 10° to the path, as shown in the diagram. The frictional force has magnitude X N. Calculate the value of X and the magnitude of the normal contact force of the path on the box.

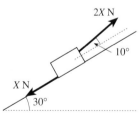

14 A plank of mass 20 kg is pulled, with a rope, up a slope inclined at 15° to the horizontal. The rope is inclined at 30° to the horizontal, as shown in the diagram.

    a Explain why the tension in the rope must certainly be greater than 53.6 N.

The tension in the rope is 65 N and the plank is moving at constant speed. Calculate

    b the magnitude of the normal contact force exerted on the plank by the ground,

    c the magnitude of the frictional force.

15 A boat on a trailer is held in equilibrium on a slipway inclined at 20° to the horizontal, by a cable inclined at $\theta°$ to a line of greatest slope of the slipway, as shown on the diagram. The combined mass of the boat and trailer is 1250 kg. The cable may break if the tension exceeds 7000 N. Find the maximum value of θ.

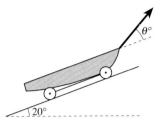

16 A glider of weight 2500 N is being towed with constant speed by a four-wheel drive vehicle. The towrope is inclined at 25° to the horizontal and the glider is inclined at 30° to the horizontal as shown in the diagram. The air resistance has magnitude R N and the lift has magnitude L N; the directions in which they act are shown in the diagram. Calculate the values of R and L, given that the tension in the rope is 3000 N.

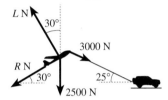

Miscellaneous exercise 4

1 A particle slides down a smooth plane inclined at an angle of $\alpha°$ to the horizontal. The particle passes through the point A with speed 1.5 m s⁻¹, and 1.2 s later it passes through the point B with speed 4.5 m s⁻¹. Find

  i the acceleration of the particle,

  ii the value of α.

          (Cambridge International AS and A level Mathematics 9709/04
                Paper 4 Q1 June 2008)

2 A particle P is in equilibrium on a smooth horizontal table under the action of horizontal forces of magnitudes F N, F N, G N and 12 N acting in the directions shown. Find the values of F and G.

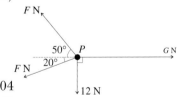

          (Cambridge International AS and A level Mathematics 9709/04
                Paper 4 Q3 June 2006)

3 Small blocks A and B are held at rest on a smooth plane inclined at 30° to the horizontal. Each is held in equilibrium by a force of magnitude 18 N. The force on A acts upwards parallel to a line of greatest slope of the plane, and the force on B acts horizontally in the vertical plane containing a line of greatest slope (see diagram). Find the weight of A and the weight of B.

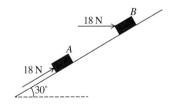

          (Cambridge International AS and A level Mathematics 9709/41
                Paper 4 Q2 November 2014)

4 Three horizontal forces of magnitudes F N, 13 N and 10 N act at a fixed point O and are in equilibrium. The directions of the forces are as shown in the diagram. Find, in either order, the value of θ and the value of F.

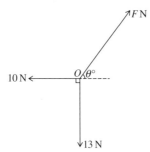

(Cambridge International AS and A level Mathematics 9709/04 Paper 4 Q3 June 2008)

5 A cyclist exerts a constant driving force of magnitude F N while moving up a straight hill inclined at an angle α to the horizontal, where $\sin \alpha = \frac{36}{325}$. A constant resistance to motion of 32 N acts on the cyclist. The total weight of the cyclist and his bicycle is 780 N. The cyclist's acceleration is $-0.2\,\mathrm{m\,s^{-2}}$.

i Find the value of F.

The cyclist's speed is $7\,\mathrm{m\,s^{-1}}$ at the bottom of the hill.

ii Find how far up the hill the cyclist travels before coming to rest.

(Cambridge International AS and A level Mathematics 9709/41 Paper 4 Q3 November 2013)

6 A, B and C are three points on a line of greatest slope of a smooth plane inclined at an angle of $\theta°$ to the horizontal. A is higher than B and B is higher than C, and the distances AB and BC are 1.76 m and 2.16 m respectively. A particle slides down the plane with constant acceleration $a\,\mathrm{m\,s^{-2}}$. The speed of the particle at A is $u\,\mathrm{m\,s^{-1}}$ (see diagram). The particle takes 0.8 s to travel from A to B and takes 1.4 s to travel from A to C. Find

i the values of u and a,

ii the value of θ.

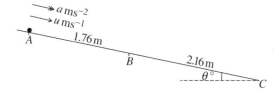

(Cambridge International AS and A level Mathematics 9709/41 Paper 4 Q4 November 2011)

7 A particle P of mass 0.5 kg lies on a smooth horizontal plane. Horizontal forces of magnitudes F N, 2.5 N and 2.6 N act on P. The directions of the forces are as shown in the diagram, where $\tan \alpha = \frac{12}{5}$ and $\tan \beta = \frac{7}{24}$.

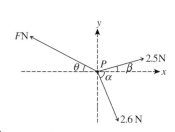

i Given that P is in equilibrium, find the values of F and $\tan \theta$.

ii The force of magnitude F N is removed. Find the magnitude and direction of the acceleration with which P starts to move.

(Cambridge International AS and A level Mathematics 9709/41 Paper 4 Q6 June 2013)

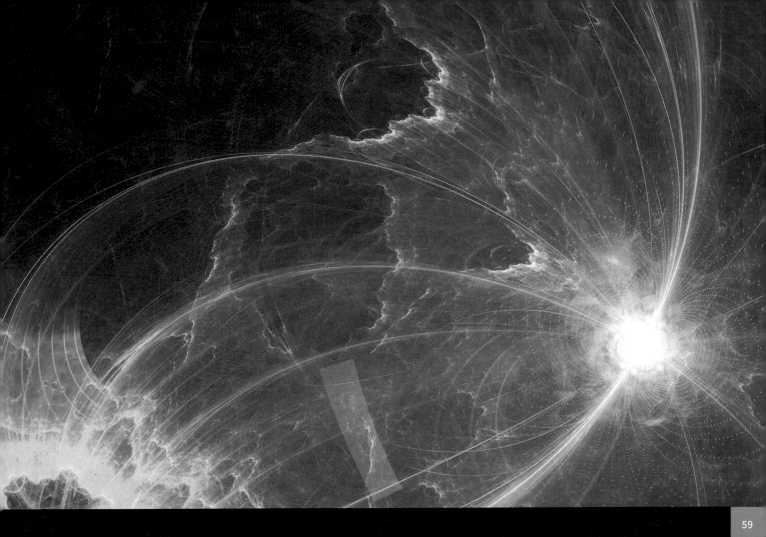

Chapter 5
Friction

In this chapter frictional force is analysed in detail. When you have completed it, you should

- be familiar with the mathematical model of friction and the properties of frictional forces
- understand the idea of limiting equilibrium
- know what is meant by the coefficient of friction and be able to use it
- be able to solve problems on motion and equilibrium in which friction is one of the forces acting on an object.

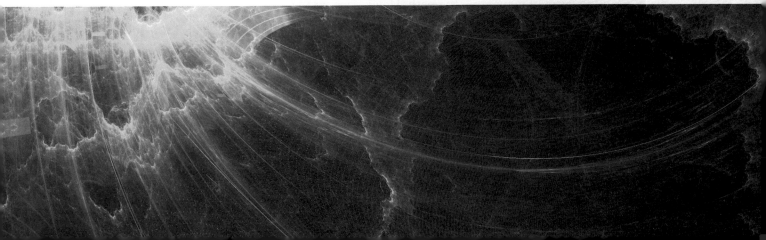

5.1 Basic properties of frictional forces

Imagine that you are trying to drag a heavy box along a horizontal platform (Fig. 5.1). One of two things may happen. If you pull hard enough, the box will start to move in the direction you are pulling in. If you don't pull so hard, the box will stay where it is. But in either case your pull will be opposed by a frictional force.

Fig. 5.1

This frictional force acts horizontally, in the plane where the base of the box is in contact with the platform. Its direction is opposite to the direction in which the box is moving, or in which it would move if it could. Fig. 5.2 shows the four forces acting on the box, whether or not it is moving.

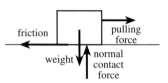

Fig. 5.2

If the box doesn't start to move, then the forces are in equilibrium. This means that the friction exactly balances the pull. If you pull a bit harder, the friction will increase; if you don't pull so hard, the friction will decrease. If you stop pulling, the friction will vanish.

If you pull hard enough for the box to move, the friction is smaller than the pull. There is a limit to the amount of friction that the base of the box and the platform can produce. If you pull with a force greater than this limit, the box will start to move.

> **When part of the surface of an object is in contact with a fixed surface, and forces are tending to move the object across the surface, these forces will be opposed by a frictional force. Its direction is opposite to the direction of motion or possible motion.**
>
> **The frictional force cannot exceed a certain magnitude, called the** limiting friction. **If the object is at rest and equilibrium is possible with a frictional force less than this limiting friction, the object will remain in equilibrium.**
>
> **If the object is at rest and the forces are in equilibrium with the limiting friction, the object is said to be in** limiting equilibrium, **and to be 'on the point of moving'.**

EXAMPLE 5.1.1

A dustbin of mass 20 kg is placed on a path which is at an angle of 13° to the horizontal. The limiting friction between the bin and the path is 50 N.

a Will the bin slide down the path?

b A force parallel to the slope is applied to the bin so that it is on the point of moving up the path. How large is this force?

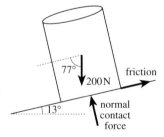

Fig. 5.3

a There are three forces on the bin: its weight, the normal contact force, and friction acting up the path (Fig. 5.3). Only the weight and the friction have any effect parallel to the path.

The weight is 200 N, and its resolved part down the path is $200 \cos 77°$, which is about 45 N. This is less than the limiting friction, so there can be equilibrium with a frictional force of 45 N up the path.

The bin will not slide down the path.

b Since the bin is on the point of sliding up the path, the friction has its limiting value of 50 N and acts in the opposite direction, down the path. Let the applied force be P N up the path. Then the forces on the bin are as in Fig. 5.4.

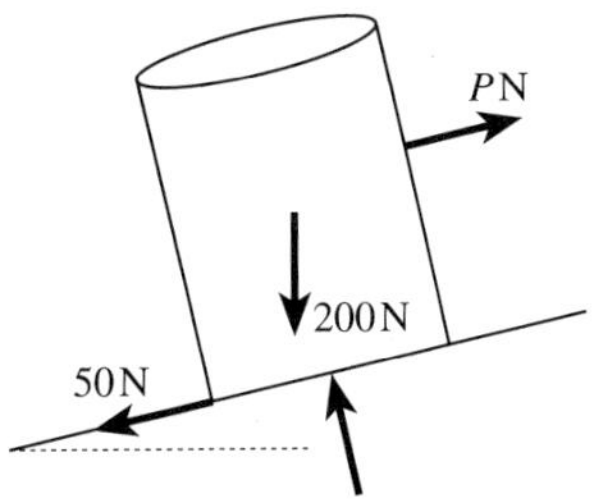

$\mathcal{R}$(up the path) $P - 50 - 200\cos 77° = 0$.

This gives $P = 50 + 45 = 95$.

If a force of 95 N is applied, the bin is on the point of sliding up the path.

Fig. 5.4

How large is the friction when the object starts to move? In theory it might stay at its limiting value, it might be smaller, or it might get larger but not so large as the force moving it. Experiments suggest that in practice the friction when there is motion is slightly smaller than limiting friction, but to a first approximation it is often taken to equal the limiting friction. This is the model you should use, unless you are told otherwise.

> **When an object slides over a fixed surface, the frictional force has its limiting value and acts in a direction opposite to the direction of motion.**

EXAMPLE 5.1.2

If, with the data in Example 5.1.1, a force of 100 N is applied to the dustbin up the path, calculate the acceleration with which the bin will move.

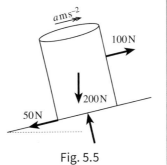

Fig. 5.5

The forces in Fig. 5.5 are the same as in Fig. 5.4, except that P is now 100. As the bin is moving, friction has its limiting value of 50 N. Let the acceleration be a m s^{-2}.

$\mathcal{R}$(up the path) $100 - 50 - 200\cos 77° = 20a$.

This gives $20a = 100 - 50 - 45 = 5$, so $a = \frac{5}{20} = 0.25$.

The bin will accelerate up the path at 0.25 m s^{-2}.

The properties of friction described in this section apply only when the surfaces in contact are dry and fairly rigid. If there is a layer of oil or water separating the surfaces, then you need to use a different model of friction.

5.2 Limiting friction

The next question to ask is, how large is the limiting friction?

This might depend on a number of factors, such as

- the materials that the surfaces in contact consist of,
- the shape and area of the region of contact between the surfaces,
- the other forces acting on the object.

The first of these is obviously important. Other things being equal, wood sliding across gravel produces much more friction than polished steel sliding across ice. Any model of friction has to take account of the difference in roughness of various materials.

Experiments suggest that shape and area do not have much effect on the size of the limiting friction. However, there are exceptions to this. For example, a new car tyre with a well-designed tread can produce more friction than a worn tyre, even though both are made of the same material.

The effect of the other forces certainly needs to be taken into account. You can show this by carrying out a simple experiment.

Take two books, one heavier than the other, and stand each upright on a table. Now clench your fists, and try to lift each book off the table, as in Fig. 5.6. To do this, you will need to push with your knuckles against the covers of the book. If the book has weight W, and the friction on each cover is F, then $2F = W$, so that $F = \frac{1}{2}W$. This means that the frictional force has to be larger for the heavier book.

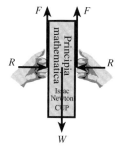

Fig. 5.6

Now reduce the forces R from your knuckles until the book is on the point of slipping. Friction is then limiting. You will find that you need to push harder on the covers to support the heavier book. This is because the limiting friction depends on the normal contact force. Since the limiting friction has to be larger for the heavier book, the normal contact force also has to be larger.

Notice that it is the same for the box pulled across the platform in Fig. 5.1. If the box is made heavier, then you need to pull harder before it starts to move. The limiting friction depends on the normal contact force, and in this case the normal contact force has the same magnitude as the weight.

If you carry out more precise experiments, you find that there is a direct proportional relationship connecting the limiting friction and the normal contact force. For example, if you double the normal force, the limiting friction is doubled. The rule for calculating limiting friction can then be summarised as follows.

> **The limiting frictional force between two surfaces is proportional to the normal contact force. If the limiting friction is F_{lim} and the normal contact force is R, then $F_{\text{lim}} = \mu R$, where μ is a constant.**
>
> **The constant μ is called the** coefficient of friction. **Its value depends mainly on the materials of which the surfaces consist.**

The symbol μ is the Greek letter 'm', pronounced 'mu'. It is always used to denote the coefficient of friction. For most surfaces, the value of μ lies between 0.3 and 0.9, but smaller or larger values (even greater than 1) can occur.

If μ is very small, you may get useful approximate results by taking μ to be 0, so that friction is ignored. In that case, the surfaces are said to be **smooth**. If μ is greater than 0, the surfaces are said to be **rough**, and you will need to consider friction. The term 'very rough' is sometimes used to describe surfaces for which μ is so large that there is no practical likelihood that one will slide over the other.

EXAMPLE 5.2.1

A person tries to pull a small cupboard across the floor. The mass of the cupboard is 76 kg and the coefficient of friction is 0.5. Describe what happens if the cupboard is pulled with a horizontal force of **a** 200 N, **b** 400 N.

The forces on the cupboard are shown in Fig. 5.7. The normal contact force, R N, is equal to the weight of the cupboard, which is 760 N.

The limiting friction is $0.5R$ N, that is 380 N.

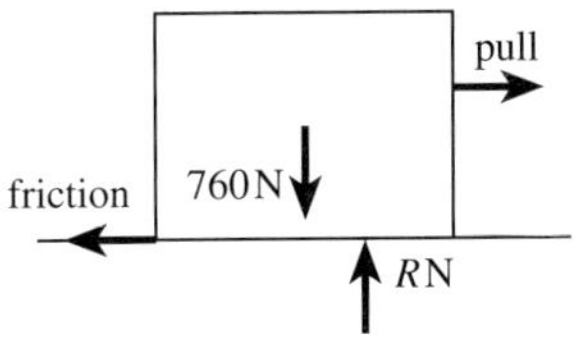

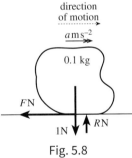

Fig. 5.7

a The pull of 200 N is less than the limiting friction. The pull is therefore opposed by a frictional force of 200 N, and the cupboard doesn't move.

b The pull of 400 N is greater than 380 N, so friction is limiting and the cupboard will start to move. Denote its acceleration by a m s^{-2}.

$$\mathcal{R}(\rightarrow) \quad 400 - 380 = 76a, \qquad \text{which gives } a = 0.263....$$

The cupboard starts to move with acceleration 0.263 m s^{-2}, to 3 significant figures.

EXAMPLE 5.2.2

A boy kicks a stone of mass 100 grams across the playground. The coefficient of friction between the stone and the playground is 0.25. If the stone comes to rest 31 m away, find the speed with which the boy kicked it.

You have to assume that the playground is flat, so that the stone stays in contact with it. The mass of the stone is 100 grams, which is 0.1 kg, so its weight is 1 N. The other forces on the stone are the normal contact force, R N, and friction, F N (see Fig. 5.8).

direction of motion

a m s^{-2}

0.1 kg

F N

1 N R N

Fig. 5.8

Resolving vertically gives $R = 1$. So long as the stone is moving, friction has its limiting value, which is 0.25×1 N $= 0.25$ N.

You can use Newton's second law to find the acceleration, a m s^{-2}.

$$\mathcal{R}(\rightarrow) \; -0.25 = 0.1\, a, \qquad \text{so} \qquad a = -2.5.$$

To finish the problem, you need a connection between velocity and distance. The acceleration is constant, so you can use the equation $v^2 = u^2 + 2as$. You have found that $a = -2.5$, so while the stone is moving $v^2 = u^2 - 5s$. You now want to find the value of u.

You are told that the stone goes 31 m, which means that $v = 0$ when $s = 31$. So $0 = u^2 - 5 \times 31$, which gives $u = \sqrt{155} = 12.4$, to 3 significant figures.

The boy kicked the stone with a speed of approximately 12.4 m s^{-1}.

63

As explained above, these results about friction are based on many experiments. Unlike Newton's second law, which defines mass by the *exact* equation $F = ma$, the formula $F_{lim} = \mu R$ is only approximate. The coefficient varies slightly, for example, depending upon whether the surfaces are stationary relative to each other or whether they are sliding past each other (when μ is slightly reduced). Likewise, the idea of smooth surfaces is also an idealisation: it is almost impossible for μ to be exactly zero in practice. Nevertheless, these approximations are good enough for most purposes, and you will use them throughout the rest of the Mechanics part of your course.

5.3 Some experiments

The model of friction described in the last two sections is based on a mixture of reasoning and experiment. Here are two experiments which you can try for yourself.

EXPERIMENT 5.3.1

You need a suitcase and a spring balance. Begin by using the spring balance to weigh the case. Then place the case flat on a table and attach the spring balance to the handle. Pull the case across the table at a steady speed with the spring balance, as shown in Fig. 5.9, and read the force on the spring balance. Repeat the experiment with various objects inside the case, and investigate the relationship between the force and the weight.

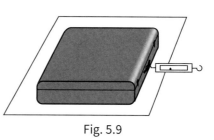

Fig. 5.9

> The forces on the case are the same as those in Fig. 5.2. Since the case is moving at a steady speed, the forces are in equilibrium. That is, the friction is equal to the pull and the normal contact force is equal to the weight. So you can find the normal contact force and the friction by measuring the weight and the pull.
>
> Also, since the case is moving, friction is limiting.
>
> One complication is that most spring balances are calibrated as if they measure mass rather than weight. (This was discussed in Section 3.4.) So when you weigh the case, if the spring balance shows x kg, the weight is $10x$ newtons.
>
> Similarly, when you measure the pull, if the spring balance reads y kg, this means that the pull is $10y$ newtons.
>
> The theory predicts that the limiting friction is proportional to the normal contact force, so that the pull is proportional to the weight. This is expressed by the equation $10y = \mu(10x)$, which gives $y = \mu x$.
>
> So if, as you carry out the experiment with different objects in the case, you plot y against x, the points should lie on a straight line through the origin. If they do, then the gradient of the line will give the value of the coefficient of friction.

EXPERIMENT 5.3.2

You need several books of different masses, with covers all made of similar materials. Take one book and place it flat on the table. Then tilt the table, gradually increasing the angle by placing equal blocks under two adjacent legs. Continue until the book is on the point of sliding down the table. Measure the height of the legs above the floor, and hence calculate the angle of tilt. Repeat the experiment with each book in turn.

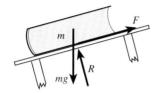

Fig. 5.10

If the book has mass m, then the forces on the book are its weight mg, the normal contact force R and the friction F, which is limiting when the book is on the point of sliding (Fig. 5.10). Theory predicts that F is equal to μR. Denote the angle of tilt by $\alpha°$.

$\mathcal{R}(\perp$ to table top$)\quad mg\cos\alpha° = R$.

$\mathcal{R}(\|$ to table top$)\quad mg\cos(90 - \alpha°) = \mu R$.

Since $\cos(90 - \alpha°) = \sin\alpha°$, this last equation can be written as

$$mg\sin\alpha° = \mu R.$$

Combining this with the first equation,

$$mg\sin\alpha° = \mu mg\cos\alpha°, \quad \text{so} \quad \sin\alpha° = \mu\cos\alpha°.$$

This can be simplified by using $\dfrac{\sin\alpha°}{\cos\alpha°} = \tan\alpha°$, to give $\tan\alpha° = \mu$.

If the theory is correct, the angles at which sliding begins should be the same for all the books, whatever their masses. If so, then the coefficient of friction is the tangent of the angle $\alpha°$.

You can extend this experiment by turning the books round on the table top, or by using books with covers of different sizes, to see if this makes any difference to the angle of tilt.

5.4 Friction and motion

You may have gained the impression that friction always acts so as to prevent motion. People often try to reduce the magnitude of the frictional force, for example by applying oil to moving parts, or by polishing surfaces which move over each other.

However, for many types of motion friction is essential. Imagine trying to run on a slippery pavement, trying to ride a bicycle on ice or driving a car in mud. In all these cases, the problem is that the magnitude of the frictional force is not large enough. It is friction which makes it possible to run, ride bicycles or drive cars.

The athlete would slip without the friction between her shoe and the ground. Pedalling causes the bicycle's back (driving) wheel to rotate, and the bicycle moves forward because of the friction between the tyre and the ground. The car's engine causes the driving wheels to rotate, and friction is needed for the car to be able to move. These situations are illustrated in Figs. 5.11, 5.12 and 5.13.

Fig. 5.11

Fig. 5.12

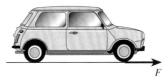

Fig. 5.13

Exercise 5A

1 The diagram shows horizontal forces of magnitudes P N and Q N acting in opposite directions on a block of mass 5 kg, which is at rest on a horizontal surface. State, in terms of P and Q, the magnitude and direction of the frictional force acting on the block when

    a $P > Q$,   **b** $Q > P$.

2 The diagram shows horizontal forces of magnitudes P N and 100 N acting in opposite directions on a block of weight 50 N, which is at rest on a horizontal surface. Given that the coefficient of friction between the block and the surface is 0.4, find the range of possible values of P.

3 The diagram shows a force of magnitude 8 N acting downwards at 30° to the horizontal on a block of mass 3 kg, which is at rest on a horizontal surface. Calculate the frictional force on the block.

4 An airline passenger pushes a 15 kg suitcase along the floor with his foot. A force of 60 N is needed to move the suitcase. Find the coefficient of friction. What force would be needed to give the suitcase an acceleration of $0.2 \, \text{m s}^{-2}$?

5 A block of mass 6 kg is accelerating at $1.25 \, \text{m s}^{-2}$, on a horizontal surface, under the action of a horizontal force of magnitude 22.5 N. Calculate the coefficient of friction between the block and the surface.

6 A horizontal cable from a winch is attached to a small boat of mass 800 kg which rests on horizontal ground. The coefficient of friction is $\frac{3}{4}$. The tension in the cable is increased in steps of 100 N. What is the frictional force when the tension is

    a 5900 N,   **b** 6000 N,   **c** 6100 N?

Describe what happens in each of these cases.

7 The diagram shows a block of weight 50 N at rest on a plane inclined at an angle $\alpha°$ to the horizontal, under the action of a force of magnitude P acting up the plane. Find, in terms of P, the magnitude and direction of the frictional force acting on the block when

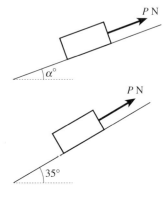

    a $P > 50 \sin \alpha°$,   **b** $P < 50 \sin \alpha°$.

8 The diagram shows a block of mass 4 kg at rest on a plane inclined at 35° to the horizontal, under the action of a force of magnitude P N acting up the plane. The coefficient of friction between the block and the plane is 0.45. Find the range of possible values of P.

9 A bowl of mass 500 grams is placed on a table, which is tilted at various angles to the horizontal. The coefficient of friction is 0.74. Calculate the net force on the bowl down a line of greatest slope of the table when the angle of tilt is

   a $36°$,   b $36\frac{1}{2}°$,   c $37°$.

   Describe what happens in each of these cases.

10 A coin of mass 5 grams is struck and slides across a horizontal wooden board. If the coefficient of friction is 0.4, and the coin is struck with a speed of $1.5\,\text{m s}^{-1}$, how far will it slide before it comes to rest?

11 A solid cylinder of mass 6 kg is lightly held, with its axis vertical, in the jaws of a vice, and is on the point of slipping downwards. The magnitude of the force exerted by each of the jaws is 70 N. Calculate the coefficient of friction between the vice and the cylinder.

12 A builder holds up a vertical piece of plate glass of weight 40 N by pressing the two sides with forces of P N from the palms of his hands. If the coefficient of friction is $\frac{1}{4}$, what is the least value of P needed if the glass is not to slip?

13 A shopper picks up a 2 kg packet of rice with the thumb and index finger of one hand. The coefficient of friction between her fingers and the wrapping is 0.3. What horizontal force must she exert to prevent the packet from slipping?

14 A cyclist and her bicycle have mass 75 kg. She is riding on a horizontal road, and positions herself so that 60% of the normal contact force acts on the back wheel and 40% on the front wheel. The coefficient of friction between the tyres and the road is 0.8. What is the greatest acceleration she can hope to achieve?

   Whilst riding at $6\,\text{m s}^{-1}$ she applies both brakes to stop the wheels rotating. In what distance will she come to a stop?

15 A crate of bottles, with total mass 6 kg, is placed on the floor of a delivery van. The coefficient of friction is 0.4. What is the greatest acceleration possible if the crate is not to slip on the floor?

16 A table of mass 15 kg stands on the floor of a restaurant. The coefficient of friction is 0.5 when there is no motion, but it drops to 0.4 when the table starts to move. A waiter pushes the table across the floor with a gradually increasing horizontal force until the table starts to move. Find the acceleration with which the table starts to move.

5.5 Problems involving friction

When you have a problem to solve which involves friction, you use the method of resolving which was described in Chapter 4, together with equations expressing the properties of friction. These can be summarised as follows, using F and R to denote friction and normal contact force.

- If motion is taking place (whether at constant speed or with acceleration), friction is limiting and in a direction opposite to the direction of motion.

- If the object is on the point of moving, friction is limiting and in a direction opposite to that in which the object is about to move.

- If friction is limiting, then $F = \mu R$.

- Whether friction is limiting or not, $F \leq \mu R$.

EXAMPLE 5.5.1

A block of weight 20 N is at rest on a horizontal surface. When a force of magnitude 12 N is applied to the block at an angle of 30° above the horizontal, it is on the point of moving. Find the coefficient of friction between the block and the surface.

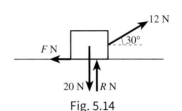

Fig. 5.14

The forces acting on the block are shown in Fig. 5.14. Since the block is about to move towards the right, friction is acting towards the left. This is a case of limiting equilibrium, so $F = \mu R$.

$$\mathcal{R}(\leftarrow) \qquad F = 12\cos 30° = 10.39....$$

$$\mathcal{R}(\uparrow) \qquad R + 12\cos 60° = 20, \qquad \text{giving} \qquad R = 14.$$

Therefore $\mu = \dfrac{F}{R} = \dfrac{10.39...}{14} = 0.74$, to 2 significant figures.

The coefficient of friction is approximately 0.74.

A common mistake in situations like this is to think that $R = 20$. When resolving vertically, you must include every force with a vertical resolved part.

EXAMPLE 5.5.2

A snow-covered hill is at an angle of 13° to the horizontal. A sledge of weight 75 N is placed on the hill. Given that the coefficient of friction between the sledge and the hill is 0.15, find whether the sledge will slide down the hill by itself.

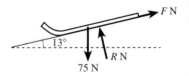

Fig. 5.15

The three forces acting on the sledge are shown in Fig. 5.15.

$$\mathcal{R}(\perp \text{to the hill}) \qquad R = 75\cos 13° = 73.07....$$

The maximum value of the friction is μR N, where

$$\mu R = 0.15 \times 73.07... = 10.96....$$

The resolved part of the weight which acts down the hill is

$$75\cos 77° \text{ N} = 16.87... \text{ N}.$$

As this force acting down the slope is greater than the maximum possible frictional force acting up the slope, the sledge will slide down the hill by itself.

EXAMPLE 5.5.3

Part of an army assault course consists of a taut cable 25 metres long fixed at 35° to the horizontal. A light rope ring is placed round the cable at its upper end. A soldier of mass 80 kg grabs hold of the ring and slides down the cable. If the coefficient of friction between the ring and the cable is 0.4, find how fast the soldier is moving when he reaches the bottom.

Fig. 5.16 shows the forces on the soldier with the ring at some point of his descent. The normal contact force is R N, the friction is F N, and the acceleration is a m s⁻². The weight of the soldier is 800 N, and the weight of the ring can be neglected.

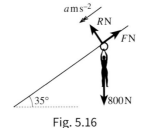

Fig. 5.16

$$\mathcal{R} \text{ (\|\ to the cable)} \qquad 800\cos 55° - F = 80a.$$

$$\mathcal{R} \text{ (}\perp\text{ to the cable)} \qquad 800\cos 35° = R.$$

Since there is motion, friction is limiting, so that $F = 0.4R$. So

$$800\cos 55° - 0.4 \times 800\cos 35° = 80a,$$

$$a = 10\cos 55° - 4\cos 35° = 2.459....$$

The acceleration is constant, and you want to find the velocity when the soldier has travelled 25 m down the cable. So use the equation $v^2 = u^2 + 2as$ with $u = 0$, $a = 2.459...$ and $s = 25$. This gives

$$v^2 = 0^2 + 2 \times 2.459... \times 25 = 122.9..., \text{giving} \qquad v = \sqrt{122.9...} = 11.08....$$

The soldier reaches the bottom of the cable at a speed of just over 11 m s⁻¹.

EXAMPLE 5.5.4

A block of weight 200 N is placed on a slope at $\beta°$ to the horizontal, where $\sin\beta° = 0.6$ and $\cos\beta° = 0.8$. It is kept from moving by a horizontal force of P newtons. For different values of the coefficient of friction μ, find the range of possible values of P.

If P is too small, the block might slide down the slope; if P is too large, the block might be pushed up the slope. So the frictional force, F N, might act either up the slope (Fig. 5.17) or down the slope (Fig. 5.18). The normal contact force is R N.

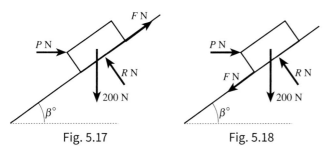

Fig. 5.17 Fig. 5.18

For Fig. 5.17:

$$\mathcal{R}(\perp \text{ to the slope}) \qquad P \times 0.6 + 200 \times 0.8 = R.$$

$$\mathcal{R} \ (\| \text{ to the slope}) \qquad P \times 0.8 + F = 200 \times 0.6.$$

Equilibrium is not necessarily limiting, so $F \leq \mu R$. This gives

$120 - 0.8P \leq \mu(0.6P + 160)$, which can be rearranged as

$$40(3 - 4\mu) \leq (0.8 + 0.6\mu)P, \qquad \text{giving} \qquad (4 + 3\mu)P \geq 200(3 - 4\mu).$$

Notice that, if μ is greater than $\frac{3}{4}$, the expression on the right is negative, but the expression on the left is positive, so the inequality is always satisfied. This links with the result of Experiment 5.3.2, where you found that the book would not slide until the table is tilted so that $\tan \alpha° = \mu$. In this example $\tan \beta° = \frac{0.6}{0.8} = \frac{3}{4}$; so if $\mu > \frac{3}{4}$, the block will not slide down the slope even if the force P is removed.

However, if μ is less than $\frac{3}{4}$, P must be at least $\dfrac{200(3 - 4\mu)}{4 + 3\mu}$ to prevent the block from sliding down the slope.

For Fig. 5.18, the equation for resolving at right angles to the slope is the same as before, but the equation $\mathcal{R}(\|$ to the slope) changes to

$$0.8P = F + 120.$$

The condition $F \leq \mu R$ then leads to the inequality

$$0.8P - 120 \leq \mu(0.6P + 160), \qquad \text{giving} \qquad (4 - 3\mu)P \leq 200(3 + 4\mu).$$

Again, there are two cases. If μ is less than $\frac{4}{3}$, P cannot be greater than $\dfrac{200(3 + 4\mu)}{4 - 3\mu}$; otherwise the block would start to slide up the slope.

But if μ is greater than $\frac{4}{3}$, the expression on the left is negative and the expression on the right is positive, so the inequality is always satisfied. This means that, however hard you push, the block can never slide up the slope.

What is happening is that, as you increase P, the normal contact force from the slope increases. If μ is large, this produces a large increase in the limiting friction. So although the resolved part of P up the slope also increases, it is not enough to overcome the available friction.

The results of this example can be illustrated with graphs. In Fig. 5.19 values of P are plotted against μ. The lower graph has equation $P = \dfrac{200(3 - 4\mu)}{4 + 3\mu}$ from $\mu = 0$ to $\mu = \frac{3}{4}$, after which $P = 0$. The upper graph has equation $P = \dfrac{200(3 + 4\mu)}{4 - 3\mu}$ from $\mu = 0$ to $\mu = \frac{4}{3}$. If, for a particular value of μ, the value of P lies between the two graphs, the block will be in equilibrium. If the value of P lies below the lower graph, the block will slide down the slope. If the value of P lies above the upper graph, the block will slide up the slope.

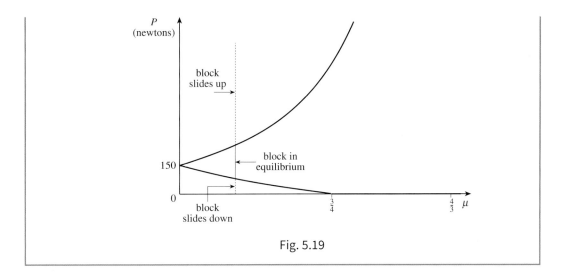

Fig. 5.19

Exercise 5B

1 A crate stands on the floor of a moving train. The crate has a tendency to slide backwards relative to the train. State the direction of the frictional force, and whether the train is accelerating or decelerating.

The acceleration or deceleration has magnitude $4\,\mathrm{m\,s^{-2}}$ and the crate is on the point of sliding. Find the coefficient of friction between the crate and the floor.

2 A cyclist and his bicycle have a total mass of $90\,\mathrm{kg}$. He is travelling along a straight horizontal road, at $7\,\mathrm{m\,s^{-1}}$, when he applies the brakes, locking both wheels. He comes to rest in a distance of $5\,\mathrm{m}$. Find the coefficient of friction between the tyres and the road surface.

3 The coefficient of friction between a waste skip of mass $500\,\mathrm{kg}$ and the horizontal ground on which it stands is 0.6. What is the maximum mass of waste material that the skip can contain if it is to be moved by a horizontal force of magnitude $7350\,\mathrm{N}$?

4 A car is travelling on a horizontal straight road at $12\,\mathrm{m\,s^{-1}}$ when its brakes are applied, locking all four wheels. The coefficient of friction between the road and the wheels is 0.8. Find the distance travelled by the car from the instant that the brakes are applied until it comes to rest.

5 The diagram shows a horizontal force of magnitude $30\,\mathrm{N}$ acting on a block of mass $2\,\mathrm{kg}$, which is at rest on a plane inclined at $50°$ to the horizontal. Find the magnitude and direction of the frictional force on the block.

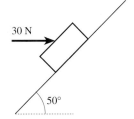

6 An ice-hockey puck is struck from one end of a rink of length $27\,\mathrm{m}$ towards the other end. The initial speed is $6\,\mathrm{m\,s^{-1}}$, and the puck rebounds from the boundary fence at the other end with a speed which is 0.75 times the speed with which it struck the fence, before just returning to its starting point. Calculate the coefficient of friction between the puck and the ice.

7 A railway engine is travelling at $50 \, \text{m s}^{-1}$, without carriages or trucks, when the power is shut off and the brakes applied, locking the wheels of the engine. The engine comes to rest in 25 seconds. Calculate the coefficient of friction between the wheels and the track.

8 A block of mass 5 kg accelerates at $0.8 \, \text{m s}^{-2}$, down a plane inclined at 15° to the horizontal, under the action of a force of magnitude 30 N acting down the plane. Calculate the coefficient of friction between the block and the plane.

9 A crate of mass 350 kg is released from rest at the top of a polished chute of length 80 m, which is inclined at an angle of 20° to the horizontal. The coefficient of friction between the crate and the chute is 0.36. Calculate the frictional force on the crate, and the speed of the crate at the bottom of the chute, given that the crate

   a is empty,

   b contains objects of total mass 150 kg.

10 A child starts from rest at the top of a playground slide and reaches a speed of $5.5 \, \text{m s}^{-1}$ at the bottom of the sloping part, which makes an angle of 35° with the horizontal. The coefficient of friction between the child and the slide is 0.25. Find the length of the sloping part of the slide, and the length of time for which the child is on the sloping part.

11 A car travels down a hill which is inclined at 6° to the horizontal, with its engine switched off. When the car's speed reaches $10 \, \text{m s}^{-1}$ the brakes are applied, locking all four wheels. The car comes to rest in a distance of 8 m. Find the coefficient of friction between the tyres and the road.

12 A small magnet of mass 0.05 kg is held against the metal door of a refrigerator and then released from rest. The magnetic effect is only partially effective and so the magnet moves vertically downwards, remaining in contact with the door. The magnet travels 1.4 m in 2 seconds. Assuming the acceleration of the magnet is constant, find the frictional force on the magnet.

   Given that the coefficient of friction between the door and the magnet is 0.3, calculate the normal contact force exerted by the door on the magnet.

13 A cyclist free-wheels down a slope inclined at 7° to the horizontal. When her speed gets to $4 \, \text{m s}^{-1}$ she applies the brakes, locking both wheels. The cyclist comes to rest 1 s after applying the brakes. Find the coefficient of friction between the tyres and the slope.

14 The diagram shows a force of magnitude 20 N acting downwards at 25° to the horizontal on a block of mass 4 kg, which is at rest in limiting equilibrium on a horizontal surface. Calculate the coefficient of friction between the block and the surface.

   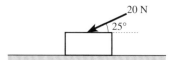

   The direction of the force of magnitude 20 N is now reversed. Calculate the acceleration with which the block starts to move.

15 The diagram shows a horizontal force of magnitude 10 N acting on a block of mass 6 kg, which is at rest in limiting equilibrium on a plane inclined at 20° to the horizontal. Calculate the coefficient of friction between the block and the plane.

   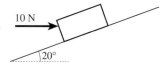

   The direction of the horizontal force is now reversed. Find the acceleration with which the block starts to move.

Miscellaneous exercise 5

1 A stone slab of mass 320 kg rests in equilibrium on rough horizontal ground. A force of magnitude X N acts upwards on the slab at an angle of θ to the vertical, where $\tan\theta = \frac{7}{24}$ (see diagram).

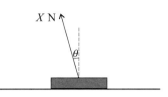

  i Find, in terms of X, the normal component of the force exerted on the slab by the ground.

  ii Given that the coefficient of friction between the slab and the ground is $\frac{3}{8}$, find the value of X for which the slab is about to slip.

(Cambridge International AS and A level Mathematics 9709/04
Paper 4 Q4 November 2005)

2 A small ring of mass 0.6 kg is threaded on a rough rod which is fixed vertically. The ring is in equilibrium, acted on by a force of magnitude 5 N pulling upwards at 30° to the vertical (see diagram).

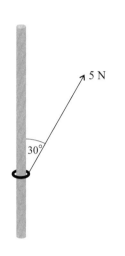

  i Show that the frictional force acting on the ring has magnitude 1.67 N, correct to 3 significant figures.

  ii The ring is on the point of sliding down the rod. Find the coefficient of friction between the ring and the rod.

(Cambridge International AS and A level Mathematics 9709/04
Paper 4 Q2 November 2006)

3 A small ring of mass 0.8 kg is threaded on a rough rod which is fixed horizontally. The ring is in equilibrium, acted on by a force of magnitude 7 N pulling upwards at 45° to the horizontal (see diagram).

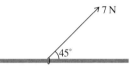

  i Show that the normal component of the contact force acting on the ring has magnitude 3.05 N, correct to 3 significant figures.

  ii The ring is in limiting equilibrium. Find the coefficient of friction between the ring and the rod.

(Cambridge International AS and A level Mathematics 9709/41
Paper 4 Q3 June 2010)

4 A particle P of mass 0.5 kg rests on a rough plane inclined at angle α to the horizontal, where $\sin\alpha = 0.28$. A force of magnitude 0.6 N, acting upwards on P at angle α from a line of greatest slope of the plane, is just sufficient to prevent P sliding down the plane (see diagram). Find

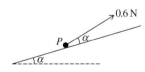

  i the normal component of the contact force on P,

  ii the frictional component of the contact force on P,

  iii the coefficient of friction between P and the plane.

(Cambridge International AS and A level Mathematics 9709/4
Paper 41 Q3 November 2012)

5 A block of weight 7.5 N is at rest on a plane which is inclined to the horizontal at angle α, where $\tan\alpha = \frac{7}{24}$. The coefficient of friction between the block and the plane is μ. A force of magnitude 7.2 N acting parallel to a line of greatest slope is applied to the block. When the force acts up the plane (see Fig. I) the block remains at rest.

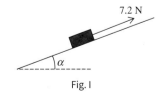

Fig. I

  i Show that $\mu \geq \frac{17}{24}$.

When the force acts down the plane (see Fig. II) the block slides downwards.

ii Show that $\mu < \frac{31}{24}$.

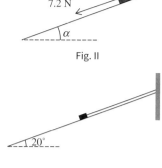

7.2 N

Fig. II

(Cambridge International AS and A level Mathematics 9709/41
Paper 4 Q3 November 2014)

6 A block of mass 8 kg is at rest on a plane inclined at 20° to the horizontal. The block is connected to a vertical wall at the top of the plane by a string. The string is taut and parallel to a line of greatest slope of the plane (see diagram).

i Given that the tension in the string is 13 N, find the frictional and normal components of the force exerted on the block by the plane.

The string is cut; the block remains at rest, but is on the point of slipping down the plane.

ii Find the coefficient of friction between the block and the plane.

(Cambridge International AS and A level Mathematics 9709/04
Paper 4 Q4 June 2009)

7 A particle of mass m kg moves up a line of greatest slope of a rough plane inclined at 21° to the horizontal. The frictional and normal components of the contact force on the particle have magnitudes F N and R N respectively. The particle passes through the point P with speed $10\,\text{m s}^{-1}$, and 2 s later it reaches its highest point on the plane.

i Show that $R = 9.336\,m$ and $F = 1.416\,m$, each correct to 4 significant figures.

ii Find the coefficient of friction between the particle and the plane.

After the particle reaches its highest point it starts to move down the plane.

iii Find the speed with which the particle returns to P.

(Cambridge International AS and A level Mathematics 9709/04
Paper 4 Q7 November 2006)

8 Particles P and Q are moving in a straight line on a rough horizontal plane. The frictional forces are the only horizontal forces acting on the particles.

i Find the deceleration of each of the particles given that the coefficient of friction between P and the plane is 0.2, and between Q and the plane is 0.25.

At a certain instant, P passes through the point A and Q passes through the point B. The distance AB is 5 m. The velocities of P and Q at A and B are $8\,\text{m s}^{-1}$ and $3\,\text{m s}^{-1}$, respectively, both in the direction AB.

ii Find the speeds of P and Q immediately before they collide.

(Cambridge International AS and A level Mathematics 9709/41
Paper 4 Q4 November 2013)

9 A ring of mass 4 kg is threaded on a fixed rough vertical rod. A light string is attached to the ring, and is pulled with a force of magnitude T N acting at an angle of 60° to the downward vertical (see diagram). The ring is in equilibrium.

i The normal and frictional components of the contact force exerted on the ring by the rod are R N and F N respectively. Find R and F in terms of T.

ii The coefficient of friction between the rod and the ring is 0.7. Find the value of T for which the ring is about to slip.

60°

T N

(Cambridge International AS and A level Mathematics 9709/04
Paper 4 Q5 November 2007)

10 A particle P of mass $0.6\,\text{kg}$ moves upwards along a line of greatest slope of a plane inclined at $18°$ to the horizontal. The deceleration of P is $4\,\text{m}\,\text{s}^{-2}$.

i Find the frictional and normal components of the force exerted on P by the plane. Hence find the coefficient of friction between P and the plane, correct to 2 significant figures.

After P comes to instantaneous rest it starts to move down the plane with acceleration $a\,\text{m}\,\text{s}^{-2}$.

ii Find the value of a.

(Cambridge International AS and A level Mathematics 9709/41
Paper 4 Q5 November 2009)

11 A block of mass $2\,\text{kg}$ is at rest on a horizontal floor. The coefficient of friction between the block and the floor is μ. A force of magnitude $12\,\text{N}$ acts on the block at an angle α to the horizontal, where $\tan\alpha = \frac{3}{4}$. When the applied force acts downwards as in Fig. I the block remains at rest.

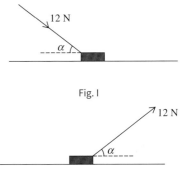

Fig. I

Fig. II

i Show that $\mu \geq \frac{6}{17}$.

When the applied force acts upwards as in Fig. II the block slides along the floor.

ii Find another inequality for μ.

(Cambridge International AS and A level Mathematics 9709/41
Paper 4 Q5 November 2011)

75

Chapter 6
Motion due to gravity

This chapter applies the constant acceleration formulae to the special case of motion due to the force of gravity, either vertical or along a slope. When you have completed it, you should

- understand that motion upwards and downwards can be covered by a single set of equations, with velocity and displacement either positive or negative
- appreciate the effect of friction for motion on a slope, and of air resistance for vertical motion.

6.1 Objects falling from a height

You know from Chapter 3 that an object falling freely under the force of gravity has a constant acceleration of about $10\,\text{m}\,\text{s}^{-2}$, often denoted by g. This acceleration is the same whatever the mass of the object, but the model is based on the assumption that the effect of air resistance is so small that it can be ignored in calculations.

Since the acceleration is constant, you can use the formulae in Section 1.5 to answer questions about the time it takes to fall a certain height, the speed after falling a certain distance, and so on.

EXAMPLE 6.1.1

At a swimming pool a girl steps from a diving board $4\,\text{m}$ above the surface of the water. How fast is she moving when her feet hit the water?

The girl's initial velocity is 0 and her acceleration in metre–second units is 10. You want a connection between the velocity v and the displacement s, so use the formula $v^2 = u^2 + 2as$ to get $v^2 = 0 + 2 \times 10 \times s$, giving $v^2 = 20s$. When $s = 4$, $v^2 = 80$, so $v = \sqrt{80}$, or 8.94…

The girl is moving at just under $9\,\text{m}\,\text{s}^{-1}$ when her feet hit the water.

EXAMPLE 6.1.2

A brick is dislodged from the top of a tall block of flats. A resident on a 10th-floor balcony sees it passing, and a second later hears it hit the ground. Each storey has a height of $2.5\,\text{m}$. How tall is the block of flats, and how fast is the brick moving when it hits the ground?

As in the previous example, $u = 0$ and $a = 10$. You are interested in the distance the brick moves in a certain time, so use the formula $s = ut + \frac{1}{2}at^2$ to get the displacement–time equation $s = 5t^2$.

Suppose that the height of the block of flats is h metres and that the brick takes T seconds to fall to the ground. The height of the balcony above ground level is 10×2.5 metres, which is 25 metres. So $s = h$ when $t = T$, and $s = h - 25$ when $t = T - 1$. Substituting these pairs of values in $s = 5t^2$ gives

$$h = 5T^2 \quad \text{and} \quad h - 25 = 5(T - 1)^2.$$

Subtract the second equation from the first. This gives

$$h - (h - 25) = 5T^2 - 5(T - 1)^2,$$

which simplifies to

$$25 = 5(2T - 1), \quad \text{so} \quad T = 3.$$

From this you can calculate $h = 5 \times 3^2 = 45$, so the block of flats is $45\,\text{m}$ high.

To find how fast the brick is moving when it hits the ground, use the formula $v = u + at$, which with the known values of u and a becomes $v = 10t$. So when $t = 3$, $v = 30$. The brick hits the ground with a speed of $30\,\text{m}\,\text{s}^{-1}$.

Exercise 6A

Air resistance may be ignored, and you may assume that the moving objects do not encounter any obstacles (such as the ground) unless specifically mentioned in the question.

1   A stone is dropped from rest. Find the velocity of the stone and the distance it has fallen after 3 seconds.

2   A ball is dropped from rest at a height 10 metres above the ground. Find the velocity of the ball just before it hits the ground.

3   A girl standing on a bridge over a river drops a stone from rest. The stone hits the water after 1.4 seconds. How high is the bridge?

4   A ball is thrown downwards with an initial velocity of $3.5\,\mathrm{m\,s^{-1}}$, and hits the ground when its velocity is $17.5\,\mathrm{m\,s^{-1}}$. From what height was the ball thrown?

5   A stone is thrown downwards from a height of 14.7 metres and hits the ground after 1.4 seconds. Find the velocity of the stone just before it hits the ground.

6.2   Objects projected upwards

In cricket, when a fielder makes a catch he often celebrates by throwing the ball vertically up into the air. To do this he has to give the ball an initial velocity, and the force producing this comes from his hands. But once the ball is in the air, the only force on it is the force of gravity.

While the ball is rising, its displacement and velocity are upwards, but the force is downwards. Gravity therefore produces a deceleration of $10\,\mathrm{m\,s^{-2}}$, so that in the constant acceleration formulae you must write $a = -10$.

EXAMPLE 6.2.1

A ball is thrown vertically upwards and rises a height of 12.8 metres. Find the speed with which it was thrown, and its velocity when it has risen 11 metres.

In this example you are not interested in the time, so use the formula which leaves out t, which is $v^2 = u^2 + 2as$. The initial velocity u is unknown, but $a = -10$. The equation connecting velocity and displacement is therefore $v^2 = u^2 - 20s$.

Since the ball rises a height of 12.8 m, its velocity is 0 when $s = 12.8$. Therefore $0 = u^2 - 20 \times 12.8$, so $u^2 = 256$, giving $u = 16$. That is, the ball was thrown with an initial velocity of $16\,\mathrm{m\,s^{-1}}$.

You can now substitute 16 for u in the velocity–displacement equation to get $v^2 = 256 - 20s$. So when $s = 11$, $v^2 = 256 - 20 \times 11 = 36$, giving $v = \sqrt{36} = 6$. That is, when it has risen 11 metres the ball is moving upwards at a speed of $6\,\mathrm{m\,s^{-1}}$.

The questions asked in this example refer only to the upward motion of the ball. But what goes up must come down, and you could go on to ask questions about the complete throw from the moment when the ball leaves the fielder's hands until the moment when he catches it again. For example, how long is it in the air for, and how fast is it moving when it is caught?

You could answer these questions by splitting the throw into two parts: the upward motion, and then the downward motion, in which the ball falls from a height of 12.8 metres. But this is not necessary. You can use just one set of equations, which hold for both the upward and the downward motion.

Consider the velocity–time equation $v = u + at$, which in this example takes the form $v = 16 - 10t$. The upward part of the throw lasts until $v = 0$, when $t = \frac{16}{10} = 1.6$; so the ball reaches its greatest height of 12.8 metres after 1.6 seconds. After that the equation gives a negative value for v.

Notice that in setting up the model for this example, and in stating that $u = 16$ and $a = -10$, it is implied that quantities measured in the upward direction are to count as positive. So if v turns out to be negative, this means that the ball is moving downwards.

This illustrates the difference between the terms 'speed' and 'velocity'. For example, if you take $t = 2$, you get $v = 16 - 10 \times 2 = -4$. You would say that the ball has a velocity of $-4\,\mathrm{m\,s^{-1}}$ in the upward direction, but that it is moving with a speed of $4\,\mathrm{m\,s^{-1}}$.

Now consider the displacement–time equation $s = ut + \frac{1}{2}at^2$, which for this example takes the form $s = 16t - 5t^2$. You can check from this that, when $t = 1.6$, $s = 25.6 - 12.8 = 12.8$, which confirms that the ball reaches its greatest height, 12.8 metres, after 1.6 seconds. After that the displacement starts to decrease. For example, when $t = 2$, you get $s = 16 \times 2 - 5 \times 4 = 12$. So after 2 seconds the ball is at a height of 12 metres.

By writing the equation for s as $s = t(16 - 5t)$, you can see that $s = 0$ when $t = \frac{16}{5} = 3.2$. This means that after 3.2 seconds the displacement s, that is the height of the ball, is zero. So the complete throw lasts for 3.2 seconds.

Finally, substituting $t = 3.2$ in the equation $v = 16 - 10t$ gives $v = 16 - 32 = -16$. This means that, when the ball is caught, its velocity is $-16\,\mathrm{m\,s^{-1}}$; that is, it is descending with a speed of $16\,\mathrm{m\,s^{-1}}$.

It is interesting to notice that the ball takes just the same time to go up as to come down, and that it is caught with the same speed as it is thrown. This is always true for an object moving under the force of gravity alone which is thrown up and caught at the same level. You are asked to prove this in Exercise 6B Question 13.

Figs. 6.1 and 6.2 show the velocity–time and displacement–time graphs for the throw. Fig. 6.1 shows that v is positive up to $t = 1.6$ and negative for t between 1.6 and 3.2, but that the whole throw can be thought of as part of one continuous motion. Fig. 6.2 shows s increasing to a maximum value of 12.8 when $t = 1.6$ and then decreasing to 0 when $t = 3.2$.

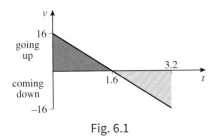

Fig. 6.1

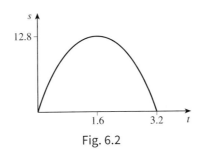

Fig. 6.2

It is important to notice how the displacement is found from the velocity–time graph. The region between the graph and the time-axis consists of two triangles, shaded dark and light grey in the figure. Both these triangles have area $\frac{1}{2} \times 1.6 \times 16 = 12.8$. The dark triangle shows that the displacement increases by 12.8 metres between $t = 0$ and $t = 1.6$. But the light triangle, which lies below the axis, shows that the displacement *decreases* by 12.8 metres between $t = 1.6$ and 3.2, so that by the time $t = 3.2$ the displacement is 12.8 + (−12.8), which is zero.

This illustrates the difference between the terms 'distance' and 'displacement'. During the throw the ball moves a distance of 12.8 + 12.8 = 25.6 metres, but since it ends up where it started the displacement at the end of the throw is zero.

EXAMPLE 6.2.2

Juliet's balcony is 3.6 metres above the ground. Romeo throws a bunch of flowers up to her with a speed of $11 \, \text{m s}^{-1}$. Juliet responds by throwing him an orange, which she throws upwards with a speed of $3 \, \text{m s}^{-1}$. Find the time for which each gift is in the air, and the speed at which it is moving when it is caught.

For Romeo's flowers you have $u = 11$ and $a = -10$, so that the displacement–time and velocity–time equations are $s = 11t - 5t^2$ and $v = 11 - 10t$. Juliet catches them when $s = 3.6$, which is when $11t - 5t^2 = 3.6$, or $25t^2 - 55t + 18 = 0$. This factorises as $(5t - 2)(5t - 9) = 0$. There are therefore two possibilities, $t = 0.4$ or $t = 1.8$.

You can see the reason for this by calculating the corresponding values of v, which are $11 - 10 \times 0.4 = 7$ and $11 - 10 \times 1.8 = -7$. Juliet has two chances of catching the flowers: either as they go past the balcony on the way up, after 0.4 seconds with a speed of $7 \, \text{m s}^{-1}$, or on the way down again, after 1.8 seconds and with the same speed.

For Juliet's orange $u = 3$ and $a = -10$, so that $s = 3t - 5t^2$ and $v = 3 - 10t$. In this case s stands for the displacement above Juliet's hands when she throws the orange, so to find when Romeo catches it you must take s to be −3.6. A negative displacement means that the object is in the negative direction from the point where it started.

This leads to the equation $3t - 5t^2 = -3.6$, or $25t^2 - 15t - 18 = 0$, which factorises as $(5t + 3)(5t - 6) = 0$. Since t cannot be negative in this model, $5t + 3$ cannot be zero, so the only possibility is $5t - 6 = 0$, or $t = 1.2$. This gives the value $v = 3 - 10 \times 1.2 = -9$. So Romeo catches the orange after 1.2 seconds, when it is coming down with a speed of $9 \, \text{m s}^{-1}$.

A detail that you should notice in this example is that 3.6 m is given as the height of the balcony above the ground, but the gifts in fact move from the hands of one of the lovers to the hands of the other. So in taking the displacement to be ±3.6 m it has been assumed that each throws the gift at the same height above the floor as the other catches it.

One final point should be made. There is nothing special about taking the positive direction to be upwards. You could equally well take it to be downwards, in which case the signs of u, a, v and s (but not t) would be reversed. But it seems more natural to take the positive direction upwards, since that is the direction in which the object is moving at first. If you look back at Section 6.1, where the motion was only downwards, the obvious choice was to take the positive direction downwards.

Exercise 6B

Air resistance may be ignored, and you may assume that the moving objects do not encounter any obstacles (such as the ground) unless specifically mentioned in the question.

1 A machine projects a tennis ball vertically upwards with an initial velocity of $25\,\text{m s}^{-1}$. Find the velocity and the height of the ball after 2 seconds.

2 A juggler throws a ball vertically upwards with an initial velocity of $6\,\text{m s}^{-1}$. Find the greatest height of the ball.

3 A ball is thrown vertically upwards and reaches a maximum height of 22 metres. Find the initial velocity of the ball.

4 A stone is thrown upwards and reaches a maximum height of 35 metres. Find the time taken to reach the maximum height.

5 A cricket ball is hit vertically upwards and reaches its maximum height after 2.2 seconds. Find the maximum height of the ball.

6 A boy throws a ball upwards with an initial velocity of $8\,\text{m s}^{-1}$ from a point 3 metres below the ceiling. Find the time between throwing the ball and the ball hitting the ceiling.

7 A stone is thrown upwards with an initial velocity of $20\,\text{m s}^{-1}$. Find the velocity and the height of the stone after 3 seconds.

8 A ball is thrown upwards and is caught (at the same height) 3.2 seconds later. Find the initial velocity of the ball.

9 A stone is thrown upwards with an initial velocity of $18\,\text{m s}^{-1}$. Find the time when the stone returns to the point of projection, and the velocity of the stone at this instant.

10 A ball is thrown upwards with an initial velocity of $15.5\,\text{m s}^{-1}$. For how long is the ball higher than 10.5 metres?

11 A ball is thrown upwards with an initial velocity of $12\,\text{m s}^{-1}$ from a point 2.5 metres above the ground. Find the time when the ball reaches the ground, and the velocity of the ball at this instant.

12 A stone is thrown upwards with an initial speed of $15\,\text{m s}^{-1}$ from the top of a cliff. It lands at the bottom of the cliff after 5.4 seconds. Find the height of the cliff.

13 An object is thrown vertically upwards with initial speed u. Show that it reaches its maximum height after time $\dfrac{u}{g}$ and show that the maximum height is $\dfrac{u^2}{2g}$.

Show that the object returns to the point of projection after total time $\dfrac{2u}{g}$ and find its velocity at this instant.

Deduce that the time moving upwards is the same as the time moving downwards, and that the speed of the object when it returns to the point of projection is equal to its initial speed.

14 A trampolinist bounces upwards and lands (at the same level) 1.8 seconds later. Find the initial velocity of the trampolinist, and her greatest height.

15 A stone is thrown upwards with an initial velocity of $25\,\mathrm{m\,s^{-1}}$ from a point 30 metres above the ground.

 a Find the maximum height of the stone (above the ground).

 b Find the time when the stone hits the ground.

 c Display the (t,v) graph for the motion of the stone (up to the time when it hits the ground).

 d Display a graph showing the height of the stone as a function of time.

6.3 Motion on a sloping plane

You can use a similar method to investigate the motion of an object sliding up and down a slope under the action of the force of gravity, but the acceleration in this case is not so large. This is illustrated by the next two examples. In the first the slope has a smooth surface, and in the second friction is introduced.

EXAMPLE 6.3.1

A path runs up a hillside, at an angle of $\alpha°$ to the horizontal, such that $\sin\alpha° = 0.6$ and $\cos\alpha° = 0.8$. A block is placed on the path, and is prevented from sliding down by a low kerbstone. The block is struck and starts to move up the path at a speed of $12\,\mathrm{m\,s^{-1}}$. The path is icy, so the effect of friction can be neglected. Find how far up the path the block moves, the speed with which it hits the kerbstone on its return, and the time it is in motion.

The only two forces on the block as it slides on the path are its weight and the normal contact force, shown in Fig. 6.3. The mass of the block is not given, so take it to be M kg. Then the weight of the block is $10M$ newtons, and the resolved part of this weight down the plane is $10M\cos(90 - \alpha)°$ newtons, which is $10M\sin\alpha° = 6M$ newtons. So if the acceleration of the block up the plane is $a\,\mathrm{m\,s^{-2}}$,

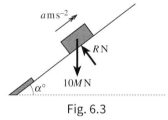

Fig. 6.3

$$\mathcal{R}(\|\text{to the plane}) \qquad -6M = Ma, \qquad \text{which gives} \qquad a = -6.$$

The first two questions can be answered from the velocity–displacement equation $v^2 = u^2 + 2as$, which with $u = 12$ and $a = -6$ takes the form $v^2 = 144 - 12s$.

At the furthest point up the path $v = 0$, so $s = \frac{144}{12} = 12$. Later, when the block hits the kerbstone again, the displacement is 0, so $v^2 = 144$. Since by this time it is sliding down the path, the velocity must be negative, so $v = -12$.

There are several ways of finding the time for which the motion lasts. One is to use the velocity–time equation $v = u + at$ in the form $v = 12 - 6t$. You know that when it hits the kerbstone $v = -12$, so $-12 = 12 - 6t$, which gives $t = \frac{24}{6} = 4$.

So the block travels 12 metres up the plane, and after 4 seconds it hits the kerbstone with a speed of $12\,\mathrm{m\,s^{-1}}$.

EXAMPLE 6.3.2

Rework Example 6.3.1 when the ice has melted. The coefficient of friction between the block and the path is now 0.45.

Fig. 6.4 shows the forces on the block while it is sliding up the path. To find the frictional force you first need to know the normal contact force, R newtons.

$$\mathcal{R}(\perp \text{to the path}) \qquad R = 10M \cos \alpha°, \qquad \text{so} \qquad R = 8M.$$

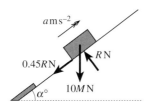

Fig. 6.4

Since the block is in motion, friction is limiting and equal to

$0.45 \times 8M$ newtons, or $3.6M$ newtons.

$$\mathcal{R}(\| \text{to the path}) \qquad -6M - 3.6M = Ma, \qquad \text{which gives} \qquad a = -9.6.$$

Using the equations $v = u + at$ and $v^2 = u^2 + 2as$ for the motion up the path, $v = 12 - 9.6t$ and $v^2 = 144 - 19.2s$. So at the highest point, when $v = 0$, $t = \frac{12}{9.6} = 1.25$ and $s = \frac{144}{19.2} = 7.5$.

For the return part of the motion the direction of the frictional force is reversed, and the forces are as shown in Fig. 6.5. It is now simpler to take the positive direction to be down the path, since the displacement and the velocity are both in that direction.

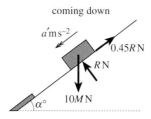

Fig. 6.5

Calling the acceleration a',

$$\mathcal{R}(\| \text{to the path}) \qquad 6M - 3.6M = Ma', \qquad \text{so} \qquad a' = 2.4.$$

For this part of the motion $u = 0$ and $a' = 2.4$, so the equations $v^2 = u^2 + 2as$ and $s = ut + \frac{1}{2}at^2$ take the forms $v^2 = 4.8s$ and $s = 1.2t^2$. The block hits the

kerbstone when $s = 7.5$, so $v = \sqrt{4.8 \times 7.5} = 6$ and $t = \sqrt{\dfrac{7.5}{1.2}} = 2.5$.

So the block now travels 7.5 metres up the path, is in motion for a total time of 1.25 + 2.5, or 3.75 seconds, and hits the kerbstone with a speed of $6 \, \text{m s}^{-1}$.

83

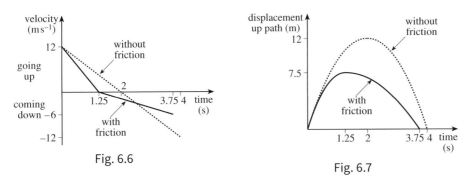

Fig. 6.6

Fig. 6.7

Fig. 6.6 and Fig. 6.7 show the velocity–time and displacement–time graphs for Example 6.3.1 (*broken line*) and Example 6.3.2 (*solid line*), with the direction up the path taken as positive. The graphs for the motion without friction take the form of a single straight line and parabola, but those for the motion with friction consist of two straight lines and two half-parabolas joined together. In Fig. 6.6, for both velocity–time graphs, the areas of the triangles above and below the time-axis are equal.

6.4 Vertical motion with air resistance

When an object is moving vertically there is no frictional force between solid surfaces, but there will usually be resistance from the air. An important difference between these forces is that, in the standard model, the size of the frictional force does not depend on the speed, but air resistance increases with the speed of the object.

The size of the air resistance force depends also on the shape of the object, the surface area, the material of which the surface is made, and the density of the air. These factors are combined to give a constant of proportion k in the equation defining the model. A useful approximation is that at low speeds the air resistance is proportional to the speed, and that at higher speeds it is proportional to the square of the speed.

For a falling object, there is a speed at which the air resistance is so large that it exactly balances the weight. When this occurs, no further acceleration is possible. This speed is called the **terminal speed**.

EXAMPLE 6.4.1

Three people step out of an aircraft, and fall vertically before opening their parachutes. The first, who has a mass of 80 kg, remains upright as he falls, and has a terminal speed of 50 m s⁻¹. The second is a soldier wearing heavy clothing and carrying equipment; his mass is 120 kg, and he also remains upright. The third is a skilled skydiver, of mass 70 kg, who takes up a horizontal position with arms and legs stretched out; this enables her to multiply the air resistance constant by a factor of 12. Find the terminal speed of the soldier and the skydiver.

84

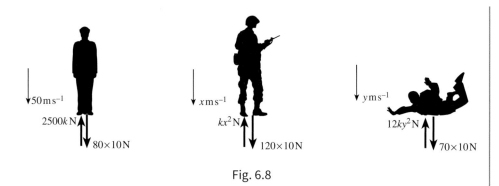

Fig. 6.8

Fig. 6.8 shows the forces on the three people. Suppose that the air resistance on the first is given by the formula kv^2 newtons, where v is his speed in m s^{-1}. The resistance on the soldier will not be very different, since he adopts the same upright position. For the skydiver the resistance is given to be $12kv^2$ newtons.

Let the terminal speeds of the soldier and the skydiver be $x\,\text{m s}^{-1}$ and $y\,\text{m s}^{-1}$ respectively. Then, equating the weight to the air resistance in each case,

$$80 \times 10 = k \times 50^2, \quad 120 \times 10 = kx^2 \quad \text{and} \quad 70 \times 10 = 12ky^2.$$

The first equation gives $k = \dfrac{80 \times 10}{50^2} = 0.32$. Substituting this in the second

and third equations gives $x = \sqrt{\dfrac{120 \times 10}{0.32}} = 61.2\ldots$ and $y = \sqrt{\dfrac{70 \times 10}{12 \times 0.32}} = 13.5\ldots$.

So the soldier will have a terminal speed of just over $60\,\text{m s}^{-1}$, but the skydiver can reduce hers to less than one-quarter of that value.

Notice that although the gravitational acceleration is the same for all three people, regardless of their mass, the soldier's greater weight causes him to fall with a faster terminal speed than the first person. On the other hand, by presenting a larger surface area to the air stream, the skydiver can reduce her terminal speed to allow much more time to enjoy the fall and to carry out spatial manoeuvres before she needs to open her parachute.

A detailed analysis of motion against air resistance involves quite advanced mathematics, which must wait until the unit M2. However, it is possible at this stage to give an approximate description of how air resistance affects vertical motion.

EXAMPLE 6.4.2

A cannonball is projected vertically upwards from a mortar with an initial velocity of $40\,\text{m s}^{-1}$. The mortar is situated at the edge of a cliff 100 metres above the sea. On the way down, the cannonball just misses the cliff. In vertical fall the cannonball would have a terminal speed of $50\,\text{m s}^{-1}$. Calculate the acceleration of the cannonball just after it leaves the mortar barrel, and at the highest point of its path. Draw graphs to compare the actual motion with the motion predicted if there were no air resistance.

For the motion without air resistance $u = 40$ and $a = -10$, so the constant acceleration formulae give $v = 40 - 10t$ and $s = 40t - 5t^2$. The cannonball would reach its highest point when $v = 0$, which is when $t = 4$, at which time $s = 80$.

It would enter the sea when $s = -100$, and you can easily check that this is when $t = 10$, that is 10 seconds after it is fired. The velocity–time graph is the broken line in Fig. 6.10.

To find the acceleration for the actual motion you need to know the formula for the air resistance. Suppose that this has the form kv^2 newtons, and that the mass of the cannonball is M kg. Then since the terminal speed in vertical fall is $50\,\mathrm{m\,s^{-1}}$, the weight $10M$ must balance the resistance kv^2 when $v = 50$. This is expressed by the equation

$$10M = 2500k, \quad \text{so} \quad k = 0.004M.$$

Fig. 6.9 shows the forces on the cannonball as it leaves the mortar barrel. Since the speed is $40\,\mathrm{m\,s^{-1}}$, the resistance is $1600k$, or $6.4M$ newtons.

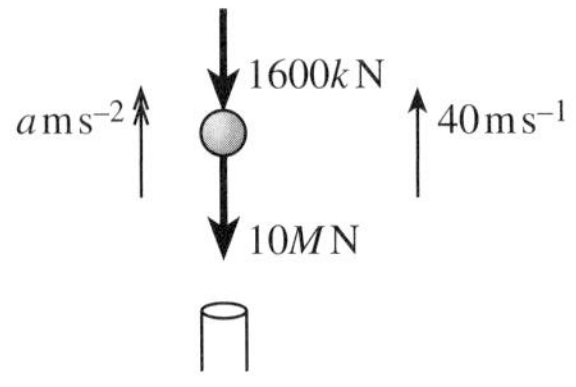

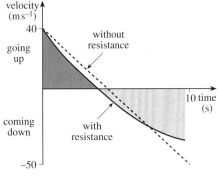

Fig. 6.9

$$\mathcal{R}(\uparrow) \qquad -10M - 6.4M = Ma,$$

so $\quad a = -16.4.$

The cannonball therefore has a deceleration of $16.4\,\mathrm{m\,s^{-2}}$ as it leaves the barrel.

At its highest point $v = 0$, so the air resistance is zero. Here, therefore, the cannonball simply has the acceleration due to gravity, $10\,\mathrm{m\,s^{-2}}$.

These calculations show that the velocity–time graph has the shape of Fig. 6.10. When $t = 0$ the gradient is -16.4, steeper than the gradient of -10 for the broken line representing the motion without resistance. But when $v = 0$, as it crosses the time-axis, the gradient is -10, so it is parallel to the broken line. Since the terminal speed is $50\,\mathrm{m\,s^{-1}}$, the graph can never go below $v = -50$.

Fig. 6.10

The greatest height of the cannonball is shown by the area of the region shaded dark grey. It looks as if this is roughly three-quarters of the corresponding area for the broken line, which is 80, so the cannonball rises to a height of about 60 m. The time when the cannonball enters the sea is shown by the value of t for which the area of the light grey region exceeds that of the dark grey region by 100. This is not so easy to estimate, but it is probably not very different from the value for the motion without resistance.

Exercise 6C

1 A particle of mass $\frac{1}{2}$ kg is placed at a point O on a track inclined at an angle $\sin^{-1} \frac{1}{2}$ to the horizontal. It is projected up the track with a speed of $12 \, \text{m s}^{-1}$. There is a frictional force of magnitude $2 \, \text{N}$, which acts in a direction opposite to the direction of motion.

    a Find the deceleration of the particle when it is moving up the track, and the acceleration when it is moving down.

    b Find how far the particle goes up the track, and how long it takes to do so.

    c Find how long it takes for the particle to return to O, and its speed when it reaches O.

    d Draw the (t,v) graph for the motion of the particle up to the time when it gets back to O, and sketch the (t,s) graph.

    What would be the answers to **b** and **c** if there were no friction? Compare the corresponding (t,v) and (t,s) graphs with those you have already drawn.

2 A smooth track is inclined to the horizontal at an angle of $\sin^{-1} \frac{3}{5}$. A particle of mass m is placed on the track at a point O, and projected directly up the track with speed $24 \, \text{m s}^{-1}$. Find how far the particle goes up the track, the speed at which it returns to O, and the time that it takes from the instant of projection until it gets back to O.

    What would the corresponding answers be if the plane were rough with coefficient of friction $\frac{9}{20}$?

3 A rock of mass $20 \, \text{kg}$ falls from a height. As it falls, it experiences air resistance of magnitude $0.08v^2$ newtons, where v is its speed in m s^{-1}. Find the terminal speed of the rock. With what acceleration will it be falling when its speed is $25 \, \text{m s}^{-1}$?

4 A cat falls from a branch of a tall tree and lands on the ground 3 seconds later. Neglecting air resistance, estimate the height of the branch and the speed at which the cat is falling just before it lands.

    If air resistance is taken into account, will the height and the speed be larger or smaller than the values you have calculated?

    The air resistance is modelled by an expression of the form kv newtons, where v is the cat's speed in m s^{-1}. If the cat has mass $2\frac{1}{2}$ kg, and its terminal speed is $50 \, \text{m s}^{-1}$, find the value of the constant k. Calculate the cat's acceleration when it is falling at $10 \, \text{m s}^{-1}$.

5 A child is on the balcony of a flat, 9.8 metres above the ground. She drops a brick over the railing, and it falls to the ground below. Neglecting air resistance, calculate how long it takes to fall, and how fast it is moving when it hits the ground.

    The mass of the brick is 1 kg, and when falling at $v \, \text{m s}^{-1}$ the air resistance has magnitude v newtons. What is the terminal speed of the brick? Find a formula for its acceleration when it is falling with speed $v \, \text{m s}^{-1}$.

    Draw a sketch to compare the (t,v) graphs for the fall, using the models without and with air resistance. What can you say about the values given by the two models for

    a the speed when the brick hits the ground,

    b the time that it takes to fall?

6 A skydiver of mass m kg steps out of an aircraft and starts to fall. The air resistance when his speed is v m s^{-1} is given by kv^2 newtons. If his terminal speed is 40 m s^{-1}, find an expression for k in terms of m.

When his speed reaches 16 m s^{-1} he adopts a position for which the air resistance is $4kv^2$ newtons. Find his new terminal speed. Find also the acceleration with which he is falling

   a just before he adopts the new position,

   b just after he adopts the new position.

7 A child throws a ball of mass 0.1 kg vertically upwards with a speed of 8 m s^{-1} from a height of 0.5 m above the ground, and catches it at the same level. Ignoring air resistance, calculate the greatest height of the ball above the ground, and the time it is in the air.

Suppose that the air resistance is modelled by the expression $0.02v$ newtons, where v is the speed of the ball in m s^{-1}. Calculate the acceleration of the ball

   a just after it is thrown,   **b** at the highest point.

With this model, what can you say about

   i the greatest height of the ball above the ground,

   ii the speed at which it is falling just before it is caught,

   iii the acceleration of the ball just before it is caught?

On another occasion the child drops the ball from the top of a high tower. What can you say about the speed at which it hits the ground?

Miscellaneous exercise 6

1 Humpty Dumpty sat on a wall 3.2 m high. When he fell off, how long did he take to reach the ground, and how fast was he moving when he hit it?

2 Two particles P and Q move vertically under gravity. The graphs show the upward velocity v m s^{-1} of the particles at time t s, for $0 \leq t \leq 4$. P starts with velocity V m s^{-1} and Q starts from rest.

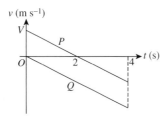

   i Find the value of V.

Given that Q reaches the horizontal ground when $t = 4$, find

   ii the speed with which Q reaches the ground,

   iii the height of Q above the ground when $t = 0$.

(Cambridge International AS and A level Mathematics 9709/41
Paper 4 Q1 November 2010)

3 The top of a cliff is 40 metres above the level of the sea. A man in a boat, close to the bottom of the cliff, is in difficulty and fires a distress signal vertically upwards from sea level. Find

   i the speed of projection of the signal given that it reaches a height of 5 m above the top of the cliff,

   ii the length of time for which the signal is above the level of the top of the cliff.

   The man fires another distress signal vertically upwards from sea level. This signal is above the level of the top of the cliff for $\sqrt{(17)}$ s.

   iii Find the speed of projection of the second signal.

   (Cambridge International AS and A level Mathematics 9709/41
   Paper 4 Q3 June 2013)

4 Bheki is standing on the flat roof of a house 6 m high, and Abel is on the ground vertically below. Abel throws a ball up to Bheki with a speed of 17 m s⁻¹, and Bheki catches it on the way down. How long is the ball in the air, and how fast is it moving as Bheki catches it?

5 A particle is projected vertically upwards with speed 9 m s⁻¹ from a point 3.15 m above horizontal ground. The particle moves freely under gravity until it hits the ground. For the particle's motion from the instant of projection until the particle hits the ground, find the total distance travelled and the total time taken.

   (Cambridge International AS and A level Mathematics 9709/41
   Paper 4 Q4 June 2014)

89

6 A particle of mass 3 kg falls from rest at a point 5 m above the surface of a liquid which is in a container. There is no instantaneous change in speed of the particle as it enters the liquid. The depth of the liquid in the container is 4 m. The downward acceleration of the particle while it is moving in the liquid is 5.5 m s⁻².

   i Find the resistance to motion of the particle while it is moving in the liquid.

   ii Sketch the velocity–time graph for the motion of the particle, from the time it starts to move until the time it reaches the bottom of the container. Show on your sketch the velocity and the time when the particle enters the liquid, and when the particle reaches the bottom of the container.

   (Cambridge International AS and A level Mathematics 9709/41
   Paper 4 Q6 November 2014)

7 A very deep shaft is drilled vertically through the earth. When a brick is dropped into the shaft, the sound of the brick hitting the bottom is heard 7.7 seconds later. Taking the speed of sound to be 350 m s⁻¹, find the depth of the shaft.

8 A helicopter is hovering 500 m above the ground. A package is dropped from the helicopter, and 2 seconds later a second package is dropped from the same position. Find expressions for the difference in height of the two packages, distinguishing the cases $0 \leq t \leq 2$, $2 < t \leq 10$, $10 < t \leq 12$ and $t > 12$. Sketch a graph to show this difference in height, and find its greatest value.

9 A parachutist with her equipment has mass 72 kg. The speed with which she lands is equal to the speed with which she would hit the ground if she jumped off a wall 3.2 m high. Taking this to be her terminal speed with the parachute open, and supposing the air resistance when she is falling at $v\,\mathrm{m\,s^{-1}}$ to be given by the expression kv newtons, find the value of k.

When she jumps from an aircraft, she falls a distance of 40 m before opening her parachute. What can you say about the speed with which she is then falling, and her deceleration when she first opens her parachute? Draw a rough sketch of the (t,v) graph for the complete drop.

10 When an object falls through a liquid, three forces act on it: its weight, the buoyancy and the resistance of the liquid. Two spheres, of mass $\frac{1}{2}$ kg and $1\frac{1}{2}$ kg respectively, have the same radius, so that they have the same buoyancy of 3.2 newtons, and the same resistance formula, $5v$ newtons when falling at speed $v\,\mathrm{m\,s^{-1}}$. Both spheres enter the liquid falling vertically at $1\,\mathrm{m\,s^{-1}}$. Calculate the terminal speeds of the two spheres, and the acceleration or deceleration when they enter the liquid. Using the same axes, sketch (t,v) graphs for the two spheres.

If the depth of the liquid is 10 m, show that the heavier sphere reaches the bottom after a time between 4 and 10 seconds. Find bounds for the time that the lighter sphere takes to reach the bottom.

11 An object of mass m kg falling from rest has terminal speed $20\,\mathrm{m\,s^{-1}}$. Two models are suggested for the air resistance force: k_1v newtons or k_2v^2 newtons, where k_1, k_2 are constant and v is the speed in $\mathrm{m\,s^{-1}}$. Find expressions for k_1 and k_2 in terms of m, and hence find expressions for the acceleration of the object at speed $v\,\mathrm{m\,s^{-1}}$ according to the two models. Using the same axes, draw graphs of these two expressions and show that, at all speeds up to $20\,\mathrm{m\,s^{-1}}$, the acceleration predicted by model 2 is greater than that predicted by model 1.

Sketch (t,v) graphs for the falling objects according to the two models. Which model predicts the shorter time to fall a given distance from rest?

Revision exercise 1

1   An iceberg breaks off from the Antarctic continent and floats due north at constant velocity. Its latitude south decreases by $1°$ in 8 days. Taking the circumference of the Earth to be 40000 km, calculate the speed of the iceberg in ms^{-1}.

2   A train increases speed from $40\,ms^{-1}$ to $60\,ms^{-1}$ in a distance of 2 km. If the acceleration is constant, find

   a   the acceleration,   b   the time it takes.

3   A motorcyclist leaves a town travelling at $15\,ms^{-1}$, and accelerates at $2.5\,ms^{-2}$. Write expressions for the distance travelled in the next t seconds, and the speed after that time. How long will he take to go 200 m, and how fast will he then be going?

4   A shopper pushes a loaded supermarket trolley of total mass 60 kg with a horizontal force of 40 N. There is a resistance to motion of 25 N. Find how long she takes to reach a walking speed of $1.5\,ms^{-1}$ from rest, and how far the trolley goes in that time.

5   An airliner of mass 60 tonnes lands at a speed of $70\,ms^{-1}$. The reverse thrust of the engines reduces this speed to $20\,ms^{-1}$ in 10 s. Neglecting air resistance, calculate the magnitude of the reverse thrust.

   Would you get a larger or smaller value than this if air resistance is taken into account?

6   A rowing crew with its boat has a total mass of 800 kg. Starting from rest, the boat reaches a speed of $5\,ms^{-1}$ in 25 s. If the resistance of the water is 320 N, find the average contribution to the forward force on the boat made by each of the eight rowers.

7   A crane lowers a container of mass 5 tonnes gently on to a quay. At a height of 10 m above the quay the container is descending at $4\,ms^{-1}$. This is reduced to zero with constant deceleration. Calculate the tension in the cable.

8   A car accelerates using three gears to reach a speed of $30\,ms^{-1}$ from rest. The speed ranges and the corresponding accelerations are given in the table for each gear. Each gearchange takes 1 second, during which time the speed of the car is constant.

Gear	first	second	third
Speed range (ms^{-1})	0 to 5	5 to 20	20 to 30
Acceleration (ms^{-2})	2.5	1.5	1

   Draw a (t,v) graph to show the motion of the car. Calculate the time the car takes to reach $30\,ms^{-1}$, and the distance travelled while it does so.

9   A loaded airport luggage trolley has a total weight of 900 N. It is being wheeled down a ramp at an angle of $8°$ to the horizontal. What force parallel to the ramp must be exerted to hold it steady?

   A similar trolley is being pushed up the ramp by a force applied at an angle of $15°$ to the ramp. What force must be exerted to keep it moving at a constant speed?

10 A car of mass 1500 kg making an emergency stop leaves skid marks 7 m long on the road. If the coefficient of friction between the tyres and the road is 1.5, calculate how fast the car was travelling when the brakes were applied.

11 A train braking with constant deceleration covers 1 km in 20 s, and a second kilometre in 30 s. Find the deceleration. What further distance will it cover before coming to a stop, and how long will this take?

12 A sailor fires a distress flare vertically upwards with a speed of 40 m s⁻¹. How high above the sea does it rise? For how long will it be more than 50 m above the sea?

13 A quarry 20 m deep is surrounded by a high fence. A boy standing on the rim behind the fence throws a brick upwards with a speed of 5 m s⁻¹, so that it goes over the fence and drops into the quarry. How long does the brick take to land on the floor of the quarry?

14 A magnetic hook of weight 0.8 N is placed on the side of a refrigerator. The force of magnetic attraction is 13 N, and the coefficient of friction between the base of the hook and the refrigerator is 0.6. What is the largest weight that the hook can support?

15 A sack of weight 600 N is being loaded on to a truck up a ramp inclined at 18° to the horizontal. A rope attached to the sack is held at an angle of 25° to the ramp. The coefficient of friction between the sack and the ramp is 0.3. What tension in the rope is needed

    a   to prevent the sack from sliding down the ramp,

    b   to pull the sack up the ramp at a steady speed?

16 A marker buoy of mass 5 kg is dropped into the sea from a helicopter at a height of 40 m. After the buoy enters the water it experiences a buoyancy force of 300 N. If there is no loss of speed as the buoy enters the water, find how far it sinks below the surface. Find also how long after it is dropped the buoy returns to the surface.

Discuss how these answers would be affected if the resistance of the air and of the water were included in the calculation.

17 A naval gun has a barrel 4 m long. When fired horizontally, a shell of mass 2 kg emerges from the muzzle at a speed of 500 m s⁻¹. The force from the expanding gases inside the barrel may be taken to have a constant value of 80 kN. Calculate the resistance to the motion of the shell from the sides of the barrel.

Would the answer be substantially different if the barrel was angled at 40° to the horizontal?

18 A hot-air balloon of mass 500 kg is descending at a speed of 5 m s⁻¹ with an acceleration of 0.2 m s⁻². What mass of ballast must be thrown out to reduce the acceleration to zero?

If twice this amount of ballast is thrown out, how much further will the balloon descend before it starts to climb?

19 The speed limit on a motorway is 120 km per hour, but because of road works there is a stretch of 2.4 km for which the speed limit is reduced to 80 km per hour. There is a warning notice 0.5 km before the restriction starts. A law-abiding

driver begins to slow down as she passes the notice, with constant deceleration, so that her speed has dropped to the required level as she reaches the road works. After the end of the restriction she accelerates back to the regular speed limit in 9 seconds. Illustrate her journey with a (t,v) graph, and find how much time she loses as a result of the road works.

20 A box of mass m has to be moved across a horizontal stage. If it is pulled with a force of $\frac{1}{2}mg\sqrt{2}$ at 45° to the upwards vertical, it will move. If it is pushed with a force of $\frac{1}{2}mg\sqrt{2}$ at 45° to the downward vertical, it won't move. What can you deduce about the coefficient of friction?

21 A bed has to be pushed across a room. If one person pushes, the bed will move with acceleration a_1. If two or three people push, it will move with acceleration a_2 or a_3 respectively. Assuming that each person pushes with force of the same magnitude, and that the resistance to motion is the same in each case, show that $a_3 = 2a_2 - a_1$.

22 A sledge accelerates down a hill with a gradient of 28% (that is, at an angle of $\sin^{-1}0.28$ to the horizontal). At the foot of the hill the ground flattens out horizontally, and the sledge comes to rest in 40 m after 10 s. Find the speed of the sledge at the bottom of the hill, and the value of the coefficient of friction.

Assuming that the coefficient of friction is the same throughout the ride, find the acceleration down the hill, and how far up the hill the sledge was to begin with.

23 A man on a bicycle, of total mass 100 kg, is free-wheeling at a constant speed of 15 m s^{-1} down a hill with a gradient of 10%. He wants to slow down to a safer speed, so he applies the brake lightly to produce a constant braking force of 84 N. The air resistance is proportional to the square of the speed.

   a Calculate the deceleration when he first applies the brake.

   b Calculate the deceleration when his speed has dropped to 12 m s^{-1}.

   c At what speed will his deceleration be reduced to zero?

   Draw a sketch of the (t,v) graph for the motion.

24 Explain why a runner's acceleration cannot exceed 10μ m s^{-2}, where μ is the coefficient of friction between her shoes and the track.

   The highest speed that a runner can keep up in an 800-metre race is 8 m s^{-1}. Show that the fastest time she can hope to achieve from a standing start is $\left(100 + \frac{2}{5\mu}\right)$ seconds. By how much could she better her time by changing running shoes, increasing μ from 0.5 to 1?

25 A valley is formed between two hills, which are at angles of $\alpha°$ and $\beta°$ to the horizontal.

   A skier starts from rest on the slope of the first hill, at a height h above the valley floor. Find his acceleration down the first hill and his deceleration up the opposite hill, supposing that there is no friction. Show that, if he exerts no force with his ski sticks, he ends up at the same height h as he started.

   Suppose now that $\alpha = 15$, $\beta = 10$ and that the coefficient of friction is 0.1. Show that he ends up at a height of about $0.4h$ above the valley floor.

Chapter 7
Newton's third law

Previous chapters have been about the equilibrium or motion of a single object. This chapter is concerned with situations in which there are two objects which interact with each other. When you have completed it, you should

- understand that forces occur in equal and opposite pairs, and be able to identify the objects on which each of the pair of forces acts
- be able to apply Newton's third law in situations involving two interacting objects
- understand what is meant by the tension in a string
- be able to solve problems on pairs of objects connected by a string, which may pass over a smooth peg or a light pulley.

7.1 Forces in pairs

Imagine two cars travelling along a motorway, one in front of the other. The front car slows down just as the car behind it accelerates. The cars collide, and both suffer damage.

The front car is damaged because it experiences a large force from behind. The rear car experiences a large force in the opposite direction, from the front. These forces are shown in Fig. 7.1. The third of Newton's laws of motion states that the two forces are equal in magnitude.

Fig. 7.1

Newton's third law   **If an object A exerts a force on an object B, then B exerts a force on A of the same magnitude in the opposite direction.**

This is neatly summarised by Newton's own statement, which (translated) was that 'action and reaction are always equal and opposite'. But in the case of the cars it is not clear which force is the 'action' and which the 'reaction'. Both drivers contributed to the accident, and each would probably say that it was the action of the other that caused it.

The important point about Newton's third law is that it applies to every kind of force. Here are some more examples.

Normal contact forces   Think of a person riding a horse. Fig. 7.2 shows the forces on the rider: her weight W and the normal contact force of magnitude R from the horse supporting her.

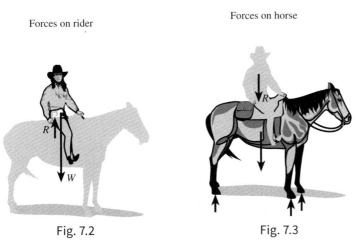

Forces on rider

Forces on horse

Fig. 7.2   Fig. 7.3

What about the horse? The forces on the horse (Fig. 7.3) similarly include its weight and normal contact forces from the ground. But the horse is also aware of the rider, because there is a normal contact force acting downwards on its back. Newton's third law states that this force also has magnitude R.

It is important to understand that this last force is *not* the weight of the rider. The definition of weight is that it is the force with which the Earth attracts the rider. It is a force on the rider, not on the horse.

If the rider is simply moving horizontally, then R would equal W, so that the force on the horse's back would have the same magnitude as the rider's weight. But if the rider is moving up and down in the saddle, then she will have some vertical acceleration, and in that case R will not equal W.

Notice that to show the forces two diagrams were needed, one for the rider and one for the horse. You shouldn't try to economise by putting all these forces on a single diagram, because it wouldn't then be clear which forces act on the rider and which on the horse.

Frictional forces   Here is an experiment for you to try. You need a trolley with a rough-ish top and a large, full teapot. Place the teapot on the trolley, and get a friend to hold the trolley still. Now place your hand on the side of the teapot facing the end of the trolley, and gradually increase the force until the teapot moves along the top of the trolley.

Now ask your friend to let go, and repeat the experiment with the trolley free to move. This time you will probably find that as you push the teapot it is the trolley which moves, and the teapot stays in the same position on the trolley.

What is the force which makes the trolley move? It can't be your push, because that is a force on the teapot, not on the trolley.

Fig. 7.4 and Fig. 7.5 analyse the forces on the teapot and on the trolley respectively. In the first part of the experiment, when your friend is holding the trolley, you have to increase your push until it exceeds the limiting friction between the teapot and the top of the trolley. Since the teapot is full, and the normal contact force equals the weight of the teapot, this limiting friction will be quite a large force.

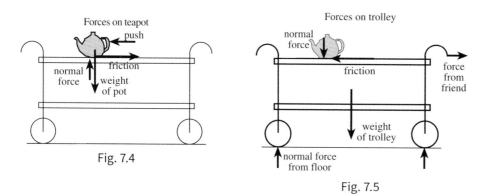

Fig. 7.4

Fig. 7.5

There are two forces from the trolley on the teapot: the normal contact force and the friction. So by Newton's third law there are equal and opposite forces from the teapot on the trolley. The frictional force on the trolley is balanced by the force exerted by your friend. As your push increases, the friction increases, so your friend's force must also increase. But once the teapot starts to move, friction has reached its limiting value, and your friend won't have to increase his force any more.

When the trolley is free to move, your push on the teapot is still opposed by friction, and there is an equal and opposite frictional force on the trolley, but there is no other horizontal force acting against it. So the trolley will start to accelerate. And because the frictional force is much less than its limiting value, the teapot will not slide on the trolley top but will also accelerate with the trolley.

Gravity forces   The force which causes the Moon to go round the Earth is the force of the Earth's gravity. If there weren't any gravity, then you know from Newton's first law that the Moon would move in a straight line rather than (approximately) in a circle.

The force on the Moon has a magnitude of about 2×10^{20} newtons. By Newton's third law, the Moon exerts a gravitational force of the same magnitude on the Earth. The most obvious evidence of this force is in the oceans; tides are caused mainly by the gravitational attraction of the Moon.

You might ask why the Moon's gravity doesn't make the Earth rotate round the Moon. The answer is that, to a small extent, it does. In fact, both the Earth and the Moon rotate about a common point; but because the Earth is so much heavier, that point is below the Earth's surface, and you would need very accurate instruments to detect the effect.

If you drop a brick, its weight is the force of attraction from the Earth. By Newton's third law, the brick also attracts the Earth with an equal force in the opposite direction. But since the Earth has mass about 10^{25} times that of the brick, the effect of this force is insignificant.

7.2   Calculations using Newton's third law

EXAMPLE 7.2.1

A pick-up truck of mass 1200 kg tows a trailer of mass 400 kg. There is air resistance of 140 N on the truck, but the resistance to the motion of the trailer is negligible. A coupling connects the trailer to the truck. Find the force from the coupling, and the driving force on the truck, when the truck and trailer accelerate at $0.5 \, \text{m s}^{-2}$.

Fig. 7.6 shows the horizontal forces on the trailer and on the truck. (To avoid complicating the diagrams, the vertical forces, weights and normal contact forces from the ground, are left out.) The only horizontal force on the trailer is the force from the coupling, denoted by C N. By Newton's third law, there is an equal force in the opposite direction on the truck. The driving force on the truck is denoted by D N.

Fig. 7.6

For the trailer,

$$\mathcal{R}(\rightarrow) \quad C = 400 \times 0.5, \quad \text{so} \quad C = 200.$$

For the truck,

$$\mathcal{R}(\rightarrow) \quad D - C - 140 = 1200 \times 0.5.$$

Since $C = 200$, this gives $D = 200 + 140 + 600 = 940$.

The force from the coupling is 200 N, and the driving force is 940 N.

EXAMPLE 7.2.2

A man of weight 750 N tries to push a bookcase of weight 1200 N across the floor. The coefficient of friction between the bookcase and the floor is 0.4. How rough must the contact between his shoes and the floor be for this to be possible?

The forces on the bookcase and on the man are shown in Fig. 7.7.

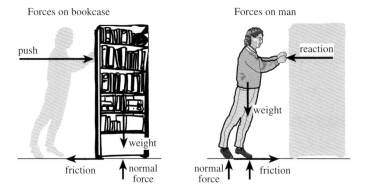

Fig. 7.7

The normal contact force on the bookcase is equal to its weight of 1200 N, so the maximum frictional force is 0.4×1200 N, which is 480 N. To move the bookcase, the man must push with a force larger than this.

There is a force equal to this in the opposite direction acting horizontally on the man, and this is balanced by the friction from the soles of his shoes. So this frictional force must be larger than 480 N.

The normal contact force on the man's shoes is equal to his weight, which is 750 N. The coefficient of friction between his shoes and the floor must therefore be greater than $\frac{480}{750}$, which is 0.64.

EXAMPLE 7.2.3

A bar magnet of mass 0.2 kg hangs from a string. A metal sphere, of mass 0.5 kg, is held underneath the magnet by a magnetic force of 20 N. The string is then pulled upwards with a force of T N. Find the largest possible value of T if the sphere is not to separate from the magnet.

As long as the sphere remains attached to the magnet, there are two forces between them: the magnetic force and a normal contact force of R N. By Newton's third law, these act in opposite directions on the magnet and the sphere. Suppose that the magnet and sphere accelerate upwards at a m s^{-2}.

Fig. 7.8 shows the forces on the sphere and on the magnet, whose weights are 5 N and 2 N respectively.

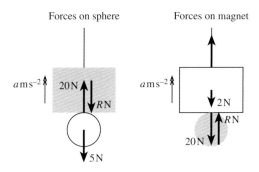

Fig. 7.8

For the sphere, $\mathcal{R}(\uparrow)$ $20 - R - 5 = 0.5a$.

For the magnet, $\mathcal{R}(\uparrow)$ $T - 2 - 20 + R = 0.2a$.

You can eliminate a from these two equations and deduce that

$$2(20 - R - 5) - 5(T - 2 - 20 + R) = 2(0.5a) - 5(0.2a) = 0,$$

so $40 - 2R - 10 - 5T + 10 + 100 - 5R = 0$, which simplifies to $5T + 7R = 140$.

Since contact is maintained, the normal contact force cannot be negative. It follows that $5T \le 140$, so $T \le 28$.

If the sphere is not to separate from the magnet, the force from the string cannot exceed 28 newtons.

EXAMPLE 7.2.4

A student has two books lying flat on the table, one on top of the other. She wants to consult the lower book. To extract it, she pushes it to the left with a force of Q N. To prevent the upper book moving as well, she exerts a force of P N on the upper book to the right. The lower book then slides out, and the upper book remains stationary. The weights of the upper and the lower books are 8 N and 7 N respectively. Between the two books the coefficient of friction is 0.25, and between the lower book and the table it is 0.4. Calculate P and Q.

The forces on each book are shown in Fig. 7.9. The motion of the lower book is opposed by two frictional forces, F N from the upper book and G N from the table, both acting to the right. By Newton's third law, there is a frictional force of F N on the upper book acting to the left.

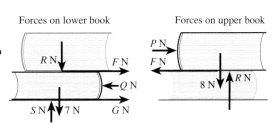

Fig. 7.9

There are normal contact forces of R N between the books, and S N on the lower book from the table. Since there is motion, the frictional forces will have their limiting values, $F = 0.25R$ and $G = 0.4S$.

If the lower book moves at a steady speed, the forces on both books will be in equilibrium.

For the upper book, $\quad \mathcal{R}(\rightarrow)\ P - F = 0, \qquad \mathcal{R}(\uparrow)\ R - 8 = 0.$

For the lower book, $\quad \mathcal{R}(\rightarrow)\ F + G - Q = 0, \quad \mathcal{R}(\uparrow)\ S - 7 - R = 0.$

From these equations you can calculate $R = 8$, $S = 15$, $F = 2$, $G = 6$, $P = 2$, $Q = 8$.

The student pushes the lower book to the left with a force of 8 newtons, and prevents the upper book from moving with a force of 2 newtons to the right.

Exercise 7A

1 A crate of weight 80 N is stacked on top of a crate of weight 100 N, on horizontal ground as shown. Make separate sketches showing the forces acting on the upper and lower crates. Indicate the magnitudes of the forces in your sketches.

2 A birdbath consists of a concrete pillar of weight 1000 N with a concrete bowl of weight 200 N on top, as shown in the diagram. State the magnitude and direction of the force exerted by

   a the pillar on the bowl,   **b** the bowl on the pillar,

   c the ground on the pillar.

3 A sack is in contact with both the base and the vertical back of an excavator scoop, as shown in the diagram. The excavator is moving forwards at constant speed in a straight line. Make separate sketches showing the forces acting on

   a the sack,   **b** the scoop.

4 A man of mass 75 kg travels upwards in a lift which is decelerating at $0.4\,\mathrm{m\,s^{-2}}$. Make a sketch showing the forces acting on the man.

Find the magnitude of the force exerted by the man on the floor of the lift.

5 A reckless truck-driver loads two identical untethered crates stacked one upon the other as shown in the diagram. No sliding takes place. Make separate sketches to show the forces acting on each crate when the truck travels on a horizontal straight road

   a with constant speed,   **b** while accelerating,

   c while decelerating.

Each crate has mass 250 kg. Calculate the magnitude of the frictional force exerted on

   i the upper crate by the lower,

   ii the lower crate by the deck of the truck, when the acceleration of the truck is $1.5\,\mathrm{m\,s^{-2}}$.

6 In an archaeological reconstruction a group of students try to drag an ancient warship along a beach. This requires a horizontal force of 5000 N. The average weight of a student is 600 N, and the coefficient of friction between each student's feet and the sand is 0.2. How many students are needed?

7   A steel block of weight W rests on a horizontal surface in an inaccessible part of a machine. The coefficient of friction between the block and the surface is μ. To extract the block, a magnetic rod is inserted into the machine and this rod is used to pull the block at a constant speed along the surface with a force F. The magnetic force of attraction between the rod and the block is M. Explain why

   a $M > \mu W$,   **b** $F = \mu W$.

8   A car of mass 1200 kg, towing a caravan of mass 800 kg, is travelling along a motorway at a constant speed of $20\,\mathrm{m\,s^{-1}}$. There are air resistance forces on the car and the caravan, of magnitude 100 N and 400 N respectively. Calculate the magnitude of the force on the caravan from the towbar, and the driving force on the car.

The car brakes suddenly, and begins to decelerate at a rate of $1.5\,\mathrm{m\,s^{-2}}$. Calculate the force on the car from the towbar. What effect will the driver notice?

9   From the instant that a pile-driver of mass 2000 kg comes into contact with a pile of mass 600 kg, they move vertically downwards together, with common deceleration $0.8\,\mathrm{m\,s^{-2}}$, until they come to rest. Make separate sketches showing the forces acting on the pile-driver and on the pile.

Find the magnitudes of all the forces exerted on the pile

   a when it is moving,   **b** after it has come to rest.

10 A drop-forge hammer, of mass 1500 kg, falls under gravity on to a piece of hot metal which rests in a fixed die. From the instant that the hammer strikes the piece of metal until it comes to rest, the hammer is decelerating at $1.5\,\mathrm{m\,s^{-2}}$. Make sketches showing the forces on the hammer and on the metal while they are in contact.

Find the magnitude of the force exerted by the hammer on the piece of metal

   a while the hammer is decelerating,

   b after the hammer has come to rest.

11 Three identical boxes, each of weight W, are to be stacked one on top of another against a vertical wall. The lowermost box is in contact with the wall, and the other two boxes are positioned as shown in the diagram. The middle box is pushed into position by the application of a horizontal force of magnitude P. Make separate sketches showing the forces acting on

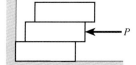

   a the uppermost box,   **b** the middle box.

Show that $P > 2\mu W$, where μ is the coefficient of friction between any two boxes.

Show also that, if $P > 4\mu W$, sliding takes place between the upper and middle boxes, and that if $P \le 4\mu W$, sliding between these boxes does not take place.

12 With the situation in Question 11, suppose that the force is first applied to the top box, until it touches the wall. How large a force will be required? Will the middle box move as well?

Once the top box is touching the wall, a force is applied to the middle box. How large a force will be needed to move it?

13 Two cylinders of equal radii each have weight W. They are at rest on a smooth slope of inclination $\alpha°$ to the horizontal, the lower of the two cylinders being in contact with a smooth vertical wall as shown in the diagram. Find, giving your answer in terms of W and $\alpha°$, the magnitude of the force exerted by

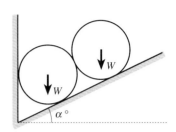

   a the slope on the upper cylinder,

   b the lower cylinder on the upper cylinder,

   c the upper cylinder on the lower cylinder,

   d the wall on the lower cylinder,

   e the slope on the lower cylinder.

7.3 Strings, ropes, chains and cables

In Fig. 7.10 one end of a string is tied to a hook in a wall. You hold the other end so that the string is horizontal, and pull on it with a force of magnitude P (in any units) to the left.

Usually the weight of the string is very small compared with the size of P. It can be left out of the calculations without much loss of accuracy. The string in the model is then described as 'light', which means that its weight, and its mass, are taken to be zero.

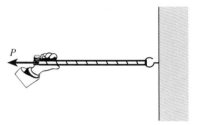

Fig. 7.10

Now consider the equilibrium of the string. There must be a force on it to counteract your pull, and that force comes from the hook. So the hook also exerts a force on the string of magnitude P to the right (see Fig. 7.11).

However you are not pulling on the hook, but on the string. You pull on the string with a force P to the left, so by Newton's third law the string exerts on you a force of magnitude P to the right.

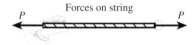

Fig. 7.11

Newton's third law applies similarly at the other end. The hook exerts on the string a force P to the right, so the string exerts on the hook a force P to the left.

For this reason, when you draw a string in a diagram, you show it with a line and arrows pointing inwards, as in Fig. 7.12. These arrows indicate the force which the string exerts on the objects attached to its two ends.

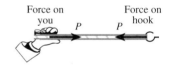

Fig. 7.12

> **A light string exerts forces of equal magnitude on the objects attached to its two ends. These forces act along the line of the string, and are directed inwards at each end. The magnitude of the force at either end is called the tension in the string.**

The same ideas apply to other objects such as ropes, chains, cables and rods, provided that their weight can be neglected by comparison with the forces which act on them.

The difference between a rod and a string, rope or cable is that it can also exert forces which are directed outwards at each end. The magnitude of such a force is called the **thrust** in the rod.

The objects at the end of the string may be stationary, as in the example just discussed, or they may move. For example, the same ideas could be applied to the cable joining two trucks in Fig. 7.13.

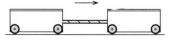

Fig. 7.13

In this case, another important property of the cable is that it remains the same length as the trucks move. The cable is then said to be 'inextensible'. It follows from this that the two trucks have the same speed, and the same acceleration.

EXAMPLE 7.3.1

Suppose that in Fig. 7.13 the truck on the left has mass 30 kg, and the truck on the right has mass 50 kg. The truck on the right is pulled along with a force of 120 N. Calculate the tension in the cable.

Let the common acceleration of the two trucks be $a\,\mathrm{m\,s^{-2}}$, and denote the tension in the cable by $T\,\mathrm{N}$. In Fig. 7.14 the middle part of the cable is shown as a light grey line. This is a reminder of what the problem is about, but separates out the forces on the two trucks. Only the horizontal forces are shown in the diagram.

For the left truck,

$$\mathcal{R}(\rightarrow)\quad T = 30a.$$

For the right truck,

$$\mathcal{R}(\rightarrow)\quad 120 - T = 50a.$$

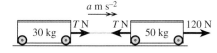

Fig. 7.14

It is probably simplest to begin by finding a, by substituting $30a$ for T in the second equation, which gives $120 - 30a = 50a$, so $a = \dfrac{120}{80} = 1.5$. Then

$$T = 30 \times 1.5 = 45.$$

The tension in the cable is 45 newtons.

7.4 Pegs and pulleys

Another property of a string is that it is flexible, so that it can be passed round a fixed peg. The string then has two straight sections and a curved section where it is in contact with the peg, as in Fig. 7.15. The argument used above to explain the force on the hook can be applied to each of the straight sections of the string. This means that the tension in each of the straight sections acts on the curved section round the peg.

If the contact between the string and the peg is rough, there could be some friction acting on the string round the circumference of the peg, and in that case the tensions in the two straight sections would be different. But if the contact is smooth, the tensions in the two straight sections are the same.

Fig. 7.15

Another possibility is for the string to pass round a pulley, which can rotate on a fixed axis. Now, if the surface is rough, the pulley will go round with the string. (The same applies when a chain passes round a cog wheel.) To make the pulley go round, the tensions in the two straight sections have to be different. But if the mass of the pulley is small, and if it runs on smooth bearings, the difference in the tensions is very small, so it can be neglected in a first approximation.

Smooth pegs and light pulleys are further examples of mathematical models often used in mechanics. You will never find them in practice, but you can often use the models in calculations with only a small loss of accuracy.

> **When a string passes round a smooth peg, or a light pulley with smooth bearings, the tension in the string is the same on either side.**

EXAMPLE 7.4.1

Repairs are being carried out in a tall building. A wheel is attached at the top of the scaffolding with its axis horizontal. A rope runs over the rim of the wheel and has buckets of mass 2 kg tied to it at both ends. One bucket is filled with 8.5 kg of rubble and then released, so that it descends to ground level. With what acceleration does it move?

As always, modelling approximations have to be made. In this example, assume that the mass of the rope and the wheel can be neglected, that the wheel rotates on smooth bearings, and that the rope doesn't stretch. Then the tension in the string will be the same at both ends, and the upward acceleration of the empty bucket will have the same magnitude as the downward acceleration of the filled bucket. Denote the tension by T N, and the acceleration by a m s^{-2}.

Fig. 7.16 shows the forces on each bucket during the motion. The weights of the buckets are 20 N and 105 N.

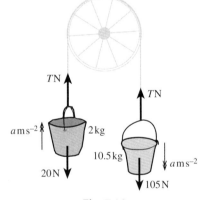

For the empty bucket,

$$\mathcal{R}(\uparrow) \quad T - 20 = 2a.$$

For the filled bucket,

$$\mathcal{R}(\downarrow) \quad 105 - T = 10.5a.$$

Adding,

$$(T - 20) + (105 - T) = 2a + 10.5a,$$

which gives $12.5a = 85$, so $a = 6.8$.

Fig. 7.16

The filled bucket descends to ground level with acceleration of 6.8 m s^{-2}.

EXAMPLE 7.4.2

A box of mass 2 kg is placed on a table. A string attached to the box passes over a smooth peg at the edge of the table, and a ball of mass 1 kg is tied to the other end. The two straight sections of the string are horizontal and vertical. If the coefficient of friction between the box and the table is 0.2, find the acceleration of the box and the ball.

Fig. 7.17 shows the forces on the box and the ball. Because the peg is smooth, the tension in the string has the same magnitude, T N, at each end. The normal contact force on the box is R N, the friction is F N, and the acceleration is a ms^{-2}. The weights are 20 N and 10 N respectively.

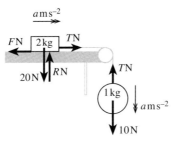

Fig. 7.17

Resolving vertically for the box gives $R = 20$. Since the system is in motion, friction will be the largest possible, so $F = 0.2 \times 20 = 4$.

For the box,　　$\mathcal{R}(\rightarrow)$　$T - F = 2a$.

For the ball,　　$\mathcal{R}(\downarrow)$　$10 - T = a$.

Adding the two equations and substituting $F = 4$ gives $10 - 4 = 3a$, so $a = 2$.

The box and the ball have an acceleration of 2 ms^{-2}.

The next example can be used as the basis of an experiment to verify the rule for finding the resolved part of a force, given in Section 4.2.

EXAMPLE 7.4.3

In the apparatus illustrated in Fig. 7.18 a mass m is attached to two strings of equal length, each of which carries a mass M at its other end. The strings are placed symmetrically over smooth nails A and B, which are at the same level. The whole system is in equilibrium. The distance between the nails is $2c$, and the mass m is at a depth d below the mid-point of AB.

Find an equation connecting M, m, c and d.

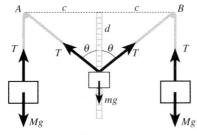

Fig. 7.18

Let the tension in each of the strings be T N, and suppose that the sloping sections of each string make an angle θ with the vertical.

For each mass M,　　$\mathcal{R}(\uparrow)$　$T - Mg = 0$.

For the mass m,　　$\mathcal{R}(\uparrow)$　$2T \cos\theta - mg = 0$.

Substituting Mg for T in the second equation and dividing by g gives $m = 2M\cos\theta$.

The sloping sections of the strings have length $\sqrt{c^2 + d^2}$, so that $\cos\theta = \dfrac{d}{\sqrt{c^2 + d^2}}$.

This gives $m = \dfrac{2Md}{\sqrt{c^2 + d^2}}$.

To use this as an experiment, keep the masses M constant but vary the mass m. Set a scale down the line of symmetry to measure the depth d, and calculate $\cos\theta = \dfrac{d}{\sqrt{c^2 + d^2}}$. If you plot $\cos\theta$ against m, you should get points which lie on a line through the origin with gradient $\dfrac{1}{2M}$.

EXAMPLE 7.4.4

On a construction site a truck of mass 400 kg is pulled up a 10° slope by a chain. The chain runs parallel to the slope up to the top, where it passes over a cog wheel of negligible mass. It then runs horizontally and is attached to the rear of a locomotive of mass 2000 kg. Neglecting any resistances, calculate the driving force needed to accelerate the truck up the slope at 0.1 m s⁻².

Fig. 7.19 shows the forces on the truck and the locomotive. Denote the tension in the chain by T N and the driving force by D N. The weight of the truck is 4000 N.

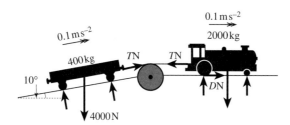

Fig. 7.19

For the truck, $\qquad\mathcal{R}(\|\text{to the slope})\qquad T - 4000\cos 80° = 400 \times 0.1,$

which gives $T = 734.5...$.

The locomotive also has acceleration 0.1 m s⁻².

For the locomotive, $\qquad\mathcal{R}(\rightarrow)\quad D - T = 2000 \times 0.1,$

so $D = 734.5... + 200 = 934.5...$.

The driving force required is about 935 N.

7.5 A way of simplifying calculations

When you have a problem to solve about two or more objects, you sometimes find that the equations have several terms which depend on the value of g. Some people find it simpler not to substitute the numerical value 10 at first, but to replace it by a letter. You can then make a single substitution of the numerical value at the end, when you calculate the answer.

Normally the letter g is used in place of the numerical value 10. For example, in Example 7.4.2, the weights of the box and the ball could be written as $2g$ newtons and g newtons respectively. The friction would then be $0.2 \times 2g$ newtons, which is $0.4g$ newtons. The two equations for the box and the ball would then be

$$\mathcal{R}(\rightarrow) \quad T - 0.4g = 2a \quad \text{and} \quad \mathcal{R}(\uparrow) \quad g - T = a,$$

which can be added to give $g - 0.4g = 3a$, so $a = 0.2g$. A single substitution of 10 for g then produces the answer $a = 2$.

In fact, using the letter g for the number 10 can be rather confusing, because in algebraic applications you have used g to stand for the quantity $10\,\mathrm{m\,s^{-2}}$, which could be written in other units such as $0.01\,\mathrm{km\,s^{-2}}$ or $1000\,\mathrm{cm\,s^{-2}}$. So in working a particular problem you need to be clear whether you are using the letter g as an abbreviation for the number 10, or whether it stands for the quantity which is the acceleration due to gravity. In the first case you need to include units in your answers, for example a force of $0.4g\,\mathrm{N}$ or an acceleration of $0.2g\,\mathrm{m\,s^{-2}}$; in the second case the units are included in the symbol for the quantity, and it would be wrong to add a unit to the symbol.

All the same, this is a useful way of avoiding over-complicated arithmetic, and you would find it useful in several of the questions in Exercise 7B. A further advantage is that in some problems the value of g cancels out, which can save you unnecessary arithmetic.

Exercise 7B

1   In the cases illustrated in the following diagrams the strings pass over small light pulleys. The contacts between the blocks and the surfaces are rough, except where they are indicated as smooth in parts **d**, **e** and **f**. The blocks are at rest and the strings taut. In each case find the tension in the string and the frictional force exerted by each surface on the block with which it is in contact.

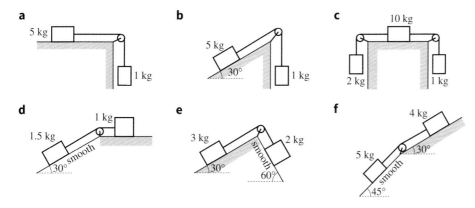

2   A tape is wound round two smooth cylinders as shown. The higher cylinder is fixed, but the lower cylinder sits in a loop formed by the tape. If the 5 kg mass descends at constant speed, calculate the mass of the lower cylinder.

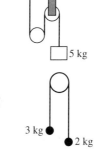

3   In the system illustrated the string passes over a smooth fixed peg. The particles are held in the positions shown, with the string taut; they are then released from rest. Find the tension in the string and the acceleration of the particles.

4 Suppose that in each of the cases illustrated in Question 1 the pulleys can rotate freely and that all the contacts between the blocks and surfaces are smooth. The blocks are held in the positions shown, with the string taut. The blocks are then released from rest. Find the acceleration of the blocks in each case.

5 A particle of mass 3 kg is attached to one end of each of two strings, s_1 and s_2. A particle of mass 2.5 kg is attached to the other end of s_1, and a particle of mass 1 kg is attached to the other end of s_2. The particles are held in the positions shown, with the strings taut and s_1 passing over a smooth fixed peg. The system is released from rest. Find the acceleration of the particles, and the tensions in s_1 and s_2.

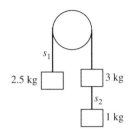

6 In the system illustrated in Question 2 suppose that the mass of the lower cylinder is 12 kg. The system is held at rest in the position shown, with the tape taut, and then released. Find the acceleration of

a the lower cylinder,   b the 5 kg mass.

7 Two particles are connected by a light inextensible string which passes over a smooth fixed peg. The heavier particle is held so that the string is taut, and the parts of the string not in contact with the pulley are vertical. When the system is released from rest the particles have an acceleration of $\frac{1}{2}g$. Find the ratio of the masses of the particles.

8 A particle of mass m is placed on a rough track which goes up at an angle $a°$ to the horizontal, where $\sin a° = 0.6$ and $\cos a° = 0.8$. The coefficient of friction is 0.5. A string is attached to the particle, and a particle of mass M is attached to the other end of the string. The string runs up the track, passes over a smooth bar at the top of the track, and then hangs vertically. Find the interval of values of M for which the system can rest in equilibrium.

Find expressions for the acceleration with which the system will move if the value of M lies outside this interval.

7.6 Internal and external forces

Suppose that a vehicle of mass 1600 kg accelerates at 0.5 m s^{-2}, and that the motion is opposed by a resistance of 140 newtons. What is the driving force, D newtons?

You can answer this question using the methods of Chapter 2. By Newton's second law, $D - 140 = 1600 \times 0.5$, so that $D = 940$.

Now compare this with Example 7.2.1, in which a pick-up truck of mass 1200 kg tows a trailer of mass 400 kg against a resistance of 140 newtons with acceleration 0.5 m s^{-2}. You found there that the driving force required is also 940 newtons.

This is hardly surprising. If the 'vehicle' in the first paragraph consists of a truck and a trailer, then it makes no difference whether you treat this as a single object or as two connected objects moving with the same velocity and acceleration.

But what you can't find by applying Newton's law to the truck-and-trailer vehicle is the force from the coupling. If you draw a diagram for the horizontal forces on the vehicle, it will look like Fig. 7.20. The only forces affecting the motion are the driving force and the resistance.

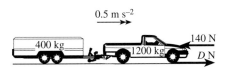

Fig. 7.20

These are called the 'external' forces on the combined vehicle. The force from the coupling on the truck and on the trailer, which had to be included in Fig. 7.6, become 'internal' forces when you are thinking of the truck-and-trailer as a single vehicle.

> **When an object is made up of two parts, each of which has the same velocity and acceleration, you can apply Newton's second law either to the object as a whole or to the parts separately.**
>
> **For the object as a whole, forces of interaction between the two parts are internal forces, and are not included in the equation.**
>
> **For the separate parts, the forces of interaction of each on the other are external forces, and are included in the equations.**

This principle also applies in Example 7.3.1. Since both trucks are moving on the same track and are connected by an inextensible cable, they have the same velocity and acceleration. You can therefore treat the two trucks together as a single object of mass 80 kg, and the only horizontal external force is the pull of 120 newtons; the tension in the cable is an internal force. The acceleration of the trucks is $\frac{120}{80}\,\mathrm{m\,s^{-2}}$, which is $1.5\,\mathrm{m\,s^{-2}}$.

But to calculate the tension in the cable you must use one or other of the Newton's law equations for the separate trucks. When you have to carry out calculations for the motion of an object which splits into two parts, you will often find it simplest to write equations for the object as a whole and for just one of the parts.

EXAMPLE 7.6.1

A dynamo of mass 1500 kg is placed in a cage of mass 500 kg, which is raised vertically by a cable from a crane. The tension in the cable is 20 400 N. Find the acceleration of the cage, and the contact force between the cage and the dynamo.

The cage and the dynamo have the same acceleration, $a\,\mathrm{m\,s^{-2}}$, so they can be treated as one object (Fig. 7.21). The only external forces are the tension in the cable and the combined weight of 2000×10 N, which is 20 000 N.

For the cage-and-dynamo,

$$\mathcal{R}(\uparrow)\ 20\,400 - 20\,000 = 2000a,$$

so $a = 0.2$.

To find the contact force, R N, you must consider either the cage or the dynamo separately. It is simpler to take the dynamo,

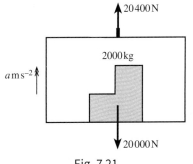

Fig. 7.21

because there are fewer forces acting on it (see Fig. 7.22). You now know that $a = 0.2$.

For the dynamo alone,

$$\mathcal{R}(\uparrow) \quad R - 15\,000 = 1500 \times 0.2,$$

so $R = 15\,300$.

The acceleration of the cage is $0.2\,\text{m}\,\text{s}^{-2}$; the contact force is $15\,300\,\text{N}$.

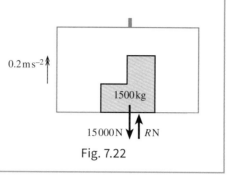

Fig. 7.22

EXAMPLE 7.6.2

Three barges travel down a river in line. Only the rear barge has an engine, which produces a forward force of $400\,\text{kN}$. The masses of the front, middle and rear barges are 1600 tonnes, 1400 tonnes and 2000 tonnes, and the water exerts on them resistances of $100\,\text{kN}$, $20\,\text{kN}$ and $30\,\text{kN}$ respectively. Find the forces in the couplings joining the barges.

The three aerial views in Fig. 7.23 show the horizontal forces on all three barges, on the front two barges and on the front barge. The acceleration is $a\,\text{m}\,\text{s}^{-2}$, and the forces in the couplings are $R\,\text{kN}$ and $S\,\text{kN}$.

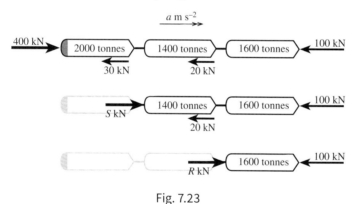

Fig. 7.23

Notice that, although tonnes (1000 kg) and kilonewtons (1000 N) are not basic SI units, they do form part of a system which is consistent with metres and seconds, so that the equation $F = ma$ can be used without any need for conversion.

There are three unknowns, but the forces in both couplings are internal forces if you take all three barges together.

For all three barges,

$\mathcal{R}$ (forwards) $400 - 100 - 20 - 30 = (1600 + 1400 + 2000)a$.

This gives $a = \dfrac{250}{5000} = 0.05$.

For the front two barges,

$\mathcal{R}$ (forwards) $S - 100 - 20 = (1600 + 1400) \times 0.05$.

For the front barge,

$\mathcal{R}$ (forwards) $R - 100 = 1600 \times 0.05$.

These equations give $S = 270$ and $R = 180$.

The forces in the front and rear couplings are $180\,\text{kN}$ and $270\,\text{kN}$ respectively.

Notice that if you use this method each equation involves just one of the unknown quantities, so you have no simultaneous equations to solve.

You can if you wish check your answers by considering the forces on one of the other barges by itself. For example, Fig. 7.24 shows the forces on the middle barge. The forces in both couplings are external forces on this barge, and the forward force is $(S - R - 20)\,\text{kN}$. With the values of R and S found, this is $70\,\text{kN}$. Since $70 = 1400 \times 0.05$, you have a check that the equation $F = ma$ is satisfied for the middle barge.

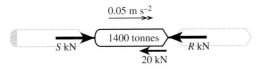

Fig. 7.24

Exercise 7C

1 A car of mass $1000\,\text{kg}$ is towing a trailer of mass $250\,\text{kg}$ along a straight road. There are constant resistances to the motion of the car and the trailer of magnitude $150\,\text{N}$ and $50\,\text{N}$ respectively. The driving force on the car has magnitude $800\,\text{N}$. Calculate the acceleration of the car and the trailer, and the tension in the towbar, when

  a the road is horizontal,

  b the road is inclined at $\sin^{-1} 0.04$ to the horizontal and the car is travelling uphill.

2 When a car of mass $1350\,\text{kg}$ tows a trailer of mass $250\,\text{kg}$ along a horizontal straight road, the resistive forces on the car and trailer have magnitude $200\,\text{N}$ and $50\,\text{N}$ respectively. Find the magnitude of the driving force on the car when the car and trailer are travelling at constant speed, and state the tension in the towbar in this case.

Find the acceleration or deceleration of the car and the trailer, and the tension in the towbar, when the driving force exerted by the car has magnitude

  a $330\,\text{N}$,   **b** $170\,\text{N}$,   **c** zero.

Find also the deceleration of the car and the trailer, and the magnitude of the force in the towbar, stating whether this force is a tension or thrust, when the driver applies the brakes and the braking force exceeds the driving force by

  d $30\,\text{N}$ **e** $70\,\text{N}$,   **f** $150\,\text{N}$.

3 A car of mass M pulls a trailer of mass m down a straight hill which is inclined at angle $\alpha°$ to the horizontal. Resistive forces of magnitudes P and Q act on the car and the trailer respectively, and the driving force on the car is F. Find an expression for the acceleration of the car and trailer, in terms of F, P, Q, M, m and α.

Show that the tension in the towbar is independent of a.

In the case when $F = P + Q$, show that the acceleration is $g\sin\alpha°$ and that the tension in the towbar is Q.

4 Five spheres, each of mass m, are joined together by four inextensible strings. The spheres hang in a vertical line as shown in the diagram, and are held at rest by a force applied to the uppermost sphere, of magnitude $5mg$, acting vertically upwards. Find the tension in each of the strings.

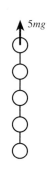

The force on the uppermost sphere is now removed. If the total air resistance acting vertically upwards on the spheres is $\frac{1}{2}mg$, find the acceleration of the system in the subsequent motion.

Find also the tension in each of the four strings if

a the air resistance on each individual sphere is $\frac{1}{10}mg$,

b the air resistance on the uppermost sphere is $\frac{3}{5}mg$ and the air resistance on each of the other four spheres is $\frac{1}{20}mg$.

Miscellaneous exercise 7

1 Particles P and Q, of masses 0.6 kg and 0.2 kg respectively, are attached to the ends of a light inextensible string which passes over a smooth fixed peg. The particles are held at rest with the string taut. Both particles are at a height of 0.9 m above the ground (see diagram). The system is released and each of the particles moves vertically. Find

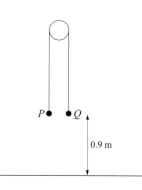

i the acceleration of P and the tension in the string before P reaches the ground,

ii the time taken for P to reach the ground.

(Cambridge International AS and A level Mathematics 9709/04 Paper 4 Q4 June 2007)

2 Particles A and B, of masses 0.2 kg and 0.3 kg respectively, are connected by a light inextensible string. The string passes over a smooth pulley at the edge of a rough horizontal table. Particle A hangs freely and particle B is in contact with the table (see diagram).

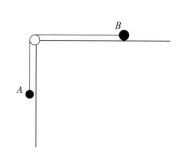

i The system is in limiting equilibrium with the string taut and A about to move downwards. Find the coefficient of friction between B and the table.

A force now acts on particle B. This force has a vertical component of 1.8 N upwards and a horizontal component of X N directed away from the pulley.

ii The system is now in limiting equilibrium with the string taut and A about to move **upwards**. Find X.

(Cambridge International AS and A level Mathematics 9709/04 Paper 4 Q4 June 2005)

3 Particles P and Q are attached to opposite ends of a light inextensible string. P is at rest on a rough horizontal table. The string passes over a small smooth pulley which is fixed at the edge of the table. Q hangs vertically below the pulley (see diagram). The force exerted on the string by the pulley has magnitude $4\sqrt{2}$ N. The coefficient of friction between P and the table is 0.8.

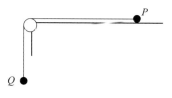

i Show that the tension in the string is 4 N and state the mass of Q.

ii Given that P is on the point of slipping, find its mass.

A particle of mass 0.1 kg is now attached to Q and the system starts to move.

iii Find the tension in the string while the particles are in motion.

(Cambridge International AS and A level Mathematics 9709/04
Paper 4 Q5 June 2006)

4 Particles A and B, of masses 0.5 kg and m kg respectively, are attached to the ends of a light inextensible string which passes over a smooth fixed pulley. Particle B is held at rest on the horizontal floor and particle A hangs in equilibrium (see diagram). B is released and each particle starts to move vertically. A hits the floor 2 s after B is released. The speed of each particle when A hits the floor is $5\,\text{m s}^{-1}$.

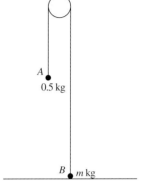

i For the motion while A is moving downwards, find

  a the acceleration of A,

  b the tension in the string.

ii Find the value of m.

(Cambridge International AS and A level Mathematics 9709/04
Paper 4 Q5 November 2008)

5 A light inextensible string has a particle A of mass 0.26 kg attached to one end and a particle B of mass 0.54 kg attached to the other end. The particle A is held at rest on a rough plane inclined at angle α to the horizontal, where $\sin\alpha = \frac{5}{13}$. The string is taut and parallel to a line of greatest slope of the plane. The string passes over a small smooth pulley at the top of the plane. Particle B hangs at rest vertically below the pulley (see diagram). The coefficient of friction between A and the plane is 0.2. Particle A is released and the particles start to move.

i Find the magnitude of the acceleration of the particles and the tension in the string.

Particle A reaches the pulley 0.4 s after starting to move.

ii Find the distance moved by each of the particles.

(Cambridge International AS and A level Mathematics 9709/41
Paper 4 Q5 June 2013)

6 Particles P and Q, of masses 0.55 kg and 0.45 kg respectively, are attached to the ends of a light inextensible string which passes over a smooth fixed pulley. The particles are held at rest with the string taut and its straight parts vertical. Both particles are at a height of 5 m above the ground (see diagram). The system is released.

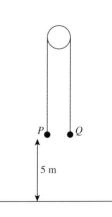

i Find the acceleration with which P starts to move

The string breaks after 2 s and in the subsequent motion P and Q move vertically under gravity.

ii At the instant that the string breaks, find

  a the height above the ground of P and of Q,

  b the speed of the particles.

iii Show that Q reaches the ground 0.8 s later than P.

(Cambridge International AS and A level Mathematics 9709/41
Paper 4 Q6 November 2009)

7 Particles *P* and *Q*, of masses 0.6 kg and 0.4 kg respectively, are attached to the ends of a light inextensible string. The string passes over a small smooth pulley which is fixed at the top of a vertical cross-section of a triangular prism. The base of the prism is fixed on horizontal ground and each of the sloping sides is smooth. Each sloping side makes an angle θ with the ground, where $\sin\theta = 0.8$. Initially the particles are held at rest on the sloping sides, with the string taut (see diagram). The particles are released and move along lines of greatest slope.

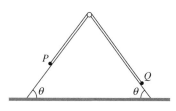

i Find the tension in the string and the acceleration of the particles while both are moving.

The speed of *P* when it reaches the ground is 2 m s^{-1}. On reaching the ground *P* comes to rest and remains at rest. *Q* continues to move up the slope but does not reach the pulley.

ii Find the time taken from the instant that the particles are released until *Q* reaches its greatest height above the ground.

(Cambridge International AS and A level Mathematics 9709/41
Paper 4 Q6 June 2012)

8 Particles *A* and *B*, of masses 0.3 kg and 0.7 kg respectively, are attached to the ends of a light inextensible string. The string passes over a fixed smooth pulley. *A* is held at rest and *B* hangs freely, with both straight parts of the string vertical and both particles at a height of 0.52 m above the floor (see diagram). *A* is released and both particles start to move.

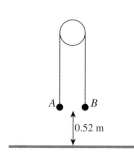

i Find the tension in the string.

When both particles are moving with speed 1.6 m s^{-1} the string breaks.

ii Find the time taken, from the instant that the string breaks, for *A* to reach the floor.

(Cambridge International AS and A level Mathematics 9709/41
Paper 4 Q6 November 2013)

9 Particles *A* of mass 0.25 kg and *B* of mass 0.75 kg are attached to opposite ends of a light inextensible string which passes over a fixed smooth pulley. The system is held at rest with the string taut and its straight parts vertical. Both particles are at a height of *h* m above the floor (see Fig. I). The system is released from rest, and 0.6 s later, when both particles are in motion, the string breaks. The particle *A* does not reach the pulley in the subsequent motion.

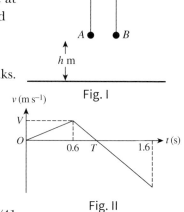

i Find the acceleration of *A* and the distance travelled by *A* before the string breaks.

The velocity–time graph shown in Fig. II is for the motion of particle *A* until it hits the floor. The velocity of *A* when the string breaks is *V* m s^{-1} and *T* s is the time taken for *A* to reach its greatest height.

ii Find the value of *V* and the value of *T*.

iii Find the distance travelled by *A* upwards and the distance travelled by *A* downwards and hence find *h*.

(Cambridge International AS and A level Mathematics 9709/41
Paper 4 Q6 June 2014)

10 Machinery of mass 300 kg is placed on the floor of a lift of mass 450 kg. The magnitudes of the tension in the cable holding the lift, and the normal contact force between the machinery and the lift floor, are *T* newtons and *R* newtons respectively. By considering the forces acting on the machinery, find the value of R when the lift is moving upwards with a deceleration of $2.2\,\text{m s}^{-2}$. By considering the motion of the machinery and the lift as one body, find the value of T for the same deceleration.

11 A rough inclined plane of length 65 cm is fixed with one end at a height of 16 cm above the other end. Particles P and Q, of masses 0.13 kg and 0.11 kg respectively, are attached to the ends of a light inextensible string which passes over a small smooth pulley at the top of the plane. Particle P is held at rest on the plane and particle Q hangs vertically below the pulley (see diagram). The system is released from rest and P starts to move up the plane.

i   Draw a diagram showing the forces acting on P during its motion up the plane.

ii Show that $T - F > 0.32$, where $T\,\text{N}$ is the tension in the string and $F\,\text{N}$ is the magnitude of the frictional force on P.

The coefficient of friction between P and the plane is 0.6.

iii Find the acceleration of P.

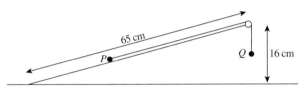

(Cambridge International AS and A level Mathematics 9709/04
Paper 4 Q7 November 2007)

12 Particles P and Q, of masses 0.2 kg and 0.5 kg respectively, are connected by a light inextensible string. The string passes over a smooth pulley at the edge of a rough horizontal table. P hangs freely and Q is in contact with the table. A force of magnitude 3.2 N acts on Q, upwards and away from the pulley, at an angle of 30° to the horizontal (see diagram).

i   The system is in limiting equilibrium with P about to move upwards. Find the coefficient of friction between Q and the table.

The force of magnitude 3.2 N is now removed and P starts to move downwards.

ii Find the acceleration of the particles and the tension in the string.

(Cambridge International AS and A level Mathematics 9709/41
Paper 4 Q7 November 2010)

13 A small ring of mass 0.2 kg is threaded on a fixed vertical rod. The end A of a light inextensible string is attached to the ring. The other end C of the string is attached to a fixed point of the rod above A. A horizontal force of magnitude 8 N is applied to the point B of the string, where $AB = 1.5\,\text{m}$ and $BC = 2\,\text{m}$. The system is in equilibrium with the string taut and AB at right angles to BC (see diagram).

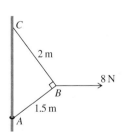

i   Find the tension in the part AB of the string and the tension in the part BC of the string.

The equilibrium is limiting with the ring on the point of sliding up the rod.

ii Find the coefficient of friction between the ring and the rod.

(Cambridge International AS and A level Mathematics 9709/41
Paper 4 Q7 June 2012)

115

Chapter 8
Work, energy and power

In this chapter the basic equations of mechanics are put together into a new form which can be applied to a wider range of problems. When you have completed it, you should

- know the definitions of work and kinetic energy
- be able to use the work–energy principle, and distinguish work done by a force from work done against a force
- know that the work–energy principle can be extended to situations in which forces are not constant
- use the fact that a force perpendicular to the direction of motion does no work
- understand the idea of power and be able to calculate it
- know and be able to use the relation between power, force and speed.

8.1 The work–energy equation

EXAMPLE 8.1.1

A car and driver have a total mass of 1000 kg. The car gains speed from 7 m s^{-1} to 13 m s^{-1} with constant acceleration over a distance of 200 metres. Calculate the driving force.

Method 1   The acceleration of the car can be found by using the equation $v^2 = u^2 + 2as$, taking $u = 7$, $v = 13$ and $s = 200$ in SI units. This gives $169 = 49 + 2a \times 200$, so $a = \frac{120}{400} = 0.3$. By Newton's second law, the driving force in newtons is given by $F = 1000 \times 0.3 = 300$.

This example is typical of many problems in mechanics, in which a force of magnitude F acts on an object of mass m over a distance s, so that the speed of the object increases from u to v. You solve it by combining Newton's second law $F = ma$ with the constant acceleration equation $v^2 = u^2 + 2as$ to show that $F = m\left(\dfrac{v^2 - u^2}{2s}\right)$, which can be rearranged as

$$Fs = \tfrac{1}{2}mv^2 - \tfrac{1}{2}mu^2$$

The expression on the left of this equation, the product of the force and the distance through which the object moves, is called the **work done by the force**. This is such an important idea in mechanics that the unit by which it is measured in the SI system has a special name, the **joule**. (James Joule was a 19th-century English physicist who played a leading part in developing the science of thermodynamics.) A joule is the work done when a force of 1 newton acts through a distance of 1 metre; that is, 1 joule = 1 newton metre. The abbreviation for joule is J.

On the right of the equation you have two terms of a similar form. If an object of mass m is moving with speed v, the quantity $\tfrac{1}{2}mv^2$ is called the **kinetic energy** of the body. So the expression on the right is the increase in the kinetic energy of the object resulting from the action of the force. Kinetic energy is also measured in joules.

Work–energy principle   **If a constant force acts on an object over a certain distance, the work done by the force is equal to the gain in the kinetic energy of the object.**

You can now use the work–energy principle to shorten the solution of Example 8.1.1.

EXAMPLE 8.1.2

Method 2   The kinetic energy increases from $\tfrac{1}{2} \times 1000 \times 7^2 \text{ J}$ to $\tfrac{1}{2} \times 1000 \times 13^2 \text{ J}$, that is by $500 \times (169 - 49) \text{ J}$, which is 60 000 J.

If the force is F newtons, the work done is $F \times 200 \text{ J}$. So $F = \dfrac{60\,000}{200} = 300$.

The driving force is 300 newtons.

117

8.2 Some generalisations

The work–energy principle can be generalised in a number of ways. This is one reason why it is so important.

First, suppose that the force doesn't act along the line of motion, but at an angle to it. Fig. 8.1, in which all the forces are horizontal, illustrates this with an object moving along a straight track, being accelerated by a force of magnitude F at an angle θ to the track. The object is prevented from leaving the track by a normal contact force N. The acceleration can be found by resolving along the track:

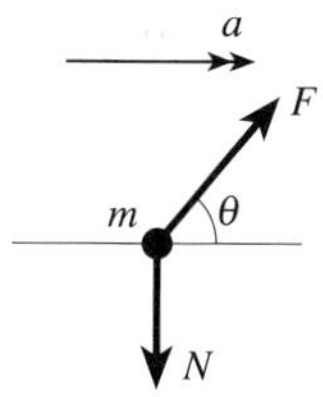

$$F \cos \theta = ma.$$

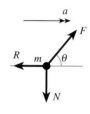

Fig. 8.1

So in the algebraic calculation in Section 8.1, F must be replaced by $F \cos \theta$, and the work–energy equation becomes

$$(F \cos \theta)s = \text{gain in kinetic energy.}$$

This means that the definition of work must be generalised as follows.

> **If an object moves through a distance s along a line under the action of a force of magnitude F at an angle θ to the line, the work done by the force is $Fs \cos \theta$.**

It is important to notice that the normal contact force N doesn't appear in the work–energy equation. This is because its direction is at right angles to the direction of motion, so the work done by this force is $Ns \cos 90°$, which is zero since $\cos 90° = 0$.

> **The work done by a force perpendicular to the direction of motion is zero.**

The next generalisation is to introduce a resisting force R, as in Fig. 8.2. Newton's second law then becomes

$$F \cos \theta - R = ma,$$

so that in the work–energy equation the term $(F \cos \theta)s$ is replaced by $(F \cos \theta - R)s$. Thus

$$Fs \cos \theta - Rs = \text{gain in kinetic energy.}$$

Fig. 8.2

The extra term, $-Rs$, can be described as the 'work done by the resistance', which is negative. But it is more usual to call the positive quantity Rs the 'work done against the resistance', and to extend the statement of the work–energy principle as follows.

> Extended work–energy principle **The work done by the force acting on an object, minus the work done against resistance, is equal to the gain in the kinetic energy of the object.**

EXAMPLE 8.2.1

A cyclist and her machine together have a mass of 100 kg. She free-wheels down a hill of gradient 5% (1 in 20) for a distance of 500 metres. If her speed at the top was 5 m s⁻¹, and there is air resistance of 40 newtons, how fast will she be going at the bottom of the hill?

The force accelerating the cyclist is the weight of 1000 N, acting at an angle to the direction of motion of $(90 - \alpha)°$, where $\cos(90 - \alpha)° = \sin \alpha° = 0.05$. The work done by the weight is $1000 \times 500 \times \cos(90 - \alpha)°$ J, which is $500\,000 \times 0.05$ J, or 25 000 J. The work done against the resistance is 40×500 J, which is 20 000 J. So the gain in kinetic energy is $(25\,000 - 20\,000)$ J, that is 5000 J.

At the top of the hill the kinetic energy was $\frac{1}{2} \times 100 \times 5^2$ J, which is 1250 J. The kinetic energy at the bottom is therefore $(5000 + 1250)$ J, that is 6250 J. If her speed is then v m s⁻¹,

$$\tfrac{1}{2} \times 100 \times v^2 = 6250,$$

so $v^2 = 125$, giving $v = 11.18\ldots$.

The speed at the bottom of the hill will be 11.2 m s⁻¹, to 3 significant figures.

There is another way in which the work–energy principle can be generalised: it enables you to talk sensibly about forces which are not constant. In the last example it is unlikely that the air resistance is constant; it will almost certainly get bigger as the cyclist gains speed. But if you think of the air resistance as having an 'average' value of 40 newtons during the descent, you can still use this to find the work done against the resistance. So the work–energy principle produces valid answers in situations when the acceleration is not constant.

Similarly, in Example 8.1.1, if the driving force is not constant, you can still use the work–energy method to deduce that the average driving force on the car is 300 newtons.

The proof of this, and a more precise definition of what is meant by the average force, involves the use of calculus. It will be discussed in more detail when motion with variable force is dealt with in M2.

EXAMPLE 8.2.2

A nail is being hammered into a plank. The mass of the hammer is 200 grams, and at each stroke the hammer is raised 15 cm above the nail. If the average force used to bring the hammer down is 10 times the average force used to raise the hammer, find the speed, to 2 significant figures, with which the hammer hits the nail.

When the hammer is raised, the kinetic energy at both the beginning and the end of the movement is zero. So the work done in raising the hammer is equal to the work done against the force of gravity.

The weight of the hammer is 0.2×10 N, which is 2 N, and the hammer rises by 0.15 m. So the work done against the weight is 2×0.15 J, which is 0.3 J.

On the downward stroke the work done is 10 times the work done in raising the hammer, so this is 3 J. Also, as the hammer falls, its weight does work of $2 \times 0.15 \, \text{J} = 0.3 \, \text{J}$. So the total work done on the downward stroke is 3.3 J.

This is equal to the kinetic energy acquired by the hammer, which is $2 \times 0.2 \times v^2$, where $v \, \text{m s}^{-1}$ is the speed with which the hammer hits the nail. This gives $0.1v^2 = 3.3$, so $v = \sqrt{33} = 5.74....$

The hammer hits the nail with a speed of $5.7 \, \text{m s}^{-1}$, to 2 significant figures.

8.3 Motion round curved paths

A further generalisation of the work–energy principle is that it is not restricted to motion along a straight line. It can also be used when an object moves round a curved path.

As an example, consider a satellite orbiting the Earth in a circular path outside the Earth's atmosphere. It is acted on by the gravitational pull from the Earth, whose direction is along the radius, perpendicular to the direction of motion. So the work done by this force is zero, which means that the kinetic energy remains constant. That is, the satellite moves at constant speed.

This is a case when it is important to distinguish between speed and velocity. The satellite doesn't, of course, move with constant velocity. It is continually changing direction because of the gravitational pull from the Earth. But in the expression for kinetic energy, v stands for the speed of the moving object. Kinetic energy is an example of what is called a 'scalar quantity'; its value doesn't depend on the direction of motion.

A similar argument applies for a particle moving on a smooth curved horizontal path, or a bead on a smooth horizontal wire. In such cases both the weight and the normal contact force are perpendicular to the velocity of the moving object. So, if there are no other forces, the particle moves with constant speed.

It should also be emphasised that the formulae you have learnt for constant acceleration (sections 1.4 and 1.5) do not apply in any of these situations, as the acceleration is not constant. You will learn more about the acceleration of objects moving in circles in the Mechanics 2 book.

Exercise 8A

1 Find the kinetic energy of

    a a football player of mass 90 kg running at $6 \, \text{m s}^{-1}$,

    b an elephant of mass 6 tonnes charging at $10 \, \text{m s}^{-1}$,

    c a racing car of mass 1.5 tonnes travelling at 300 km per hour,

    d a bullet of mass 20 grams moving at $400 \, \text{m s}^{-1}$,

    e a meteorite of mass 20 kg as it enters the Earth's atmosphere at $8 \, \text{km s}^{-1}$.

2 An object of mass 20 kg is pulled 7 metres at a constant speed across a rough horizontal floor by means of a horizontal rope. The tension in the rope is 100 N. Calculate the work done by the rope. State the work done by the weight of the object and the normal contact force between the object and the floor. State also the work done against resisting forces.

3 A gardener moves a wheelbarrow 30 metres along a level, straight path. The work done by the gardener is 120 J, and the barrow is initially and finally at rest. Calculate the average force resisting the motion.

4 A crate is moved at a steady speed in a straight line by means of a towrope. The work done in moving the crate 16 metres is 800 J. Calculate the resolved part of the tension in the rope in the direction of motion.

5 A ball of mass 1.2 kg moving with initial speed 20 m s^{-1} comes to rest after travelling 30 metres across a horizontal surface. Find the work done against resisting forces, and hence calculate the mean resisting force.

6 An aircraft of mass 1.8 tonnes landing on an aircraft carrier at 144 kilometres per hour is brought to rest by a parachute brake and an arrester cable. If 30% of the work is done by the parachute, calculate the work done by the cable.

7 A father pulls his children on a wagon along a level path. The rope by which the wagon is pulled makes an angle of 20° with the horizontal, and has tension 30 N. Calculate the work done in moving the wagon 40 metres at constant speed.

8 A bicycle of mass 30 kg is pushed up a hill inclined at 15° to the horizontal. Calculate the work done in moving the bicycle 70 metres, starting and finishing with the bicycle at rest.

9 A car of mass 600 kg is pushed along a horizontal road. Initially the car is at rest, and its final speed is 4 m s^{-1}. Calculate the work done in accelerating the car.

10 A box of mass 20 kg is pulled up a ramp inclined at 30° to the horizontal. The work done in moving the box 10 metres is 1200 J. Calculate the magnitude of the average resisting force.

11 A cyclist free-wheels down a slope inclined at 15° to the horizontal, increasing his speed from 4 m s^{-1} to 10 m s^{-1} over a distance of 50 metres. Calculate the mean resistance on the cyclist, given that the mass of the cyclist and his bicycle is 60 kg.

12 A car of mass 700 kg accelerates from 10 m s^{-1} to 30 m s^{-1} over a distance of 120 metres. Neglecting resistances, calculate the work done by the car engine if the road is

   a horizontal,   **b** rising at 10° to the horizontal,

   c dropping at 5°.

Comment on the work done if the gradient of the road is 20° below the horizontal.

13 A parachutist of mass 70 kg falls from a stationary helicopter at an altitude of 1 km. She has speed 8 m s^{-1} on reaching the ground. Calculate the work done against air resistance.

14 A tractor of mass 500 kg pulls a trailer of mass 200 kg up a rough slope inclined at 17° to the horizontal. The resistance to the motion is 4 N per kg. Calculate the work done by the tractor engine, given that the vehicle travels at a constant speed of 1.4 m s^{-1} for 2 minutes.

8.4 Power

Competitors in a long-distance canoe race have to get past a series of waterfalls by dragging their canoes up the riverside path, a distance of 60 metres. One competitor takes 90 seconds to do this, another takes 100 seconds. The combined force of the friction and the resolved part of the weight down the path is 75 N for both canoes. Both competitors therefore do the same amount of work in raising their canoes, 75 × 60 J, which is 4500 J. But the first canoeist is more powerful; he does this work in a shorter time.

The rate at which a person or an engine works is called **power**. The unit of power is the joule per second; this is given a special name, the **watt**, abbreviated to W. Thus 1 W = 1 J s^{-1}. James Watt was a Scottish engineer in the second half of the 18th century, most famous for his contribution to the development of the steam engine.

In the example of the two canoeists, the first expends power of $\dfrac{4500}{90}$ joules per second, on average, which is 50 watts; the second expends power of $\dfrac{4500}{100}$ joules per second, which is 45 watts.

EXAMPLE 8.4.1

A hotel lift, of total mass 1200 kg, rises a distance of 60 metres in 20 seconds. What is the power output of the motor?

The weight of the lift is 12 000 N, so the work done in raising it 60 metres is 12 000 × 60 J, which is 720 000 J. To do this work in 20 seconds requires power of $\dfrac{720\,000}{20}$ W , which is 36 000 W.

The power output of the motor is 36 000 W, or 36 kilowatts (kW).

EXAMPLE 8.4.2

A car of mass 1500 kg arrives at the foot of a straight hill travelling at 30 m s^{-1}. It reaches the top of the hill 40 seconds later travelling at 10 m s^{-1}. The length of the hill is 1000 metres, and the gain in height is 120 metres. The average resistance to motion is 500 N. Find the average power developed by the engine.

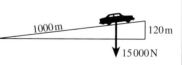

Fig. 8.3

The work done against the resistance is 500 × 1000 J. From Fig. 8.3 the resolved part of the weight of 15 000 N down the hill is $15\,000 \times \dfrac{120}{1000}$ N, which is 1800 N, so the work done against the weight is 1800 × 1000 J = 1 800 000 J. The total work done against the external forces is therefore (500 000 + 1 800 000) J, which is 2 300 000 J.

Some of this work is accounted for by the loss in kinetic energy, which is $(\frac{1}{2} \times 1500 \times 30^2 - \frac{1}{2} \times 1500 \times 10^2)$ J = 600 000 J.

This leaves (2 300 000 − 600 000) J = 1 700 000 J to be provided by the engine.

So the engine has to produce 1 700 000 J in 40 seconds, which means that the average power developed is $\dfrac{1\,700\,000}{40}$ W, which is 42 500 W, or 42.5 kW.

8.5 Power, force and velocity

Suppose that a vehicle is travelling on a level road with constant velocity v, so that the driving force F from the engine exactly balances the resistance R. Then over an interval of time t the vehicle will travel a distance vt, and the work done by the driving force is $F \times (vt)$. The power developed by the engine is therefore $\dfrac{Fvt}{t}$, that is Fv.

It can be shown that this formula still holds if the velocity of the vehicle is not constant. The general result is:

> **If an engine drives an object at velocity v by means of a force F in the direction of motion, the power developed by the engine is Fv.**

In many cases, both for mechanical engines and for athletes, the greatest power of which they are capable is roughly constant over a range of speeds. This means that, when v gets larger, F decreases; and by Newton's second law, it follows that the acceleration decreases.

This is a familiar experience to anyone who drives a car, rides a bicycle or runs sprint races. If you are producing maximum power, then you can achieve higher acceleration at low speeds than at high speeds.

EXAMPLE 8.5.1

A swimmer of mass 50 kg pushes off from the side of a pool with a speed of 0.8 m s^{-1}. She can develop power of 200 W, and the resistance of the water is 220 N.

a At what rate can she accelerate away from the side of the pool?

b Assuming the resistance remains the same, what is her greatest possible speed?

   a At a speed of 0.8 m s^{-1} the largest force she can produce is given by power ÷ speed, which is $\frac{200}{0.8}$ N $= 250$N . The net force available for acceleration is $(250 - 220)$ N, or 30 N. Therefore, by Newton's second law, her greatest possible acceleration is $\frac{30}{50}$ m s^{-2}, which is 0.6 m s^{-2}.

   b At her greatest possible speed the forward force is equal to the resistance of 220 N. Swimming at her full power of 200 W, her greatest speed is given by power ÷ force, which is $\frac{200}{220}$ m s^{-1}, or 0.909... m s^{-1}.

At a speed of 0.8 m s^{-1} she can accelerate away from the side at 0.6 m s^{-2}, and reach a maximum speed of about 0.9 m s^{-1}.

EXAMPLE 8.5.2

A racing car of mass 1830 kg is being tested out at high speeds. Running at full power, it is found that the greatest speed the car can achieve is 80 m s^{-1}. With the same power output, at a speed of 64 m s^{-1}, the car accelerates at 0.5 m s^{-2}. Assuming that the resistance to motion is proportional to the square of the speed, find the acceleration of the car at full power when its speed is 75 m s^{-1}.

   Let the power output of the car be P watts, and suppose that the resistance when the car is travelling at v m s^{-1} is kv^2 newtons.

At 80 m s^{-1}, the driving force is $\frac{1}{80}P$ newtons. At the car's top speed the driving force is equal to the resistance of $k \times 80^2$ newtons. So

$$\frac{1}{80}P = k \times 80^2, \qquad \text{which gives} \qquad P = 512\ 000k.$$

At 64 m s^{-1}, the driving force is $\frac{1}{64}P$ newtons and the resistance is $k \times 64^2$ newtons, so by Newton's second law

$$\frac{1}{64}P - k \times 64^2 = 1830 \times 0.5.$$

Substituting 512 000k for P, this equation becomes

$$8000k - 4096k = 915,$$

giving $3904k = 915$, so $k = \frac{915}{3904}$, and $P = 512\ 000k = 120\ 000$.

If the acceleration at 75 m s^{-1} is a m s^{-2}, Newton's second law gives

$$\frac{1}{75} \times 120\ 000 - \frac{915}{3904} \times 75^2 = 1830a,$$

so $\qquad a = \dfrac{1600 - 1318.3...}{1830} = 0.154$, to 3 significant figures.

At full power, the acceleration of the car when its speed is 75 m s^{-1} is 0.154 m s^{-2}.

Exercise 8B

1 A crane is used to raise a block of mass 2 tonnes to a height of 75 metres in 45 seconds. What is the average power output of the motor?

2 A mountaineer and her pack have mass 90 kg. She climbs a 1200 metre mountain in 160 minutes. At what average power is she working?

3 A child of mass 30 kg runs up a flight of stairs in 6 seconds. The top of the flight is 3 metres above the bottom, and at the top he is running at 2 m s^{-1}. What average power does he need to produce?

4 A chair-lift runs at constant speed. Each passenger starts from rest at the lower station, and is delivered to the upper station with the speed of the lift. The lift raises 30 passengers a minute, of average mass 75 kg. The top of the lift is 300 metres higher than the bottom, and the ride takes 3 minutes. What power do the motors produce?

5 The power developed by a motorcycle, as it travels on a horizontal straight road at a constant speed of 20 m s^{-1}, is 12 kW. Calculate the resistance to the motion of the motorcycle.

6 Calculate the power of the engine of a car which maintains a steady speed of 40 m s^{-1} when the motion is opposed by a constant force of 400 N.

7 A cyclist maintains a steady speed of 11 m s^{-1} when opposed by a force of 80 N. Calculate the power produced by the cyclist.

8 A motorcyclist is travelling on a straight level road, with the engine working at a rate of 8 kW. The total mass of the motorcyclist and the machine is 160 kg. Ignoring any resistance, find the acceleration at an instant when the speed is 20 m s^{-1}.

9   A winch operating at 1 kW pulls a box of weight 980 N up a smooth slope at a constant speed of 2 m s⁻¹. Calculate the angle the slope makes with the horizontal.

10 A car of mass 800 kg travels on a horizontal straight road. The resistance to motion is a constant force of magnitude 300 N. Find the power developed by the car's engine at an instant when the car has a speed of 10 m s⁻¹ and acceleration of 0.6 m s⁻².

11 A winch is used to raise a 200 kg load. The maximum power of the winch is 5 kW. Calculate the greatest possible acceleration of the load when its speed is 2 m s⁻¹, and the greatest speed at which the load can be raised.

12 A car of mass of 950 kg moves along a horizontal road with its engine working at a constant rate of 25 kW. The car accelerates from 14 m s⁻¹ to 18 m s⁻¹. Assuming that there is no resistance to motion, calculate the time taken.

13 The engine of a car of mass 1200 kg works at a constant rate of 18 kW. The car is moving on a horizontal road. Find the acceleration of the car at the instant when its speed is 25 m s⁻¹ and the resistance to motion has magnitude 200 N.

14 A locomotive of mass 50 000 kg pulls a train of mass 80 000 kg up a straight slope inclined at 0.5° to the horizontal, at a constant speed of 9 m s⁻¹. The resistance to motion is a constant force of magnitude 5000 N. Calculate the power generated by the locomotive.

15 A car of mass 1200 kg is moving along a horizontal road. The engine of the car is working at a constant power of 24 kW. The frictional resistance to motion has magnitude of 400 N. When the speed of the car is v m s⁻¹, show that the acceleration is $\dfrac{60-v}{3v}$ m s⁻².

16 A car of mass of 960 kg moves along a straight horizontal road with its engine working at a constant rate of 20 kW. Its speed at the point A on the road is 10 m s⁻¹. Assuming that there is no resistance to motion, calculate the time taken for the car to travel from A until its speed reaches 20 m s⁻¹.

    Assume now that there is a constant resistance to motion and that the car's engine continues to work at 20 kW. It takes 12 seconds for the car's speed to increase from 10 m s⁻¹ to 20 m s⁻¹. During this time the car travels 190 metres. Calculate the work done against the resistance and hence find the magnitude of the resistance.

17 A car of mass 900 kg descends a straight hill which is inclined at 2° to the horizontal. The car passes through the points A and B with speeds 14 m s⁻¹ and 28 m s⁻¹ respectively. The distance AB is 500 metres. Assuming there are no resisting forces, and that the driving force produced by the car's engine is constant, calculate the power of the car's engine at A and at B.

18 A pump, taking water from a large reservoir, is used to spray a jet of water with speed 20 m s⁻¹ and radius 0.05 metres, from a nozzle level with the surface of the reservoir. Calculate the power of the pump.

Miscellaneous exercise 8

1   A car travels along a horizontal straight road with increasing speed until it reaches its maximum speed of 30 m s^{-1}. The resistance to motion is constant and equal to R N, and the power provided by the car's engine is 18 kW.

   i   Find the value of R.

   ii Given that the car has mass 1200 kg, find its acceleration at the instant when its speed is 20 m s^{-1}.

   (Cambridge International AS and A level Mathematics 9709/04 Paper 4 Q3
   June 2007)

2   A car of mass 1150 kg travels up a straight hill inclined at 1.2° to the horizontal. The resistance to motion of the car is 975 N. Find the acceleration of the car at an instant when it is moving with speed 16 m s^{-1} and the engine is working at a power of 35 kW.

   (Cambridge International AS and A level Mathematics 9709/41 Paper 4 Q1
   June 2010)

3   A small block is pulled along a rough horizontal floor at a constant speed of 1.5 m s^{-1} by a constant force of magnitude 30 N acting at an angle of $\theta°$ upwards from the horizontal. Given that the work done by the force in 20 s is 720 J, calculate the value of θ.

   (Cambridge International AS and A level Mathematics 9709/04 Paper 4 Q1
   June 2005)

4   A crate of mass 50 kg is dragged along a horizontal floor by a constant force of magnitude 400 N acting at an angle $\alpha°$ upwards from the horizontal. The total resistance to motion of the crate has constant magnitude 250 N. The crate starts from rest at the point O and passes the point P with a speed of 2 m s^{-1}. The distance OP is 20 m. For the crate's motion from O to P, find

   i   the increase in kinetic energy of the crate,

   ii the work done against the resistance to the motion of the crate,

   iii the value of α.

   (Cambridge International AS and A level Mathematics 9709/04 Paper 4 Q2
   November 2005)

5   A cyclist travels along a straight road working at a constant rate of 420 W. The total mass of the cyclist and her cycle is 75 kg. Ignoring any resistance to motion, find the acceleration of the cyclist at an instant when she is travelling at 5 m s^{-1},

   i   given that the road is horizontal,

   ii given instead that the road is inclined at 1.5° to the horizontal and the cyclist is travelling up the slope.

   (Cambridge International AS and A level Mathematics 9709/04 Paper 4 Q3
   November 2006)

6   A car of mass 800 kg is moving on a straight horizontal road with its engine working at a rate of 22.5 kW. Find the resistance to the car's motion at an instant when the car's speed is 18 m s^{-1} and its acceleration is 1.2 m s^{-2}.

   (Cambridge International AS and A level Mathematics 9709/41 Paper 4 Q1
   November 2014)

7 A car of mass 1200 kg travels along a horizontal straight road. The power provided by the car's engine is constant and equal to 20 kW. The resistance to the car's motion is constant and equal to 500 N. The car passes through the points A and B with speeds 10 m s^{-1} and 25 m s^{-1} respectively. The car takes 30.5 s to travel from A to B.

  i Find the acceleration of the car at A.

  ii By considering work and energy, find the distance AB.

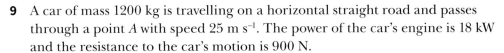

      (Cambridge International AS and A level Mathematics 9709/04 Paper 4 Q7 June 2005)

8 A block B lies on a rough horizontal plane. Horizontal forces of magnitudes 30 N and 40 N, making angles of α and β respectively with the x-direction, act on B as shown in the diagram, and B is moving in the x-direction with constant speed. It is given that $\cos\alpha = 0.6$ and $\cos\beta = 0.8$.

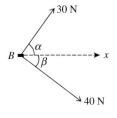

  i Find the total work done by the forces shown in the diagram when B has moved a distance of 20 m.

  ii Given that the coefficient of friction between the block and the plane is $\frac{5}{8}$, find the weight of the block.

      (Cambridge International AS and A level Mathematics 9709/41 Paper 4 Q2 November 2013)

9 A car of mass 1200 kg is travelling on a horizontal straight road and passes through a point A with speed 25 m s^{-1}. The power of the car's engine is 18 kW and the resistance to the car's motion is 900 N.

  i Find the deceleration of the car at A.

  ii Show that the speed of the car does not fall below 20 m s^{-1} while the car continues to move with the engine exerting a constant power of 18 kW.

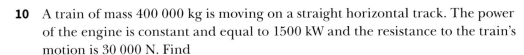

      (Cambridge International AS and A level Mathematics 9709/04 Paper 4 Q3 November 2008)

10 A train of mass 400 000 kg is moving on a straight horizontal track. The power of the engine is constant and equal to 1500 kW and the resistance to the train's motion is 30 000 N. Find

  i the acceleration of the train when its speed is 37.5 m s^{-1},

  ii the steady speed at which the train can move.

      (Cambridge International AS and A level Mathematics 9709/41 Paper 4 Q4 June 2013)

11 A particle of mass 0.8 kg slides down a rough inclined plane along a line of greatest slope AB. The distance AB is 8 m. The particle starts at A with speed 3 m s^{-1} and moves with constant acceleration 2.5 m s^{-2}.

  i Find the speed of the particle at the instant it reaches B.

  ii Given that the work done against the frictional force as the particle moves from A to B is 7 J, find the angle of inclination of the plane.

When the particle is at the point X its speed is the same as the average speed for the motion from A to B.

  iii Find the work done by the frictional force for the particle's motion from A to X.

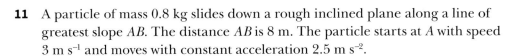

      (Cambridge International AS and A level Mathematics 9709/41 Paper 4 Q5 November 2010)

12 A particle P of mass 0.6 kg is projected vertically upwards with speed 5.2 m s^{-1} from a point O which is 6.2 m above the ground. Air resistance acts on P so that its deceleration is 10.4 m s^{-2} when P is moving upwards, and its acceleration is 9.6 m s^{-2} when P is moving downwards. Find

i the greatest height above the ground reached by P,

ii the speed with which P reaches the ground,

iii the total work done on P by the air resistance.

(Cambridge International AS and A level Mathematics 9709/04 Paper 4 Q6 June 2008)

13 A car of mass 1200 kg moves in a straight line along horizontal ground. The resistance to motion of the car is constant and has magnitude 960 N. The car's engine works at a rate of 17 280 W.

i Calculate the acceleration of the car at an instant when its speed is 12 m s^{-1}.

The car passes through points A and B. While the car is moving between A and B it has constant speed V m s^{-1}.

ii Show that $V = 18$.

At the instant that the car reaches B the engine is switched off and subsequently provides no energy. The car continues along the straight line until it comes to rest at the point C. The time taken for the car to travel from A to C is 52.5 s.

iii Find the distance AC.

(Cambridge International AS and A level Mathematics 9709/41 Paper 4 Q7 November 2012)

14 A car manufacturer plans to bring out a new model with a top speed of 65 m s^{-1} to be capable of accelerating at 0.1 m s^{-2} when the speed is 60 m s^{-1}. Wind-tunnel tests on a prototype suggest that the air resistance at a speed of v m s^{-1} will be $0.2v^2$ newtons. Find the power output (assumed constant) of which the engine must be capable at these high speeds, and the constraint which the manufacturer's requirement places on the total mass of the car and its occupants.

15 If the air resistance to the motion of an airliner at speed v m s^{-1} is given by kv^2 newtons at ground level, then at 6000 metres the corresponding formula is $0.55kv^2$, and at 12 000 metres it is $0.3kv^2$. If an airliner can cruise at 220 m s^{-1} at 12 000 metres, at what speed will it travel at 6000 metres with the same power output from the engines?

Suppose that $k = 2.5$ and that the mass of the airliner is 250 tonnes. As the airliner takes off its speed is 80 m s^{-1} and it immediately starts to climb with the engines developing three times the cruising power. At what angle to the horizontal does it climb?

Chapter 9
Potential energy

This chapter makes a distinction between two kinds of force, conservative and non-conservative, and shows how the former can be regarded as the source of a store of energy. When you have completed the chapter, you should

- know how to calculate the work done by a constant force acting on an object which moves in a curved path
- know the difference between conservative and non-conservative forces
- know that the work done against a conservative force creates potential energy
- understand and be able to apply the principle of conservation of energy
- know that the total energy (potential and kinetic) can be changed by the work done by non-conservative forces.

9.1 Another expression for work

In Section 8.2 the work done by a force was defined as $(F\cos\theta) \times s$; that is, the product of the resolved part of the force and the distance moved by the object it acts on. Another way of writing this product is to link the factor $\cos\theta$ with s rather than F, as $F \times (s\cos\theta)$.

This is illustrated in Fig. 9.1. If the object moves from A to B under the action of the force, then $s\cos\theta$ is the distance AK, where K is the foot of the perpendicular from B to the line of action of the force. That is, AK is the displacement of the object in the direction of the force.

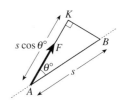

Fig. 9.1

So if an object moves along a line under the action of a force of magnitude F, the work done by the force is equal to the product of F and the distance that the object moves in the direction of the force.

If you know about scalar products of vectors (see P1 Section 13.8), you will recognise this as the scalar product $\mathbf{F}.\mathbf{r}$, where $\mathbf{r}$ denotes the displacement $\overrightarrow{AB}$ (please note that the scalar product is not part of the M1 syllabus).

Fig. 9.1 shows this only when the object moves in a straight line, but it is also true if the object moves in a curved path, as in Fig. 9.2. To show this, you can divide the path up into a lot of small steps AB, BC, CD, ... , for each of which the straight chord can't be distinguished from the curve. In these steps the displacements of the object in the direction of F are AK, KL, LM, ... So the work done is

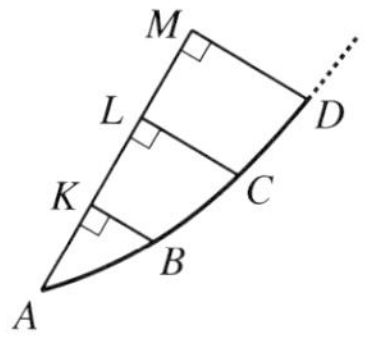

Fig. 9.2

$$F \times AK + F \times KL + F \times LM + \ldots = F(AK + KL + LM + \ldots).$$

This means that, in the statement in the third paragraph in this section, you can replace the word 'line' by 'curve':

> **If an object moves along a curve under the action of a constant force of magnitude F, the work done by the force is equal to the product of F and the distance that the object moves in the direction of the force.**

EXAMPLE 9.1.1

A small sphere of mass m is suspended from a hook by a thread of length l. The sphere is pulled sideways, so that the thread makes an angle of 60° with the downward vertical, and then released from rest. How fast is the sphere moving when the thread becomes vertical?

Fig. 9.3 shows that, after the sphere is released, there are two forces on the sphere, its weight and the tension in the thread. Since the sphere goes round part of a circle, it is always moving at right angles to the direction of the thread, so the work done by the tension is zero.

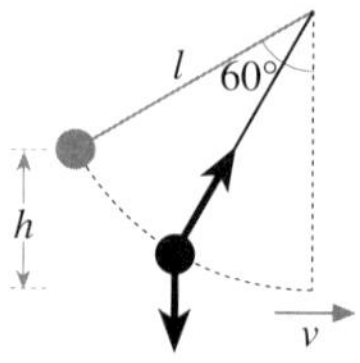

Fig. 9.3

The weight mg acts vertically downwards, so the work done by the weight is equal to mg times the distance that the sphere moves in the vertical direction. This distance is just the vertical height h of the initial position above the lowest point of the circle.

The speed v of the sphere at the lowest point can be found by using the work–energy principle,

$$(mg)h = \tfrac{1}{2}mv^2.$$

This gives $v^2 = 2gh$, so $v = \sqrt{2gh}$.

Now you can find h by trigonometry. From the right-angled triangle in Fig. 9.4, the initial position of the sphere is a distance $l\cos 60°$ below the hook. So

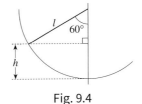

$$h = l - l\cos 60° = l\left(1 - \frac{1}{2}\right) = \frac{1}{2}l.$$

Fig. 9.4

Substituting this in $v = \sqrt{2gh}$ gives

$$v = \sqrt{2g\left(\tfrac{1}{2}l\right)} = \sqrt{gl}.$$

When the thread is vertical the speed of the sphere is $\sqrt{gl}$.

9.2 Three problems with one answer

Here are two problems which you already know how to solve.

1 A stone is thrown vertically upwards with initial speed u. Find its speed v when it has risen to a height h.

2 A block is hit and starts to move up a smooth path at an angle α to the horizontal. If its initial speed is u, find its speed v when it is at a height h above its starting point.

The solutions are as follows.

1 This is a straight application of the constant acceleration equation $v^2 = u^2 + 2as$. Writing $a = -g$ and $s = h$ gives

$$v^2 = u^2 - 2gh.$$

2 Fig. 9.5 shows the two forces acting on the block, its weight mg and the normal contact force N. By Newton's second law,

$$R(\parallel \text{ to the path}) \qquad -mg\sin\alpha = ma,$$

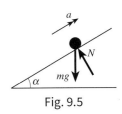

Fig. 9.5

so the block has constant acceleration $-g\sin\alpha$ up the path. To reach a height h above its starting point the block must travel a distance $\dfrac{h}{\sin\alpha}$ up the path.

So, using the constant acceleration formula $v^2 = u^2 + 2as$,

$$v^2 = u^2 + 2\left(-g\sin\alpha\right) \times \frac{h}{\sin\alpha} = u^2 - 2gh.$$

The work–energy principle provides the explanation why both these problems lead to the same answer. If you multiply each term of the equation $v^2 = u^2 - 2gh$ by $\tfrac{1}{2}m$, you get

$$\tfrac{1}{2}mv^2 = \tfrac{1}{2}mu^2 - mgh.$$

The terms $\frac{1}{2}mu^2$ and $\frac{1}{2}mv^2$ are the kinetic energy of the object initially and after it has risen a height h. It remains to see why the kinetic energy is reduced by the same amount, $-mgh$, in each case.

The stone thrown vertically upwards moves a distance h in the direction opposite to the weight mg, so mgh is the work done against the force of gravity.

For the block moving up the smooth path there are two forces. The normal contact force does no work, because it acts at right angles to the direction in which the block is moving. The result in Section 9.1 provides the explanation why the work done against the force of gravity is mgh.

Here is another problem to which the work–energy principle can be applied to give the same answer.

3 A ball is thrown at an angle to the horizontal with speed u. Neglecting the effect of air resistance, find how fast it will be moving when it is at a height h above the ground.

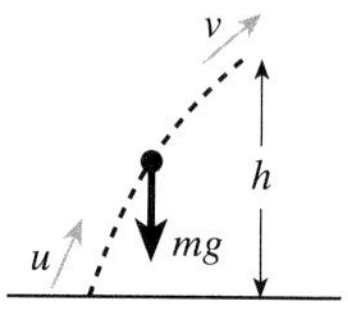

Fig. 9.6

In this example the ball travels in a curved path, so the initial and final velocities are in different directions (see Fig. 9.6).

The only force on the ball is its weight mg, which always acts vertically downwards. You can therefore again use the result in Section 9.1 to show that the work done by the force of gravity is $mg \times (-h)$. So, applying the work–energy principle,

$$-mgh = \tfrac{1}{2}mv^2 - \tfrac{1}{2}mu^2,$$

which again leads to the equation

$$v^2 = u^2 - 2gh.$$

These examples illustrate how you can economise by using the work–energy principle.

It provides a general theory which can be applied in a large number of situations that seem to be quite different.

9.3 Conservative and non-conservative forces

Here is a fourth problem which could have the same answer as those in the last section.

4 A brick is set in motion with speed u across a rough floor. The frictional force is F. Find the speed at which it is moving when it has gone a distance h horizontally.

Newton's second law gives $-F = ma$, so the acceleration has the constant value $-\dfrac{F}{m}$. Using the formula $v^2 = u^2 + 2as$ with $a = -\dfrac{F}{m}$ and $s = h$ gives

$$v^2 = u^2 - 2\frac{F}{m}h.$$

Now suppose that F has the value mg. The equation would then become $v^2 = u^2 - 2gh$. This can again be expressed in work–energy form, as $\tfrac{1}{2}mv^2 = \tfrac{1}{2}mu^2 - mgh$, but this time the term mgh is the work done against the frictional force mg over the horizontal displacement h.

But there is an important difference between this example and those in Section 9.2. For the objects thrown into the air or hit up the smooth path, kinetic energy has been temporarily lost, but you will eventually get it all back when they return to the same level as they started. For this reason the force of gravity is called a **conservative** force. You can think of gaining height as a way in which an object can store up energy, which it can use later to recover its original kinetic energy.

It is quite different with the frictional force. In the fourth example, if the brick is allowed to continue across the floor, it will go on losing speed until it stops. The kinetic energy which it had to start with is lost, and there is no way of getting it back. The frictional force is said to be **non-conservative**.

Another example of a non-conservative force is air resistance. If air resistance had been taken into account in the third example in Section 9.2, it would act along the tangent to the path of the ball in a direction opposite to the velocity. The work done against the resistance would have the effect of reducing the final velocity. So when the ball returns to its original level, its speed will be smaller than u.

9.4 The conservation of energy

Fig. 9.7 shows part of a roller-coaster ride in an amusement park. Consider an idealised model in which there is no friction or air resistance. At four points A, B, C and D on the ride the car has speeds p, q, r and s, and it is at heights a, b, c and d above ground level. The car has mass m and weight W, where $W = mg$.

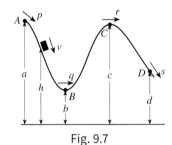

Fig. 9.7

The two forces on the car (with passengers) are its weight and the normal contact force from the track. The contact force does no work, because it always acts at right angles to the direction in which the car is moving.

Between A and B the car is descending with increasing speed. The car loses height of amount $a - b$, so the work done by the weight is $W(a - b)$. Therefore, by the work–energy principle,

$$W(a - b) = \tfrac{1}{2}mq^2 - \tfrac{1}{2}mp^2.$$

This equation can be rearranged as

$$Wa + \tfrac{1}{2}mp^2 = Wb + \tfrac{1}{2}mq^2.$$

Between B and C the car climbs and the speed decreases. Work is done *against* the weight of amount $W(c - b)$, so there is a decrease of kinetic energy of amount

$$\tfrac{1}{2}mq^2 - \tfrac{1}{2}mr^2 = W(c - b).$$

Rearranging,

$$Wb + \tfrac{1}{2}mq^2 = Wc + \tfrac{1}{2}mr^2.$$

Between C and D the car descends again, so

$$Wc + \tfrac{1}{2}mr^2 = Wd + \tfrac{1}{2}ms^2.$$

133

What these equations show is that, as the car goes up and down, its height h and speed v at any point vary so that the sum

$$Wh + \frac{1}{2}mv^2$$

remains constant. As h increases, v decreases and vice versa.

The quantity Wh represents the car's store of energy, which can be traded in for increased kinetic energy by reducing h. It is called **potential energy**, and the property illustrated by the roller-coaster example is called the conservation of energy principle.

> Conservation of energy principle   **For an object moving along a path, if there is no work done by external forces other than the force of gravity, the sum of the potential energy and the kinetic energy is constant.**

The terms 'potential energy' and 'kinetic energy' are often abbreviated to their initials p.e. and k.e.

The idea of storing energy in the form of potential energy has many practical applications. For example, in mountainous areas valleys are often dammed to create a reservoir of water at a height above the surrounding land. This allows water to be released when required so that, as it loses height, it gains speed which can be used to drive a turbine and generate electricity.

Another example is in clock mechanisms. Some clocks work by means of a heavy weight attached to a chain. The energy needed to keep the clock going is provided by raising the weight to the top of its case, thus creating a store of potential energy.

You can also think of Example 9.1.1 in terms of the conservation of energy. When the sphere is pulled aside, so that it is at a height $\frac{1}{2}l$ above the lowest point of the circle, potential energy of amount $mg(\frac{1}{2}l)$ is created. When the sphere is released, this is converted into kinetic energy of amount $\frac{1}{2}mv^2$.

EXAMPLE 9.4.1

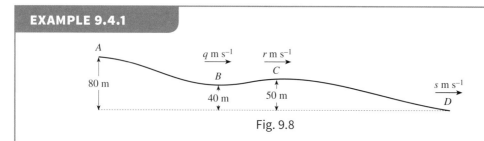

Fig. 9.8

Fig. 9.8 shows the profile of a hill. The points A, B and C are at heights 80, 40 and 50 metres respectively above D. A lightweight truck of mass 250 kg starts from rest at A and descends the hill without power. Neglecting any resistances, calculate how fast it is travelling at B, C and D.

Denote the speeds at B, C and D by $q\,\text{m s}^{-1}$, $r\,\text{m s}^{-1}$ and $s\,\text{m s}^{-1}$ respectively. The weight of the truck is 2500 N, so the potential energy at a height of h metres is $2500h$ joules.

When the speed is $v\,\text{m s}^{-1}$, the kinetic energy is $\frac{1}{2} \times 250 \times v^2$ joules, which is $125v^2$ joules. The conservation of energy principle gives the equations

$$2500 \times 80 = 2500 \times 40 + 125q^2 = 2500 \times 50 + 125r^2 = 125s^2.$$

Notice that at the beginning there is no kinetic energy, and at the end there is no potential energy. At B and C there is both potential and kinetic energy.

From these equations you can calculate $q^2 = 800$, $r^2 = 600$ and $s^2 = 1600$, so $q = 28.2\ldots$, $r = 24.4\ldots$ and $s = 40$.

At B, C and D the truck is travelling at about $28\,\text{m s}^{-1}$, $24\,\text{m s}^{-1}$ and $40\,\text{m s}^{-1}$ respectively.

In working this example all the heights have been taken to be measured above D, so that the potential energy at D is zero. But in fact you can take any level to be at 'zero height', so long as you are consistent right through the calculation. For example, D might be 600 m above sea level; if you choose to take the potential energy above sea level, then the potential energy terms in the equations would be 2500×680, 2500×640, 2500×650 and 2500×600.

Alternatively, you could choose to take the potential energy above B. In that case the heights at A, B, C and D would be 40, 0, 10 and -40. The conservation of energy equations would then be

$$2500 \times 40 = 125q^2 = 2500 \times 10 + 125r^2 = 2500 \times (-40) + 125s^2.$$

You can easily check that in either case you get the same answers as before. This is because, in a conservation of energy equation, measuring from a different level simply adds or subtracts the same amount on both sides of the equation, which doesn't affect the answer.

For instance, in Example 9.1.1 you could measure all the heights from the level of the hook. The sphere is initially $\frac{1}{2}l$ below the hook, and you want the speed v when it is l below the hook. The conservation of energy equation would then be

$$mg\left(-\tfrac{1}{2}l\right) = mg(-l) + \tfrac{1}{2}mv^2,$$

which gives the answer $v = \sqrt{gl}$, as before.

Exercise 9A

1   A particle of mass 2 kg falls freely from rest. Calculate the kinetic energy of the particle after it has descended 20 metres.

2   A stone of mass 0.8 kg is thrown vertically upwards with speed $10\,\text{m s}^{-1}$. Calculate the initial kinetic energy of the stone, and the height to which it will rise.

3   A helicopter of mass 800 kg rises to a height of 170 metres in 20 seconds, before setting off in horizontal flight. Calculate the potential energy gain of the helicopter, and hence estimate the mean power of its engine. State a form of kinetic energy that has been ignored in this model.

4 A child of mass 25 kg slides 15 metres down a water-chute inclined at 30° to the horizontal, starting from rest. Calculate the speed the child would have at the foot of the chute, assuming no energy is lost during the descent.

5 A mountaineer of mass 65 kg scales a peak 3.2 km high. Calculate her gain in potential energy.

6 If no mechanical energy were lost, a skate-boarder descending a straight 40 metre slope would arrive at its foot with speed 15 m s⁻¹. Calculate the angle the slope makes with the horizontal.

7 In an amusement park, a boy reaches the foot of a slide with speed 7 m s⁻¹, after starting from rest. Because of friction, only 25% of his initial potential energy has been converted into kinetic energy. Calculate the vertical distance the boy has descended.

8 A 160 kg barrel of bricks is raised vertically by a 2 kW engine. Calculate the distance the barrel will move in 7 seconds travelling at a constant speed.

9 A stone of mass 0.5 kg is attached to one end of a light inextensible string of length 0.4 metres. The other end of the string is attached to a fixed point O. The stone is released from rest with the string taut and inclined at an angle of 40° below the horizontal through O. Calculate the speed of the particle as it passes beneath O. Calculate also the speed of the stone when the string makes an angle of 20° with the vertical through O.

10 A simple pendulum is modelled as a thread of length 0.7 metres, fixed at one end and with a particle (called the 'bob') attached to the other end. As the pendulum swings, the greatest speed of the bob is 0.6 m s⁻¹. Calculate the angle through which the pendulum swings.

11 A particle of mass 0.2 kg is attached to one end of a light rod of length 0.6 metres. The other end of the rod is freely pivoted at a fixed point O. The particle is released from rest with the rod making an angle of 60° with the upward vertical through O. Calculate the speed of the particle when the rod is

a horizontal,   b vertical.

12 A bead is threaded on a smooth circular wire hoop. The radius of the hoop is a metres. The bead is projected from the lowest point of the hoop with speed u m s⁻¹, and just reaches the top of the hoop. Express u in terms of a and g.

13 A particle is projected with speed 4 m s⁻¹ up a line of greatest slope of a smooth ramp inclined at 30° to the horizontal. It reaches the top of the ramp with speed 1.2 m s⁻¹. Calculate the length of the ramp.

14 A cyclist of mass 90 kg arrives at the top of a hill travelling at 4 m s⁻¹. Free-wheeling, he descends to a bridge and then climbs up to his house on the other side of the valley. The heights above sea level of the three points are 432, 350 and 387 metres respectively. Use a model which neglects resistances to estimate the cyclist's speed as he crosses the bridge and as he reaches his house. (See Exercise 9B Question 9.)

9.5 Application to systems of connected objects

Conservation of energy can also be used to solve problems about a pair of objects connected by a string.

EXAMPLE 9.5.1

A toy has the form of a truck of mass 4 kg which can run on a track at an angle of 30° to the horizontal. A light chain attached to the truck runs parallel to the track, passes over a light pulley at its upper end, and then hangs vertically (see Fig. 9.9). A counterweight of mass 3 kg is attached to the free end of the chain. The system is released from rest with the counterweight at a height $\frac{1}{2}$ m above the floor. Find how fast the truck is moving when the counterweight hits the floor.

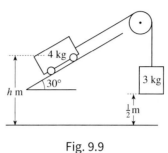

Fig. 9.9

Suppose that the truck is originally h metres above the floor. Let the speed with which the truck is moving as the counterweight hits the floor be $v\,\mathrm{m\,s^{-1}}$. If the chain is inextensible, the counterweight will also be moving at $v\,\mathrm{m\,s^{-1}}$.

At the start there is no kinetic energy, but both the truck and the counterweight have potential energy, of amounts $(4g)h$ joules and $(3g)\frac{1}{2}$ joules respectively, where $g = 10$. When the counterweight hits the floor, the truck has moved a distance $\frac{1}{2}$ m up the track, so it has gained a height of $\frac{1}{2}\sin 30°$ m, which is $\frac{1}{4}$ m . So, equating the total energy at the beginning and the end,

$$4gh + \tfrac{3}{2}g = 4g\left(h + \tfrac{1}{4}\right) + \tfrac{1}{2} \times 4 \times v^2 + \tfrac{1}{2} \times 3 \times v^2,$$

which can be simplified as

$$\left(\tfrac{3}{2} - 1\right)g = \tfrac{7}{2}v^2, \quad \text{so} \quad v^2 = \tfrac{1}{7}g, \quad \text{and} \quad v = 1.195\ldots$$

The truck is moving at about $1.2\,\mathrm{m\,s^{-1}}$ as the counterweight hits the floor.

In this example you might wonder whether the tension in the chain contributes to the energy equation. The answer is that when you consider the system as a whole the tension does no work. As the truck and the counterweight move $\frac{1}{2}$ m , the tension of T newtons acting up the plane on the truck does work $T \times \frac{1}{2}$ J, and the tension of T newtons acting upwards on the counterweight does work $(-T) \times \frac{1}{2}$ J. These add up to zero.

You can, though, find the tension by writing a work–energy equation for the truck by itself. During the motion the truck gains potential energy $4g \times \frac{1}{4}$ J and kinetic energy $\frac{1}{2} \times 4 \times v^2$ J. So, equating the gain in energy to the work done by the tension,

$$\tfrac{1}{2}T = g + 2\left(\tfrac{1}{7}g\right),$$

which gives $T = \frac{18}{7}g = 25.71\ldots$. The tension in the chain is therefore 25.7 N, to 3 significant figures.

You can check for yourself that this is the same answer as you get using the method described in Chapter 7.

9.6 Including non-conservative forces in the equation

The speeds calculated in Example 9.4.1 are unrealistic, since resistance is not taken into account. Because some of this will be air resistance, it is likely to be greater at higher speeds. The next example tries to model the motion of the lightweight truck more realistically.

EXAMPLE 9.6.1

Suppose that in Example 9.4.1 the distances AB, BC and CD measured along the hill are 200 m, 100 m and 300 m. The average resistances to motion along these stretches of the hill are estimated to be 95 N, 140 N and 210 N. For the uphill stretch from B to C the motor is activated, producing a driving force of 700 N. Calculate the speeds at B, C and D using this model.

Between A and B the work done against the resistance is 95×200 J, and the effect of this is to reduce the total energy (potential and kinetic) at B. So the first equation in Example 9.4.1 is replaced by

$$2500 \times 80 - 95 \times 200 = 2500 \times 40 + 125q^2.$$

Between B and C there are two extra terms in the equation, the work done by the driving force, which is 700×100 J, and the work done against the resistance, which is 140×100 J. So the equation is

$$2500 \times 40 + 125q^2 + 700 \times 100 - 140 \times 100 = 2500 \times 50 + 125r^2.$$

For the final stretch the work done against the resistance is 210×300 J, so

$$2500 \times 50 + 125r^2 - 210 \times 300 = 125s^2.$$

These equations give $125q^2 = 81\,000$, $125r^2 = 112\,000$ and $125s^2 = 174\,000$, so $q = \sqrt{648} = 25.4\ldots$, $r = \sqrt{896} = 29.9\ldots$ and $s = \sqrt{1392} = 37.3\ldots$.

At B, C and D the truck is moving at about $25\,\mathrm{m\,s^{-1}}$, $30\,\mathrm{m\,s^{-1}}$ and $37\,\mathrm{m\,s^{-1}}$.

This example shows that the conservation of energy principle has to be modified to take account of the driving force and the resistance, which are the non-conservative forces in the situation. Notice, though, that the work done by the weight no longer appears as a separate term in the equations, since this has already been included in the form of the potential energy.

> **For an object moving along a path, the total energy (potential and kinetic) is increased by the work done by the non-conservative external forces.**

In Example 9.6.1 the work done by the driving force between B and C is positive, but the work done by the resistance is negative, equal to minus the work done against the resistance.

Notice that potential energy can be used up either by conversion into kinetic energy, or in overcoming resistance. In Examples 9.4.1 and 9.5.1, all the potential energy lost is converted into kinetic energy. In Example 9.6.1 some of it is converted into kinetic energy and some is lost in work done against resistance. In the example of the clock, raising the weight inside the case doesn't make the clock run faster; the potential energy created when the weight is raised is all used to overcome the resistance inside the clock mechanism.

EXAMPLE 9.6.2

Abe and Dev have mass 30 kg and 40 kg respectively. Abe is standing on the ground holding one end of a rope. Dev is 5 metres up a tree. Abe tosses the other end of his rope over a high branch. Dev grabs it, pulls it tight and then uses it to descend to the ground. As he does so, Abe keeps hold of the rope and goes up. As Dev reaches ground level, both boys are moving at $3\,\mathrm{m\,s^{-1}}$. How much work is done against the frictional force between the rope and the branch?

In the descent Dev loses potential energy of $40 \times 10 \times 5\,\mathrm{J}$, and Abe gains potential energy of $30 \times 10 \times 5\,\mathrm{J}$, so the net loss of potential energy is $(40 - 30) \times 10 \times 5\,\mathrm{J}$, which is $500\,\mathrm{J}$.

Both boys gain kinetic energy. Abe gains $\frac{1}{2} \times 30 \times 3^2\,\mathrm{J}$, and Dev gains $\frac{1}{2} \times 40 \times 3^2\,\mathrm{J}$, so the total gain is $\frac{1}{2} \times (30 + 40) \times 3^2\,\mathrm{J}$, which is $315\,\mathrm{J}$.

The only non-conservative force is the friction between the rope and the branch, so the loss of energy of $185\,\mathrm{J}$ must be accounted for by the work done against this frictional force.

Notice that in this example various minor complications have been neglected, such as the mass of the rope, air resistance and the possibility that the rope might stretch. None of these factors is likely to have much effect, and the calculated answer would give a good estimate of the loss of energy due to the friction.

In some questions in the following exercises, you are given the work done by or against a force. You might be tempted to work out the forces involved and then use constant acceleration formulae. However, unless you are told that the forces involved are constant, you cannot assume that they are, and so you must use energy methods instead.

Exercise 9B

1   Two particles of mass 0.3 kg and 0.5 kg are connected by a light inextensible string passing over a smooth rail. The particles are released from rest with the string taut and vertical except where it is in contact with the rail. Calculate the velocity of the particles after they have moved 1.3 metres.

2   Particles of mass 1.2 kg and 1.4 kg hang at the same level, connected by a long light inextensible string passing over a small smooth peg. They are released from rest with the string taut. Calculate the separation of the particles when they are moving with speed $0.5\,\mathrm{m\,s^{-1}}$.

3   A particle of mass 1.2 kg is at rest 2 metres from the edge of a smooth horizontal table. It is connected by a light inextensible string, passing over a light pulley on smooth bearings at the edge of the table, to a particle of mass 0.7 kg which hangs freely. The system is released from rest. Calculate

   a   the distance moved by the particles when their speed is $3\,\mathrm{m\,s^{-1}}$,

   b   the speed of the particles just before the heavier particle reaches the pulley.

4   An object of mass 1.6 kg rests on a smooth slope inclined at 10° to the horizontal. It is connected by a light inextensible string passing over a smooth rail at the top of the slope to an object of mass 0.8 kg which hangs freely. After their release from rest, calculate

   a   their speed when they have moved 0.5 metres,

   b   the distance they have moved when their speed is $3\,\mathrm{m\,s^{-1}}$.

5   Two particles of mass 0.1 kg and 0.2 kg are attached to the ends of a light inextensible string which passes over a smooth peg. Given that the particles move vertically after being released from rest, calculate their common speed after each has travelled 0.6 m. Deduce the work done on the lighter particle by the string, and use this to calculate the tension in the string.

6   A particle of mass 2.2 kg rests on a smooth slope inclined at 30° to the horizontal. It is connected by a light inextensible string passing over a smooth rail at the top of the slope to a particle of mass 2.7 kg which hangs freely. The particles are set in motion by projecting the lighter down a line of greatest slope with speed $4\,\mathrm{m\,s^{-1}}$. Find the distance the particles travel before their direction of motion is reversed. Find the total energy gained by the hanging mass during this part of the motion, and hence find the tension in the string.

7   An airliner of mass 300 tonnes is powered by four engines, each developing 15 000 kW. Its speed at take-off is $75\,\mathrm{m\,s^{-1}}$, and it takes 11 minutes to reach its cruising speed of $210\,\mathrm{m\,s^{-1}}$ at a height of 10 000 metres. Calculate the work done against air resistance during the climb.

8   *A* and *B* are two points 1 km apart on a straight road, and *B* is 60 metres higher than *A*. A car of mass 1200 kg passes *A* travelling at $25\,\mathrm{m\,s^{-1}}$. Between *A* and *B* the engine produces a constant driving force of 1600 newtons, and there is a constant resistance to motion of 1150 newtons. Calculate the speed of the car as it passes B.

9   In Exercise 9A Question 14 a more realistic model for the cyclist's motion includes a resistance force of constant magnitude, which produces a value of $15\,\mathrm{m\,s^{-1}}$ for the speed of the cyclist as he crosses the bridge. The road lengths of the downhill and uphill stretches of his ride are 820 metres and 430 metres respectively. Calculate the resistance force. Show that he won't be able to complete the journey without pedalling, and find the constant force necessary on the uphill stretch to produce the energy to reach his house.

Miscellaneous exercise 9

1 A crate C is pulled at a constant speed up a straight inclined path by a constant force of magnitude F N, acting upwards at an angle of 15° to the path. C passes through points P and Q which are 100 m apart (see diagram). As C travels from P

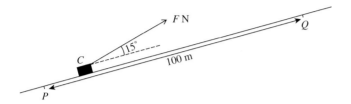

to Q the work done against the resistance to C's motion is 900 J, and the gain in C's potential energy is 2100 J. Write down the work done by the pulling force as C travels from P to Q, and hence find the value of F.

> (Cambridge International AS and A level Mathematics 9709/04
> Paper 4 Q2 June 2009)

2 A load of mass 1250 kg is raised by a crane from rest on horizontal ground, to rest at a height of 1.54 m above the ground. The work done against the resistance to motion is 5750 J.

i Find the work done by the crane.

ii Assuming the power output of the crane is constant and equal to 1.25 kW, find the time taken to raise the load.

> (Cambridge International AS and A level Mathematics 9709/41
> Paper 4 Q2 June 2011)

3 A load of mass 160 kg is pulled vertically upwards, from rest at a fixed point O on the ground, using a winding drum. The load passes through a point A, 20 m above O, with a speed of 1.25 m s^{-1} (see diagram). Find, for the motion from O to A,

i the gain in the potential energy of the load,

ii the gain in the kinetic energy of the load.

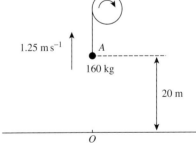

The power output of the winding drum is constant while the load is in motion.

iii Given that the work done against the resistance to motion from O to A is 20 kJ and that the time taken for the load to travel from O to A is 41.7 s, find the power output of the winding drum.

> (Cambridge International AS and A level Mathematics 9709/41
> Paper 4 Q3 June 2012)

4 Two bodies, of mass 3 kg and 5 kg, are attached to the ends of a light inextensible string. The string passes over a smooth fixed rail and the particles are moving vertically with both vertical parts of the string taut. Find the speed of the particles when they have travelled 0.4 metres, and deduce the magnitude of their acceleration.

5 A cyclist and his machine have a total mass of 80 kg. The cyclist starts from rest at the top *A* of a straight path *AB*, and free-wheels (moves without pedalling or braking) down the path to *B*. The path *AB* is inclined at 2.6° to the horizontal and is of length 250 m (see diagram).

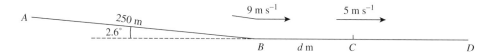

i Given that the cyclist passes through *B* with speed 9 ms⁻¹, find the gain in kinetic energy and the loss in potential energy of the cyclist and his machine. Hence find the work done against the resistance to motion of the cyclist and his machine.

The cyclist continues to free-wheel along a horizontal straight path *BD* until he reaches the point *C*, where the distance *BC* is *d* m. His speed at *C* is 5 ms⁻¹. The resistance to motion is constant, and is the same on *BD* as on *AB*.

ii Find the value of *d*.

The cyclist starts to pedal at *C*, generating 425 W of power.

iii Find the acceleration of the cyclist immediately after passing through *C*.

(Cambridge International AS and A level Mathematics 9709/04 Paper 4 Q5 June 2009)

6 Particles, of mass 1.5 kg and 2 kg, are attached to the ends of a light inextensible string. The string passes over a light pulley on smooth bearings, fixed at the top of the smooth, sloping face of a fixed wedge. The 2 kg mass is at rest on the sloping face, which is inclined at 30° to the horizontal. The 1.5 kg mass hangs freely and the string is taut. The particles are released. Find the speed of the particles when they have travelled 0.7 metres, and state the direction of motion of the 1.5 kg mass.

7 Loads *A* and *B*, of masses 1.2 kg and 2.0 kg respectively, are attached to the ends of a light inextensible string which passes over a fixed smooth pulley. *A* is held at rest and *B* hangs freely, with both straight parts of the string vertical. *A* is released and starts to move upwards. It does not reach the pulley in the subsequent motion.

i Find the acceleration of *A* and the tension in the string.

ii Find, for the first 1.5 metres of *A*'s motion,

   a *A*'s gain in potential energy,

   b the work done on *A* by the tension in the string,

   c *A*'s gain in kinetic energy.

B hits the floor 1.6 seconds after *A* is released. *B* comes to rest without rebounding and the string becomes slack.

iii Find the time from the instant the string becomes slack until it becomes taut again.

(Cambridge International AS and A level Mathematics 9709/41 Paper 4 Q7 June 2011)

8 A smooth wire is bent into the shape of the graph of $y = \frac{1}{6}x^3 - \frac{3}{2}x^2 + 4x$ for $0 < x < 6$, the units being metres. Points A, B and C on the wire have coordinates $(0, 0)$, $(3,3)$ and $(6,6)$. A bead of mass $m\,\text{kg}$ is projected along the wire from A with speed $u\,\text{m s}^{-1}$ so that it has enough energy to reach B but not C. Prove that u is between 8.16 and 10.95, to 2 decimal places, and that the speed at B is at least $2.58\,\text{m s}^{-1}$.

If $u = 10$, the bead comes to rest at a point D between B and C. Find

a the greatest speed of the bead between B and D,

b the coordinates of D, to 1 decimal place.

What happens after the bead reaches D?

9 A block of mass M is placed on a rough horizontal table. A string attached to the block runs horizontally to the edge of the table, passes round a smooth peg, and supports a sphere of mass m attached to its other end. The motion of the block on the table is resisted by a frictional force of magnitude F, where $F < mg$. The system is initially at rest.

a Show that, when the block and the sphere have each moved a distance h, their common speed v is given by $v^2 = \dfrac{2(mg - F)h}{M + m}$.

b Show that the total energy lost by the sphere as it falls through the distance h is $\dfrac{m(Mg + F)h}{M + m}$. Hence find an expression for the tension in the string.

c Write down an expression for the energy gained by the block as it moves through the distance h. Use your answer to check the expression for the tension which you found in part **b**.

10 A tube is bent into the form of a semicircle with centre O and radius r. It is fixed in a vertical plane with its diameter horizontal, as shown in the diagram. A steel ball is held at one end A, and released into the tube. Throughout its motion the ball experiences a resistance of constant magnitude R. The ball first comes to rest at B, where OB makes an angle of $\frac{1}{3}\pi$ with the vertical. It then runs back down the tube and next comes to rest at C, where OC makes an angle α with the vertical.

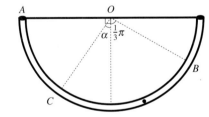

a Show that $R = \dfrac{3mg}{5\pi}$.

b Find the speed of the ball at the lowest point of the tube

   i as it moves from A to B,

   ii as it moves from B to C.

c Show that $0.6\alpha = \pi(\cos\alpha - 0.7)$.

d Explain why the ball will continue to oscillate after reaching C if $\alpha > \sin^{-1}\left(\dfrac{0.6}{\pi}\right)$, and determine whether this condition is satisfied.

Chapter 10
Force as a vector quantity

This chapter deals with force as an example of a vector quantity, and shows how forces may be combined or taken apart. When you have completed it, you should

- understand the terms 'resultant' and 'component'
- be able to find the resultant of two or more forces
- be able to find the components of a force in two given directions
- appreciate that when a force is split into perpendicular components their magnitudes are equal to the resolved parts of the force in the given directions
- be familiar with the notation of vector addition and with the representation of forces by column vectors
- understand how the equilibrium of two or three forces can be expressed in vector notation
- be able to represent the equilibrium of three forces with a triangle of forces.

10.1 Combining forces geometrically

You have now met a number of different mechanics concepts, such as displacement, velocity, acceleration and force. What these all have in common is that to describe them you have to give both a magnitude and a direction. They are all examples of **vector quantities**.

Contrast this with mass and kinetic energy, which are completely described by their magnitude, and which have no direction associated with them. These are examples of **scalar quantities**.

When you want to show that a symbol stands for a vector quantity, it is usual to write it with a wavy line under the letter. Thus, a force of 10 N on a bearing of 020° might be denoted by the symbol P̰. In print, in place of the wavy line, the symbol is written in bold type, as **P**.

You are already used to showing vector quantities in diagrams as arrows. This is fine for indicating the direction, but you also need a way of showing the magnitude. A simple way of doing this is with the length of the arrow. Choose a scale, such as 1 centimetre to 5 newtons; then the force **P** would be represented by an arrow of length 2 cm pointing on a bearing of 020°, as in Fig. 10.1. Another force, **Q**, of 15 N on a bearing of 080°, would be represented by an arrow of length 3 cm. Now suppose that **P** and **Q** act on a particle at the same time. In which direction will the particle accelerate? To answer this, you want to find a single force which has the same effect on the particle as **P** and **Q** together. This is done by taking the two arrows representing the forces, and placing them so that the head of **P** coincides with the tail of **Q**, as in Fig. 10.2. Then join the tail of **P** to the head of **Q** with a third arrow. This arrow then represents (on the same scale) the single force **R** which has the same effect as **P** and **Q** together. The force **R** is called the **resultant** of **P** and **Q**.

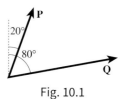

Fig. 10.1

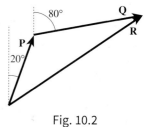

Fig. 10.2

145

If you draw this to scale, you will find that the length of the third arrow is about 4.4 cm, and that it makes an angle of about 37° with the **P** arrow. Now 4.4 cm represents 4.4 × 5 N, or 22 N. So the resultant of **P** and **Q** is a force of magnitude 22 N on a bearing of 057°.

To see why this works, look at Fig. 10.3. The lines *AB*, *BC* and *AC* correspond to the three arrows in Fig. 10.2. Draw a line *AL* in any direction you like, and draw *BM* and *CN* perpendicular to *AL*, and *BK* parallel to *AL*.

Then you can see that

$$AN = AM + MN = AM + BK.$$

Now *AB*, which has length 2 cm, represents the force **P**, of magnitude 10 newtons. So *AM*, of length $2\cos\angle BAL$ cm, represents a force of magnitude $10\cos\angle BAL$ newtons. You will recognise this as the resolved part of **P** in the direction *AL*. In just the same way, *BK* and *AN* represent the resolved parts of **Q** and **R** in the direction *AL*. So the equation $AM + BK = AN$ shows that the effect of **P** and **Q** (taken together) in the direction *AL* is equal to the effect of **R** in that direction.

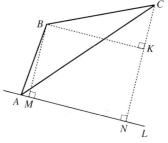

Fig. 10.3

Since *AL* was drawn in any direction you like, the same argument shows that the effect of **P** and **Q** together in any direction is the same as the effect of **R** in that direction.

> Triangle law for combining forces **If two forces P and Q are represented by arrows (on some scale) and the arrow representing R is obtained from these as in Fig. 10.2, then the single force R has exactly the same effect on a particle as the two forces P and Q acting together.**

A figure like Fig. 10.2 is called a **force diagram**.

To find **R** by calculation rather than by scale drawing, you have to use trigonometry. In that case you do not need to choose a scale; you can simply use the magnitudes of the forces as if they were the lengths of the sides of a triangle.

EXAMPLE 10.1.1

Find the resultant **R** of the two forces **P** and **Q** in Fig. 10.1 by calculation.

It is convenient to use the letters P, Q and R, printed in italic but not bold, to stand for the magnitudes of **P**, **Q** and **R**. (In handwriting, you would use P, Q and R without a wavy line underneath.) In Fig. 10.4 these are used as the lengths of the sides of a triangle XYZ, so that $XY = 10$, $YZ = 15$ and $XZ = R$. Also the angle between the directions of **P** and **Q** is $80° - 20° = 60°$, so $\angle XYZ = 180° - 60° = 120°$.

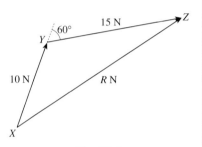

Fig. 10.4

Using the cosine rule,

$$R^2 = 10^2 + 15^2 - 2 \times 10 \times 15 \times \cos 120° = 100 + 225 - 300 \times (-0.5)$$
$$= 475, \quad \text{so} \quad R = \sqrt{475} = 21.79\ldots.$$

To find the direction of **R**, you can use the sine rule to calculate $\angle YXZ$.

$$\frac{15}{\sin \angle YXZ} = \frac{R}{\sin 120°} \quad \text{gives} \quad \sin \angle YXZ = \frac{15 \sin 120°}{21.79\ldots},$$

so $\quad \sin \angle YXZ = 0.596\ldots, \quad$ and $\quad \angle YXZ = 36.58\ldots°.$

(Alternatively you could use the cosine rule a second time, in the form $15^2 = 10^2 + R^2 - 2 \times 10 \times R \times \cos \angle YXZ$.)

The resultant is therefore about 22 N on a bearing of approximately $020° + 37°$, which is $057°$.

An important special case is when two forces **P** and **Q** are at right angles to each other. The force diagram then takes the form of Fig. 10.5. From this you can calculate

$$R - \sqrt{P^2 + Q^2} \quad \text{and} \quad \tan \angle YXZ = \frac{Q}{P}.$$

Fig. 10.5

The resultant of two forces with magnitudes P and Q in perpendicular directions is a force of magnitude $\sqrt{P^2+Q^2}$ which makes an angle $\tan^{-1}\dfrac{Q}{P}$ with the direction of the force P.

This calculation is easy if your calculator has a rectangular–polar conversion key. Enter the values of P and Q, and you can read off the magnitude of the resultant and the angle.

10.2   Splitting a force into components

Suppose that you are trying to shift a heavy object but don't have the strength to do it by yourself. You get a friend to help, and hope that your combined efforts will produce the resultant force needed. How much force will you each have to exert?

This is the reverse of the problem in Section 10.1. You know **R**, and you want to find **P** and **Q**. The forces **P** and **Q** are called **components** of **R**.

If you know the directions in which these components act, it is easy to construct the force diagram in reverse. Draw the arrow to represent **R** on the chosen scale, and then draw lines through the tail and head of that arrow, one in each of the given directions, far enough so that they intersect. Then insert arrowheads on the two lines so that they form two vectors which combine to give **R**.

Again you can do the calculation using trigonometry. You know all the angles of the triangle and the magnitude of one side, so you can use the sine rule to find the other two sides.

EXAMPLE 10.2.1

Two people are pushing a piano across a stage. This needs a force of 240 N. One person pushes at 20° to the left of the desired direction of motion, the other pushes at 30° to the right of it. How hard must each person push?

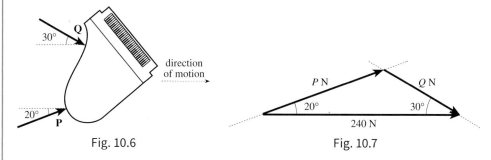

Fig. 10.6   Fig. 10.7

Fig. 10.6 illustrates the actual situation, and Fig. 10.7 is the triangle construction for calculating the forces. Two of the angles of the triangle are 20° and 30°, so the third angle is 130°. By the sine rule,

$$\frac{P}{\sin 30^\circ}=\frac{Q}{\sin 20^\circ}=\frac{240}{\sin 130^\circ}.$$

This gives $P=\dfrac{240\sin 30^\circ}{\sin 130^\circ}=156.6\ldots$ and $Q=\dfrac{240\sin 20^\circ}{\sin 130^\circ}=107.1\ldots$.

The two people must push with forces of about 157 N and 107 N respectively.

EXAMPLE 10.2.2

A ship is towed along a narrow channel by cables attached to two tugboats. The more powerful tugboat produces a force of 800 kN; its cable is at 10° to the direction of the channel. The other tugboat is to produce as small a force as possible. What should be the direction of the second tugboat's cable, and how large is the net forward force on the ship?

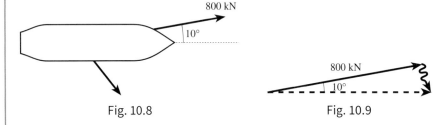

Fig. 10.8   Fig. 10.9

Fig. 10.8 illustrates the ship and the two cables, and Fig. 10.9 is the beginning of the construction of the force diagram. The arrow representing the force in the second cable is drawn with a wavy line, since its direction is unknown. But the arrow representing the resultant force has to lie along the broken line, parallel to the direction of the channel.

For the force in the second cable to be as small as possible, it must be drawn perpendicular to the direction of the channel. The triangle can then be completed as in Fig. 10.10. From this you can calculate the magnitude of the resultant; it is $800 \cos 10°$ kN, or $787.8\ldots$ kN.

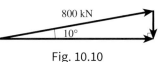

Fig. 10.10

The second tugboat's cable should be at right angles to the direction of the channel, and the net forward force on the ship is then about 788 kN.

An important special case is when a force is split into two components in perpendicular directions. This is illustrated in Fig. 10.11. If the directions make angles of $A°$ and $(90-A)°$ with the resultant force **R**, then the magnitudes of the two components are $R \cos A°$ and $R \sin A°$, which is $R \cos (90-A)°$.

Notice that these expressions are the same as the resolved parts of the force in the two directions. This is an important result.

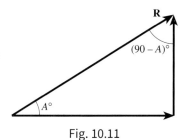

Fig. 10.11

> **If a force is split into components in two perpendicular directions, the magnitude of each component is the resolved part of the force in that direction.**

When you read mechanics books or articles, you will notice that authors sometimes use the word 'component' instead of the more correct 'resolved part'. Strictly, a phrase like 'the vertical component of **R**' shouldn't be used without specifying the direction of the other component. But if you do come across it, you should assume that the other component is at right angles (in this case, horizontal), in which case the words 'component' and 'resolved part' are interchangeable.

You can find perpendicular components of a force very quickly if your calculator has a polar–rectangular conversion key. Simply enter the values of R and the angle A, and you can read off the magnitudes of the two components.

In solving problems it is sometimes helpful to show two perpendicular components of a force separately on a diagram, rather than just the single force. For example, if you are dealing with an object of weight 80 N on a slope inclined at 20° to the horizontal, you could replace the weight (Fig. 10.12) by two components (Fig. 10.13), of $80\cos 20°\,\text{N}$ perpendicular to the slope and $80\sin 20°\,\text{N}$ down the slope. These two figures are precisely equivalent ways of showing the same information.

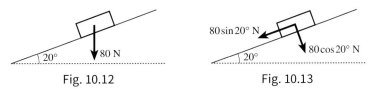

Fig. 10.12   Fig. 10.13

Exercise 10A

1   Use scale drawing to find the resultant of the forces **P** and **Q** in the following cases. Confirm your answer in each case by calculation.

   a   **P** has magnitude 15 N and bearing 025°, **Q** has magnitude 10 N and bearing 075°.

   b   **P** has magnitude 20 N and bearing 030°, **Q** has magnitude 15 N and bearing 115°.

   c   **P** has magnitude 25 N and bearing 045°, **Q** has magnitude 20 N and bearing 200°.

   d   **P** has magnitude 10 N and bearing 065°, **Q** has magnitude 5 N and bearing 310°.

2   A car is being pushed by two people. The magnitude and direction of the horizontal force exerted by each is shown in the diagram. Find the resultant of the two forces.

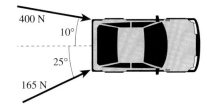

3   A particle *P* of weight 4 N is attached to one end of a light inextensible string. The other end of the string is attached to a fixed point *O*. With the string taut *P* travels in a circular path in a vertical plane. The string exerts a force **T** on the particle in the direction *PO* as shown in the diagram. The resultant of **T** and the weight of *P* is denoted by **R**.

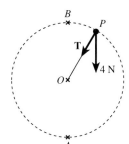

   a   The magnitude of **T** is 28 N when *P* is at *A*, the lowest point of the circular path.

   State the direction of **R** when *P* is in this position, and find its magnitude.

   b   The magnitude of **T** is 4 N when *P* is at *B*, the highest point of the circular path.

   State the direction of **R** when *P* is in this position, and find its magnitude.

   c   The magnitude of **T** is 16 N when *OP* is horizontal. Find the magnitude and direction of **R**.

4   Use scale drawing to find the magnitude of the resultant of the forces **P** and **Q** in the following cases. Confirm your answer in each case by calculation.

  a   **P** has magnitude 20 N and bearing 030°, **Q** has bearing 065° and the resultant has bearing 045°.

  b   **P** has magnitude 25 N and bearing 035°, **Q** has bearing 125° and the resultant has bearing 060°.

  c   **P** has magnitude 15 N and bearing 050°, **Q** has bearing 210° and the resultant has bearing 100°.

  d   **P** has magnitude 30 N and bearing 075°, **Q** has bearing 330° and the resultant has bearing 035°.

5

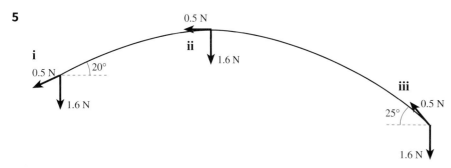

A cricket ball has weight 1.6 N. At any instant between being struck by the bat and reaching the ground the ball is subject to a resistive force of constant magnitude 0.5 N. The diagram shows the directions in which the resistive force acts

  i   immediately after the ball leaves the bat,

  ii   at the highest point of the flight,

  iii   immediately before the ball reaches the ground.

The resultant of the resistive force and the weight of the cricket ball is denoted by **R**. Find the magnitude and direction of **R** in each of the three cases.

Assuming that the resistive force always acts in a direction opposite to that in which the cricket ball is moving, state at which stage of the flight

  a   the magnitude of the resultant is greatest,

  b   the angle between the resultant and the vertical is greatest.

6   A child has weight 450 N. Whilst on a fairground ride the child is subject to a force **P** acting at 35° to the upward vertical, as shown in the diagram. Given that the resultant of **P** and the child's weight acts horizontally,

  a   find the magnitude of this resultant,

  b   state the direction of the child's acceleration,

  c   find the magnitude of the child's acceleration.

7   A package of weight 6 N slides down a smooth chute which is inclined at 50° to the horizontal. The chute exerts a force **C** on the package, which acts in a direction at right angles to the chute, as shown in the diagram. Given that the resultant of **C** and the weight of the package acts in a direction down the chute, find

  a   the magnitude of this resultant,

  b   the magnitude of the acceleration of the package.

150

8   Horizontal forces **P** and **Q** act on a particle of mass 0.8 kg which is free to move on a horizontal plane. **P** has magnitude 0.5 N and bearing 020°, and **Q** has magnitude 0.7 N and bearing 100°. Find the distance travelled by the particle while its speed increases from rest to 4 m s⁻¹.

9   Use scale drawing to find the magnitude of the resultant of the forces **P** and **Q** in the following cases. Confirm your answer in each case by calculation.

  a   **P** has magnitude 15 N and bearing 035°, **Q** has magnitude 20 N and the resultant has bearing 050°.

  b   **P** has magnitude 20 N and bearing 040°, **Q** has magnitude 25 N and the resultant has bearing 075°.

  c   **P** has magnitude 10 N and bearing 055°, **Q** has magnitude 15 N and the resultant has bearing 110°.

  d   **P** has magnitude 25 N and bearing 080°, **Q** has magnitude 30 N and the resultant has bearing 040°.

10   A rock-climber has weight 550 N. A rope attached to her waist-belt passes through a ring which is fixed at a point higher up the cliff. She loses her foothold and starts to move in a direction at 20° to the horizontal. The tension in the rope at this instant is 560 N.

  Calculate the angle that the rope makes with the vertical.

11   Find the magnitudes of the components **P** and **Q** of the force **R** in the following cases.

  a   **R** has magnitude 20 N due north, **P** and **Q** have bearings 040° and 320°.

  b   **R** has magnitude 25 N due east, **P** and **Q** have bearings 110° and 310°.

  c   **R** has magnitude 30 N due south, **P** and **Q** have bearings 075° and 225°.

  d   **R** has magnitude 35 N due west, **P** and **Q** have bearings 220° and 300°.

12   A force **F** acts in an easterly direction. It has components **P** and **Q**; **P** is known and the magnitude of **Q** is to be as small as possible. Describe the component **Q** when

  a   **P** has magnitude 20 N and bearing 050°,

  b   **P** has magnitude 20 N and bearing 120°.

13   An object can slide on a path inclined at 15° to the horizontal. It is acted on by a force of magnitude 50 N, acting at an angle of 5° to the upward vertical, as shown in the diagram. Find the components of the force

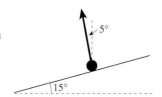

  a   in directions parallel to and at right angles to the path,

  b   in horizontal and vertical directions,

  c   in directions parallel to the path and horizontally,

  d   in directions at right angles to the path and horizontally,

  e   in directions parallel to the path and vertically,

  f   in directions at right angles to the path and vertically.

151

14

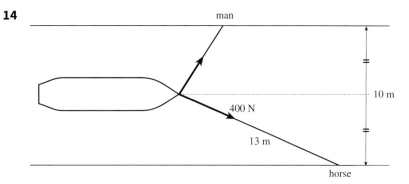

A barge moves in a straight line parallel to and midway between the banks of a canal of width 10 m. A horse on one bank and a man on the other bank pull the barge with taut horizontal towropes. The length of the towrope pulled by the horse is 13 m and the tension in it is 400 N, as shown in the diagram. Assuming the resultant of the two tensions is in the direction of motion of the barge, state the direction in which the man must pull to exert the least effort. Find the corresponding tension.

15 A particle of mass 0.2 kg moves in a straight line AB on a horizontal surface, under the influence of horizontal forces **P** and **Q**. The direction of **P** makes an angle of $30°$ with AB. The distance AB is 1.5 m and the speed of the particle is $1 \, \mathrm{m \, s^{-1}}$ at A and $2 \, \mathrm{m \, s^{-1}}$ at B. If the magnitude of **Q** is as small as possible, find the magnitude of **P**.

10.3 Combining forces by perpendicular components

The process of splitting and combining forces in perpendicular directions suggests another method of calculating the resultant of two or more forces.

Step 1 Choose two directions at right angles.

Step 2 Split each force into components in these directions.

Step 3 For each direction, find the sum of the components you have calculated.

Step 4 Find the resultant of the two sums.

EXAMPLE 10.3.1

Use this procedure to calculate the resultant of **P** and **Q** in Fig. 10.1 (page 145).

The solution shows the procedure in use with two different choices of directions.

Choice 1   Choose the directions to be north and east, as shown in Fig. 10.14. The calculation is set out in Table 10.15; the first two lines of figures correspond to Step 2, and the third line is Step 3.

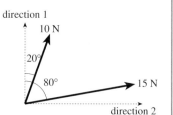

Fig. 10.14

Table 10.15

Force	Component in	
	direction 1 (north)	direction 2 (east)
P	$10 \cos 20° = 9.39...$	$10 \sin 20° = 3.42...$
Q	$15 \cos 80° = 2.60...$	$15 \sin 80° = 14.77...$
R	$12.00...$	$18.19...$

The resultant of 12.00... N north and 18.19... N east is a force of magnitude $\sqrt{12.00...^2 + 18.19...^2}$ N, or 22 N to the nearest whole number. It acts at an angle $\tan^{-1}\dfrac{18.19...}{12.00...}$, or 57° to the nearest degree, to the north direction.

Choice 2   The calculation is simpler if you choose one of the directions to be parallel to one of the forces, say **P**. This is shown in Fig. 10.16, and the calculation is set out in Table 10.17.

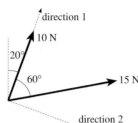

Fig. 10.16

Table 10.17

Force	Component in	
	direction 1 ($\parallel$ to **P**)	direction 2 ($\perp$ to **P**)
P	10	0
Q	$15\cos 60° = 7.5$	$15\sin 60° = 12.99...$
R	17.5	12.99...

The resultant of 17.5 N parallel to **P** and 12.99... N perpendicular to **P** is a force of magnitude $\sqrt{17.5^2 + 12.99...^2}$ N, or 22 N, at an angle $\tan^{-1}\dfrac{12.99...}{17.5}$, or 37°, to the direction of **P** (both to the nearest whole number). So the bearing is $(020 + 037)° = 057°$.

With this method you need to take care when calculating the direction of the resultant. Using $\tan^{-1}$ to find the angle leaves you with two possible ways in which the resultant could point. If the components of **R** in directions 1 and 2 are denoted by R_1 and R_2, then the angle which the resultant makes with direction 1 could be either $\tan^{-1}\dfrac{R_2}{R_1}$ or $\tan^{-1}\dfrac{R_2}{R_1} \pm 180°$. Draw for yourself diagrams with the four possible sign combinations:

$$R_1 > 0,\ R_2 > 0;\quad R_1 > 0,\ R_2 < 0;\quad R_1 < 0,\ R_2 > 0;\quad R_1 < 0,\ R_2 < 0.$$

You will see that in the first two cases the resultant makes an acute angle with direction 1.

The angle is therefore given by $\tan^{-1}\dfrac{R_2}{R_1}$, since by definition the angle $\tan^{-1} x$ lies between $-90°$ and $90°$. But in the last two cases the resultant makes an obtuse angle with direction 1, so the angle is $\tan^{-1}\dfrac{R_2}{R_1} \pm 180°$.

The rule is therefore that if $R_1 > 0$ (as it is in Example 10.3.1), the angle is $\tan^{-1}\dfrac{R_2}{R_1}$; but if $R_1 < 0$ you have to add or subtract 180°.

It is not worthwhile remembering this rule. In a numerical example it is easy to check with a sketch whether you have chosen the correct angle. But it is important to remember that you have to make the decision.

The advantage of the splitting and combining method is greatest when you want to find the resultant of several forces. The next example solves such a problem by scale drawing and by the component method.

EXAMPLE 10.3.2

The following four forces act on a particle (see Fig. 10.18). Find their resultant **V**.

P 6 N in the *x*-direction

Q 8 N at 50° to the *x*-direction

S 12 N in the negative *y*-direction

U 10 N at 160° to the *x*-direction

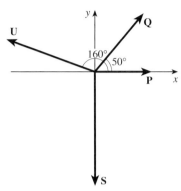

Fig. 10.18

Method 1 The force diagram is drawn in Fig. 10.19 on a scale of 1 cm to 4 N. It contains a chain of four arrows, **P**, **Q**, **S** and **U**. The resultant **V** is represented by the arrow from the tail of **P** to the head of **U**.

To see why, draw in the broken arrows **R** and **T**. **R** is the resultant of **P** and **Q**. **T** is the resultant of **R** and **S**; that is, of **P**, **Q** and **S**. **V** is the resultant of **T** and **U**; that is, of **P**, **Q**, **S** and **U**.

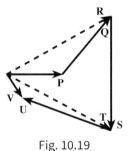

Fig. 10.19

By measurement the arrow labelled **V** has length 0.75 cm and is at an angle of 55° below the *x*-axis. So the resultant is about 3 N at an angle of −55° to the *x*-axis.

Method 2 Table 10.20 shows the components in the *x*- and *y*-directions of the forces and of their resultant.

Table 10.20

Force	Component in	
	x-direction	*y*-direction
P	6	0
Q	$8\cos 50° = 5.14\ldots$	$8\sin 50° = 6.12\ldots$
S	0	−12
U	$10\cos 160° = -9.39\ldots$	$10\sin 160° = 3.42\ldots$
V	1.74…	−2.45…

The resultant of 1.74… N in the *x*-direction and −2.45… N in the *y*-direction has magnitude $\sqrt{1.74\ldots^2 + (-2.45\ldots)^2}$ N, or 3.01 N, and makes an angle $\tan^{-1}\dfrac{-2.45\ldots}{1.74\ldots}$, or −54.5°, with the *x*-axis.

In solving this example, the first method is fine, but you will often want greater accuracy than you can achieve with scale drawing. You don't need to include in the diagram the intermediate resultant forces **R** and **T**. The figure formed by **P**, **Q**, **S**, **U** and the resultant **V** is called a **force polygon**.

However, if you want to calculate the resultant accurately with this method you have to use the sine and cosine rules in three triangles, one after the other. This is very laborious. The second method, using components, is the only sensible way to find the resultant by calculation when there are forces in more than two directions.

10.4   Using algebraic notation

The process of finding a resultant **R** of two forces **P** and **Q** is called **vector addition**, and is expressed by the equation **R** = **P** + **Q**. This is of course a different operation from addition of numbers, though there are many similarities between the two. Notice that the magnitude of the resultant is not the sum of the magnitudes of the components. For instance, in Example 10.1.1 (working in newtons) $P = 10$ and $Q = 15$, but $R = 21.79...$, not 25.

If you use the component method for finding the resultant, the most obvious perpendicular directions to take are those of the x- and y-axes, as in method 2 of Example 10.3.2. In that case, it is usual to represent a force as a column of two numbers, called a **column vector**. A force with components X in the x-direction and Y in the y-direction is denoted by $\begin{pmatrix} X \\ Y \end{pmatrix}$.

Putting these two ideas together, you could write out the solution in method 2 of Example 10.3.2 in algebraic form:

$$\mathbf{V} = \mathbf{P} + \mathbf{Q} + \mathbf{S} + \mathbf{U} = \begin{pmatrix} 6 \\ 0 \end{pmatrix} + \begin{pmatrix} 8\cos 50° \\ 8\sin 50° \end{pmatrix} + \begin{pmatrix} 0 \\ -12 \end{pmatrix} + \begin{pmatrix} 10\cos 160° \\ 10\sin 160° \end{pmatrix}$$

$$= \begin{pmatrix} 6 \\ 0 \end{pmatrix} + \begin{pmatrix} 5.14... \\ 6.12... \end{pmatrix} + \begin{pmatrix} 0 \\ -12 \end{pmatrix} + \begin{pmatrix} -9.39... \\ 3.42... \end{pmatrix}$$

$$= \begin{pmatrix} 6 + 5.14... + 0 + (\pm 9.39...) \\ 0 + 6.12... + (-12) + 3.42... \end{pmatrix} = \begin{pmatrix} 1.75 \\ -2.45 \end{pmatrix}, \text{ to 3 significant figures.}$$

There is nothing essentially new here that is not in Table 10.20. You may use whichever layout you prefer. However, more advanced mechanics uses vector operations other than addition. The advantages of using column-vector notation then become apparent. So you may like to get some practice in using it now in simple applications.

Exercise 10B

1   Rework Exercise 10A Question 1 using the splitting and combining method, taking components in directions north and east.

2   Repeat Question 1, taking components parallel to and at right angles to **P**.

3   Rework Exercise 10A Question 2 using the splitting and combining method, taking components parallel and at right angles to the direction in which the car is facing.

4 Find the magnitude and direction of the resultant of the four forces $\begin{pmatrix} -5 \\ 12 \end{pmatrix}$N,

$\begin{pmatrix} -18 \\ -8 \end{pmatrix}$N, $\begin{pmatrix} 4 \\ 9 \end{pmatrix}$N and $\begin{pmatrix} 4 \\ -5 \end{pmatrix}$N.

5 Express each of the three forces shown in the diagram in column-vector form. Find the resultant of the three forces in column-vector form, and hence find the magnitude and direction of the resultant.

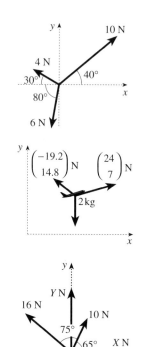

6 The diagram represents a model aircraft of mass 2 kg. Its engine produces a force of $\begin{pmatrix} 24 \\ 7 \end{pmatrix}$N, and the force of the air on its wings is $\begin{pmatrix} -19.2 \\ 14.8 \end{pmatrix}$N. Find the magnitude and direction of the acceleration of the aircraft.

7 In the first diagram, the resultant of the four forces is $\begin{pmatrix} 7 \\ 24 \end{pmatrix}$N. By expressing this in the notation of vector addition, find the values of X and Y. New directions are now chosen parallel and perpendicular to the resultant force, as shown in the second diagram. Rewrite the equation of vector addition in column vectors relative to the new directions, and check that this equation is satisfied by the values of X and Y that you have found.

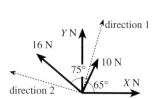

8 A particle of mass 2.6 kg moves in a straight line on a horizontal surface under the influence of horizontal forces $\begin{pmatrix} X \\ 0.2 \end{pmatrix}$N and $\begin{pmatrix} 0.7 \\ 0.3 \end{pmatrix}$N. The velocity of the particle increases from $2\,\mathrm{m\,s^{-1}}$ to $3.5\,\mathrm{m\,s^{-1}}$ in 3 seconds. Find the two possible values of X.

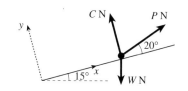

9 A particle of weight W N moves up an inclined track under the action of a pull of magnitude P N at 20° to the track. The track is at 15° to the horizontal. The normal contact force has magnitude C N. Taking axes parallel and perpendicular to the track, find the resultant force on the particle, in terms of W, P and C, in column-vector form.

Given that the resultant force is parallel to the track, express C and the magnitude of the resultant force in terms of P and W.

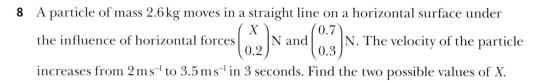

10 Find the magnitude and the direction of the resultant of $\begin{pmatrix} 2 \\ 7 \end{pmatrix}$N, $\begin{pmatrix} 8 \\ -5 \end{pmatrix}$N and $\begin{pmatrix} -5 \\ 10 \end{pmatrix}$N.

11 A load of weight 285 N is supported by two ropes. They exert on the load tension forces of $\begin{pmatrix} 84 \\ 288 \end{pmatrix}$N and $\begin{pmatrix} -40 \\ 30 \end{pmatrix}$N, where the components are in the horizontal and vertical directions. Find the magnitude of the resultant force on the load, and the angle which its direction makes with each of the ropes.

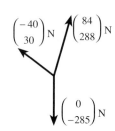

12 A particle of mass m moves in a straight line on a horizontal surface under the influence of horizontal forces $\begin{pmatrix} 2mx \\ -m \end{pmatrix}, \begin{pmatrix} m \\ mx \end{pmatrix}, \begin{pmatrix} mx \\ 2mx \end{pmatrix}$. The particle has an initial velocity of $1.5\,\mathrm{m\,s^{-1}}$, and travels 7 m in 2 seconds. Find the two possible values of x.

10.5 Equilibrium

i Two forces in equilibrium

Fig. 10.21 shows two people pulling the two ends of a rope. The person on the right pulls with a force **P**, the person on the left with a force **Q**. Until it breaks, the rope remains at rest. The weight of the rope is negligible compared with the pulling forces.

Fig. 10.21

The two people are pulling with forces of equal magnitude, so the force diagram for the resultant of **P** and **Q** has the form of Fig. 10.22. Since the tail of **P** coincides with the head of **Q**, the resultant force is zero. This is expressed algebraically by the equation **P** + **Q** = **0**, where **0** denotes the zero vector.

Fig. 10.22

Alternatively, you can write **Q** = −**P**, where the symbol −**P** stands for the force with the same magnitude as **P** but in the opposite direction.

ii Three forces in equilibrium

Consider the following two problems.

> A crate is being unloaded from a ship on to a dock down a ramp inclined at 5° to the horizontal. It is placed on a wheeled trolley, so that friction is negligible. The total mass of the trolley and crate is 80 kg. The crate is held steady by a member of the crew, who supports it with a force at 30° to the horizontal, as shown in Fig. 10.23. How large a force must he exert?

Fig. 10.23

> In a military exercise a soldier of mass 80 kg is lowered over a river by a cable from a helicopter. She catches a lifeline which is used to pull her towards the river bank, as shown in Fig. 10.24. When the cable is at 5° to the vertical, the lifeline is at 30° to the horizontal. How large is the tension in the lifeline?

At first sight these appear to be quite different problems, but you will see from Fig. 10.25 that, when the crate and the soldier are modelled as particles acted on by forces, the two models are identical. It is unimportant that in the first problem the force **U** is provided by the push from the crewman's hand and the force **V** is the normal contact force from the ramp, but that in the second case **U** and **V** are the tensions in the lifeline and the helicopter cable. Also, what matters is not the point at which each force is applied, but only the line along which it acts, which in this model must pass through the point representing the particle. This is called the **line of action** of the force.

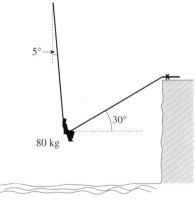

Fig. 10.24

It would be possible to complete the solution by resolving in two directions, but this is not easy unless you choose the two directions rather cleverly. A simpler method is to use vector ideas and to calculate the forces by trigonometry.

So in both problems you have a weight **W** of 800 N supported by two forces, **U** at 30° to the horizontal and **V** at 5° to the vertical. The resultant of **U** and **V** must therefore be equal and opposite to the weight. Algebraically,

$$\mathbf{U} + \mathbf{V} = -\mathbf{W}, \qquad \text{or} \qquad \mathbf{U} + \mathbf{V} + \mathbf{W} = \mathbf{0}.$$

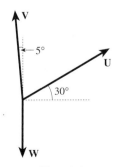

Fig. 10.25

This equation is represented by Fig. 10.26. This is an example of a **triangle of forces**.

> **Triangle of forces**   **If three forces X, Y and Z are in equilibrium, then the corresponding vectors can be represented by the sides of a closed triangle in which at each vertex the head of one vector arrow meets the tail of another.**

You can now find the magnitude, U N, of the force **U**, either by scale drawing or by applying the sine rule to the triangle of forces. From Fig. 10.27, this gives

$$\frac{U}{\sin 5°} = \frac{800}{\sin 115°}, \quad \text{so} \quad U\frac{800 \sin 5°}{\sin 115°} = 76.9\ldots.$$

So the crewman can steady the crate by pushing with a force of about 77 N, and the tension in the lifeline is also about 77 N.

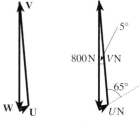

Fig. 10.26   Fig. 10.27

EXAMPLE 10.5.1

Three strings are knotted together at one end, and parcels of weights 5 N, 7 N and 9 N are attached to the other ends. The first two strings are placed over smooth horizontal pegs, and the third parcel hangs freely, as shown in Fig. 10.28. The system is in equilibrium. Find the angles which the first two strings make with the vertical between the knot and the pegs.

Since the pegs are smooth, the tensions in the strings at the knot are 5 N, 7 N and 9 N as shown in Fig. 10.29, and these forces are in equilibrium. The three vectors therefore form a closed triangle of forces, as in Fig. 10.30.

Fig. 10.28

You can complete the solution either by scale drawing or by trigonometry. If you use scale drawing, begin by drawing the 9 N arrow to your chosen scale, since you know its direction. Then find the third vertex of the triangle as

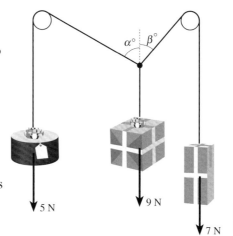

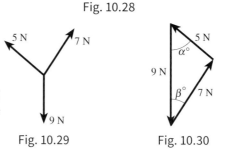

Fig. 10.29   Fig. 10.30

the intersection of arcs with radii proportional to 5 N and 7 N on the same scale.

To calculate the angles $\alpha°$ and $\beta°$ which the 5 N and 7 N strings make with the vertical by trigonometry, use the cosine rule in the forms

$$7^2 = 5^2 + 9^2 - 2 \times 5 \times 9 \times \cos \alpha° \quad \text{and} \quad 5^2 = 7^2 + 9^2 - 2 \times 7 \times 9 \times \cos \beta°.$$

These equations give $\cos \alpha° = \frac{57}{90}$ and $\cos \beta° = \frac{105}{126}$, so $\alpha = 50.7\ldots$ and $\beta = 33.5\ldots$.

The 5 N and 7 N strings make angles of about 51° and 34° with the vertical respectively.

158

EXAMPLE 10.5.2

A trough is formed from two rectangular planks at angles of 30° and 40° to the horizontal, joined along a horizontal edge. A cylindrical log of weight 400 N is placed in the trough with its axis horizontal. Calculate the magnitudes P N and Q N of the normal contact forces from each plank on the log

a using a triangle of forces,

b by resolving.

Fig. 10.31 shows the forces on the log. The log has no tendency to slip, so there is equilibrium without any frictional force, and the contact forces act along radii of the log.

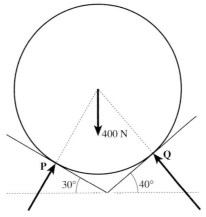

Fig. 10.31

a The forces **P** and **Q** are at 30° and 40° to the vertical, so the triangle of forces has the form of Fig. 10.32. By the sine rule,

$$\frac{P}{\sin 40°} = \frac{Q}{\sin 30°} = \frac{400}{\sin 110°},$$

so $P = \dfrac{400 \sin 40°}{\sin 110°} = 273.6\ldots$

and $Q = \dfrac{400 \sin 30°}{\sin 110°} = 212.8\ldots$

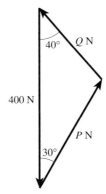

Fig. 10.32

The forces **P** and **Q** have magnitude 274 N and 213 N respectively, to 3 significant figures.

b If you resolve horizontally and vertically you get two simultaneous equations for P and Q, with unpleasant coefficients, which are awkward to solve. But you can get the answers directly by resolving parallel to each of the planks.

Since **P** is at 60° to the horizontal, it is at $(60-40)° = 20°$ to the right plank. The weight is at $(90-40)° = 50°$ to the right plank.

$\mathcal{R}(\parallel$ to right plank) $\qquad P \cos 20° = 400 \cos 50°.$

Since $\cos 20° = \sin 70° = \sin 110°$ and $\cos 50° = \sin 40°$,

$P = \dfrac{400 \sin 40°}{\sin 110°}$, as before.

Check for yourself that resolving parallel to the left plank leads to the same expression for Q as that found from the triangle of forces.

The reason why you get simpler equations by resolving parallel to the planks is that, in each case, one of the forces does not come into the equation. For example, **Q** acts at right angles to the right plank, so its resolved part parallel to the right plank is zero. The only unknown force in the equation is therefore P N.

This is a useful general rule.

> **If two forces of unknown magnitude act on a particle in equilibrium, they can be found directly by resolving in directions perpendicular to each force.**

Notice that in Example 10.5.2 this involves resolving in two directions which are not perpendicular to each other. Although many problems are best solved by resolving in two perpendicular directions, it is sometimes better to use non-perpendicular directions.

The next example uses a geometrical trick: a triangle similar to the triangle of forces is constructed in the diagram.

EXAMPLE 10.5.3

A coordinate grid is marked on a vertical wall. Small smooth pegs are driven into the wall at the points (–3,11) and (9,7) and a hoop of weight W and radius $\sqrt{130}$ rests on the pegs with its centre at the origin. Find the magnitudes of the contact forces at the pegs in terms of W.

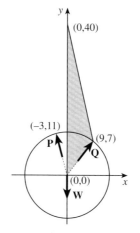

Fig. 10.33

Since the pegs are smooth, contact forces of magnitudes P and Q act along the radii, as shown in Fig. 10.33. Therefore, in the triangle of forces, one arrow must point in the negative y-direction and the other two have gradients $-\frac{11}{3}$ and $\frac{7}{9}$.

If you draw a line with gradient $-\frac{11}{3}$ through the point (9,7), you can verify that it cuts the y-axis at the point (0,40). So a triangle with vertices (0,0), (9,7) and (0,40) is similar to the triangle of forces, with sides proportional to P, Q and W.

The lengths of the sides of this triangle are $\sqrt{(-9)^2 + 33^2} = 3\sqrt{130}, \sqrt{9^2 + 7^2} = \sqrt{130}$ and 40. Therefore

$$\frac{P}{3\sqrt{130}} = \frac{Q}{\sqrt{130}} = \frac{W}{40},$$

so $P = \frac{3}{40}\sqrt{130}\,W$ and $Q = \frac{1}{40}\sqrt{130}\,W$.

Another approach to solving problems involving three forces acting on a particle is to use Lami's Theorem. You are not required to know this theorem for the Module M1 examination, but you are permitted to use it when answering questions if you wish to.

If three non-parallel forces A, B and C are in equilibrium, with the angle between A and B being $\gamma°$ and so on, as shown in figure 10.34, then

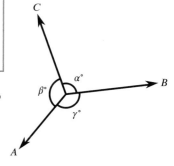

Fig. 10.34

$$\frac{A}{\sin\alpha^\circ} = \frac{B}{\sin\beta^\circ} = \frac{C}{\sin\gamma^\circ}.$$

Note that this formula is identical to the sine rule formula, though the meanings of the letters is different in this case.

We can prove Lami's theorem using a triangle of forces. If we redraw the figure to make a triangle of forces, we obtain the diagram shown in Figure 10.35.

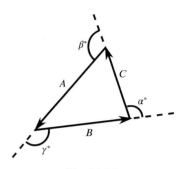

Fig. 10.35

We can now apply the sine rule to this triangle to obtain

$$\frac{A}{\sin(180^\circ - \alpha^\circ)} = \frac{B}{\sin(180^\circ - \beta^\circ)} = \frac{C}{\sin(180^\circ - \gamma^\circ)}.$$

Since $\sin(180^\circ - x^\circ) = \sin x^\circ$ for all angles, x°, Lami's theorem follows.

As an example of using this theorem, consider Example 10.5.2 again.

The forces $P\,\text{N}$, $Q\,\text{N}$ and $400\,\text{N}$ passing through the centre of the log can be shown as in Figure 10.36.

Then from this diagram, Lami's theorem gives

$$\frac{P}{\sin140^\circ} = \frac{Q}{\sin150^\circ} = \frac{400}{\sin70^\circ}$$

from which we deduce

$$P = \frac{400}{\sin70^\circ} \times \sin140^\circ = 273.6\ldots$$

and $Q = \dfrac{400}{\sin70^\circ} \times \sin150^\circ = 212.8\ldots$ as before.

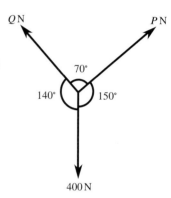

Fig. 10.36

iii More forces in equilibrium

There is no difficulty in extending the triangle of forces to situations in which there are more than three forces. If four forces are in equilibrium, then the arrows representing them form a closed quadrilateral, and so on. The problem arises when you want to do calculations with the sides and angles of the quadrilateral, since this usually involves splitting the quadrilateral into two triangles.

This means, in effect, beginning by combining two of the forces into a single force, and then using a triangle of forces.

Exercise 10C

You should use a geometrical method to work the problems in this exercise.

1 An object is in equilibrium under the action of three horizontal forces **P**, **Q** and **R**. Use a triangle of forces to find the magnitudes of **Q** and **R** respectively in each of the following cases.

    a **P** has magnitude $10\,\text{N}$ and bearing 090°, **Q** and **R** have bearings 210° and 340° respectively.

    b **P** has magnitude $20\,\text{N}$ and bearing 020°, **Q** and **R** have bearings 090° and 240° respectively.

    Confirm your answers by resolving in directions perpendicular to **R** and to **Q**.

161

2   A cable car is connected to a cable by two rigid supports which make angles of 75° and 35° with the upward vertical, as shown in the diagram. Find the tensions in the supports when the total weight of the cable car and its passengers is 8000 N and the cable car is stationary.

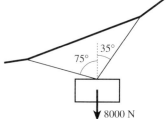

3   An object of mass 5 kg is held at rest on a smooth plane, inclined at an angle of 20°, by a force of magnitude P N acting directly up the plane.

   a   State the direction of the force exerted by the plane on the object, and find its magnitude.

   b   Hence state the magnitude and direction of the force exerted by the object on the plane.

   c   Find the value of P.

4   A skier of weight 700 N is pulled at constant speed up a smooth slope, of inclination 15°, by a force of magnitude P N acting at 25° upwards from the slope, as shown in the diagram. Find the value of P.

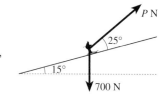

5   A small sign of weight 6 N is suspended by two chains AC and BC, as shown in the diagram.

   A and B are attached to fixed points which are 60 cm apart and at the same horizontal level. The lengths of AC and BC are 40 cm and 30 cm. Calculate the tensions in the chains.

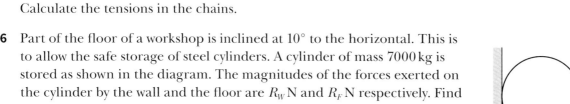

6   Part of the floor of a workshop is inclined at 10° to the horizontal. This is to allow the safe storage of steel cylinders. A cylinder of mass 7000 kg is stored as shown in the diagram. The magnitudes of the forces exerted on the cylinder by the wall and the floor are R_W N and R_F N respectively. Find the values of R_W and R_F.

   If the sloping part of the floor was inclined at $\alpha°$ $(0 < \alpha < 45)$ instead of at 10°, show that

   a $R_W < 70000 < R_F$, whatever the value of α,

   b R_W and R_F both increase with α.

7   A body is in equilibrium under the action of three horizontal forces **P**, **Q** and **R**. Find the angle between the direction of **P** and the direction of **Q**, and the angle between the direction of **P** and the direction of **R**, in each of the following cases.

   a   **P**, **Q** and **R** have magnitudes 16 N, 24 N and 25 N respectively.

   b   **P**, **Q** and **R** have magnitudes 7 N, 20 N and 25 N respectively.

8   A child of weight 300 N is seated on a swing which is supported by the tension in the rope of magnitude 320 N. The child and the swing are held at rest by a restraining force of magnitude 130 N, as shown in the diagram. Find the angles that

   a   the rope,   **b**   the restraining force,

   make with the upward vertical.

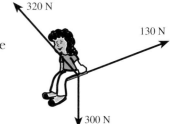

9   A tanker is being steered at constant speed along a channel by two tugs. The cables from the tugs have tensions of 45 000 N and 20 000 N and the motion of the tanker is resisted by a drag force of 52 000 N. Find the angle between each cable and the direction of motion of the tanker.

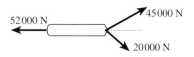

162

10 A particle of mass m hangs by a thread from a hook. It is pulled aside with the thread at an angle of $\alpha°$ from the vertical by a force. In what direction should the force be applied for its magnitude to be as small as possible? Find an expression for its magnitude in this case in terms of m, g and α.

11 The diagram shows three strings, which are tied in a knot K. Two of the strings pass over smooth pulleys and have particles of mass $0.3\,kg$ and $0.5\,kg$ attached to them at the ends opposite to K. The other string has a particle of mass $m\,kg$ attached to it at the end opposite to K. The system is at rest.

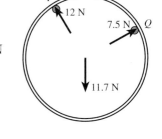

a In the case $m = 0.7$, find the angle made by the sloping part of each string with the upward vertical.

b Give a reason why $m < 0.8$.

c In the case when $m = 0.4$, show that part of one of the strings is horizontal.

d If the pulleys were at the same horizontal level, give a reason why $m > 0.4$.

12 A particle is in equilibrium under the action of three horizontal forces $\mathbf{P}$, $\mathbf{Q}$ and $\mathbf{R}$. The magnitudes of $\mathbf{P}$, $\mathbf{Q}$ and $\mathbf{R}$ are $25\,N$, $Q\,N$ and $R\,N$ respectively, and the cosine of the angle between $\mathbf{P}$ and $\mathbf{Q}$ is -0.96. Show that $R^2 = (Q - 24)^2 + 7^2$. Hence find

a the least possible value of R,

b the corresponding angle between $\mathbf{Q}$ and $\mathbf{R}$.

13 A hoop of diameter $1.5\,m$ and weight $11.7\,N$ hangs on two smooth horizontal pegs P and Q. The forces exerted on the hoop by P and Q have magnitudes $12\,N$ and $7.5\,N$ respectively. Find the directions of these forces.

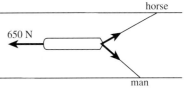

The x- and y-axes are taken to be horizontal and vertical respectively, and the origin O is the centre of the hoop. Find the (x,y) coordinates of P and Q.

14 A barge moves, at constant speed, in a straight line midway between the parallel banks of a canal. The banks are $8\,m$ apart. A horse on one bank and a man on the other bank exert pulling forces on the barge, through taut horizontal towropes. The length of the towrope pulled by the horse is $16.25\,m$. A horizontal drag force of magnitude $650\,N$ acts on the barge in a direction opposite to its motion, as shown in the diagram. State the angle between the towropes which minimises the effort exerted by the man. Find the magnitudes of the corresponding pulling forces.

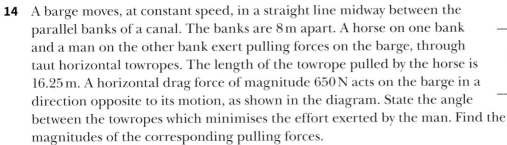

Miscellaneous exercise 10

1 Three coplanar forces act at a point. The magnitudes of the forces are $5\,N$, $6\,N$ and $7\,N$, and the directions in which the forces act are shown in the diagram. Find the magnitude and direction of the resultant of the three forces.

(Cambridge International AS and A level Mathematics 9709/04 Paper 4 Q2 June 2005)

2 Particles A of mass $0.65\,kg$ and B of mass $0.35\,kg$ are attached to the ends of a light inextensible string which passes over a fixed smooth pulley. B is held at rest with the string taut and both of its straight parts vertical. The system is released from rest and the particles move vertically. Find the tension in the string and the magnitude of the resultant force exerted on the pulley by the string.

(Cambridge International AS and A level Mathematics 9709/41 Paper 4 Q2 November 2011)

163

3 A particle is in equilibrium on a smooth horizontal table when acted on by the three horizontal forces shown in the diagram.

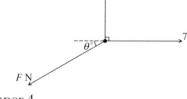

   i Find the values of F and θ.

   ii The force of magnitude 7 N is now removed. State the magnitude and direction of the resultant of the remaining two forces.

                           (Cambridge International AS and A level Mathematics 9709/04 Paper 4
                                           Q3 November 2007)

4 Forces of magnitudes 7 N, 10 N and 15 N act on a particle in the directions shown in the diagram.

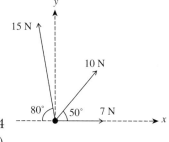

   i Find the component of the resultant of the three forces

        a in the x-direction,

        b in the y-direction.

   ii Hence find the direction of the resultant.

                           (Cambridge International AS and A level Mathematics 9709/04 Paper 4
                                            Q3 June 2009)

5 Each of three light strings has a particle attached to one of its ends. The other ends of the strings are tied together at a point A. The strings are in equilibrium with two of them passing over fixed smooth horizontal pegs, and with the particles hanging freely. The weights of the particles, and the angles between the sloping parts of the strings and the vertical, are as shown in the diagram. Find the values of W_1 and W_2.

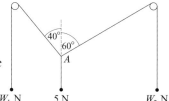

                       (Cambridge International AS and A level Mathematics 9709/04 Paper 4
                                          Q3 November 2005)

6 The diagram shows three particles A, B and C hanging freely in equilibrium, each being attached to the end of a string. The other ends of the three strings are tied together and are at the point X. The strings carrying A and C pass over smooth fixed horizontal pegs P_1 and P_2 respectively. The weights of A, B and C are 5.5 N, 7.3 N and W N respectively and the angle P_1XP_2 is a right angle. Find the angle AP_1X and the value of W.

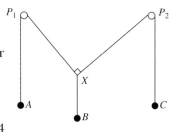

                       (Cambridge International AS and A level Mathematics 9709/41 Paper 4
                                        Q3 November 2010)

7 A small smooth ring R of weight 8.5 N is threaded on a light inextensible string. The ends of the string are attached to fixed points A and B, with A vertically above B. A horizontal force of magnitude 15.5 N acts on R so that the ring is in equilibrium with angle $ARB = 90°$. The part AR of the string makes an angle θ with the horizontal and the part BR makes an angle θ with the vertical (see diagram). The tension in the string is T N. Show that $T\sin\theta = 12$ and $T\cos\theta = 3.5$ and hence find θ.

                     (Cambridge International AS and A level Mathematics 9709/41 Paper 4
                                         Q3 June 2011)

8 Each of two forces has magnitude X N, and the resultant of the two forces has magnitude 12 N. When the magnitude of one of the forces is increased by 70%, the magnitude of the resultant of the two forces becomes 21 N. Find X and the angle between the two forces.

9 A force **F** of magnitude 12 N has components **P** and **Q**. The sum of the magnitudes of **P** and **Q** is 18 N. The direction of **Q** is at right angles to **F**. Find the magnitude of **Q**.

10 Forces **X**, **Y** and **Z** have magnitudes 10 N, $5(\sqrt{3}-1)$ N and $5(\sqrt{3}+1)$ N. The forces **Y** and **Z** act in the same direction, as shown in the diagram. The resultant of **X** and **Y** and the resultant of **X** and **Z** have the same magnitude. Find $\theta°$, the angle between **X** and **Y**.

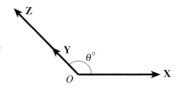

11 A particle of mass 0.7 kg is free to move on a horizontal surface under the influence of horizontal forces of magnitudes 1 N and 1.7 N. The particle starts from rest and reaches a speed of 3 m s⁻¹ in a distance of 1.5 m. Find the angle between the directions of the forces.

12 Three coplanar forces of magnitudes 15 N, 12 N and 12 N act at a point A in directions as shown in the diagram.

   i Find the component of the resultant of the three forces

      a in the direction of AB,

      b perpendicular to AB.

   ii Hence find the magnitude and direction of the resultant of the three forces.

   (Cambridge International AS and A level Mathematics 9709/41 Paper 4
   Q3 November 2011)

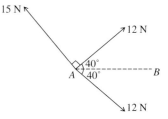

13 A particle P of weight 5 N is attached to one end of each of two light inextensible strings of lengths 30 cm and 40 cm. The other end of the shorter string is attached to a fixed point A of a rough rod which is fixed horizontally. A small ring S of weight W N is attached to the other end of the longer string and is threaded on to the rod. The system is in equilibrium with the strings taut and $AS = 50$ cm (see diagram).

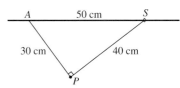

   i By resolving the forces acting on P in the direction of PS, or otherwise, find the tension in the longer string.

   ii Find the magnitude of the frictional force acting on S.

   iii Given that the coefficient of friction between S and the rod is 0.75, and that S is in limiting equilibrium, find the value of W.

   (Cambridge International AS and A level Mathematics 9709/41 Paper 4
   Q4 November 2009)

14 Two loads X and Y, of weights 800 N and 400 N respectively, are connected by a rope which passes over a pulley A. The forces acting on X, Y and A are as shown in the diagram. Find the magnitude and direction of the resultant force acting on each of X, Y and A.

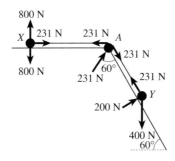

15 A concrete pyramid of weight 300 N is being lifted vertically upwards. The forces on the pyramid are a pulling force of magnitude 320 N, exerted by a wire which passes over a fixed pulley, and a restraining force of magnitude F N exerted by a rope being pulled by a man. The directions of the forces are as shown in the diagram. The values of F, θ and ϕ vary as the pyramid moves upwards, but the direction of the resultant force is always vertical. Find the value of F and the magnitude of the resultant, stating whether the resultant acts upwards or downwards, when

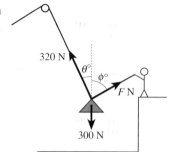

  a $\theta = 15$ and $\phi = 53$,   **b** $\theta = 19$ and $\phi = 90$,   **c** $\theta = 26$ and $\phi = 127$.

16 Forces of magnitudes P N and 25 N act at right angles to each other. The resultant of the two forces has magnitude R N and makes an angle of $\theta°$ with the x-axis (see diagram). The force of magnitude P N has components -2.8 N and 9.6 N in the x-direction and the y-direction respectively, and makes an angle of $\alpha°$ with the negative x-axis.

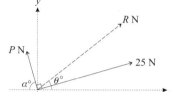

  i Find the values of P and R.

  ii Find the value of α, and hence find the components of the force of magnitude 25 N in

    a the x-direction,

    b the y-direction.

  iii Find the value of θ.

(Cambridge International AS and A level Mathematics 9709/04 Paper 4
Q6 November 2006)

17 Three coplanar forces of magnitudes 8 N, 12 N and 2 N act at a point. The resultant of the forces has magnitude R N. The directions of the three forces and the resultant are shown in the diagram. Find R and θ.

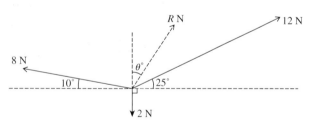

(Cambridge International AS and A level Mathematics 9709/41 Paper 4
Q4 November 2012)

Chapter 11
General motion in a straight line

This chapter extends the study of kinematics to include objects moving with acceleration which is not constant. When you have completed it, you should

- know how to use differentiation and integration to find expressions for acceleration, velocity and displacement as functions of time.

11.1 Velocity and acceleration

So far you have mostly met examples of objects moving with constant acceleration. And as acceleration is proportional to the force applied, the forces have also been constant.

But forces are often not constant. For example, on a bicycle you can't exert as much force on the pedals when you are going fast as you can at low speeds. If you are driving on a slippery road, it is wise to apply the brakes gently to start with and then gradually increase the pressure. If the force is variable, then so is the acceleration. How can you deal with this mathematically?

When the idea of acceleration was introduced in Section 1.3, it was described as the rate at which velocity increases. The clue lies in the word 'rate'. In P1 Section 7.4, it is shown that the rate at which a variable y increases with respect to an independent variable x is measured by the derivative $\dfrac{\mathrm{d}y}{\mathrm{d}x}$. In this mechanics application you want the rate at which the velocity v increases with respect to the time t, so this is measured by the derivative $\dfrac{\mathrm{d}v}{\mathrm{d}t}$.

Notice that this fits in with the rule you have already used for motion with constant acceleration, that the acceleration is the gradient of the velocity–time graph.

EXAMPLE 11.1.1

A car starts to accelerate as soon as it leaves a town. After t seconds its velocity $v\,\mathrm{m\,s^{-1}}$ is given by the formula $v = 14 + 0.45t^2 - 0.03t^3$, until it reaches maximum velocity. Find a formula for the acceleration. How fast is the car moving when its acceleration becomes zero?

The acceleration a is found by differentiating the formula for v, so

$$a = \frac{\mathrm{d}v}{\mathrm{d}t} = 0.9t - 0.09t^2.$$

This can be factorised as $a = 0.09t\,(10 - t)$, so the acceleration becomes zero when $t = 10$. This is when the car reaches its maximum velocity. After that the model no longer applies.

To find the maximum velocity, substitute $t = 10$ in the formula for v. This gives $v = 14 + 0.45 \times 100 - 0.03 \times 1000 = 14 + 45 - 30 = 29$.

The car reaches a maximum velocity of $29\,\mathrm{m\,s^{-1}}$ after 10 seconds.

Notice that in this example the acceleration is also zero when $t = 0$, but this is not relevant to the question asked. You can easily see that at time $t = 0$, $v = 14$. That is, the initial velocity of the car as it leaves the town is $14\,\mathrm{m\,s^{-1}}$.

Sketch for yourself the velocity–time graph for this example. Notice that when the acceleration is zero there is a stationary point on the graph.

11.2 Displacement and velocity

Just as acceleration is the rate of increase of velocity with respect to time, so velocity is the rate of increase of displacement.

If the displacement is constant, then the object is not moving, and the velocity is zero. The more rapidly the displacement changes, the faster the object is moving.

So if x denotes the displacement of the object from a fixed point of the line along which it is moving, the velocity is measured by the derivative $\dfrac{\mathrm{d}x}{\mathrm{d}t}$.

> **EXAMPLE 11.2.1**
>
> A space probe is launched by rockets. For the first stage of its ascent, which is in a vertical line and lasts for 40 seconds, the height x metres after t seconds is modelled by the equation $x = 50t^2 + \frac{1}{4}t^3$. How high is the probe at the end of the first stage, and how fast is it then moving?
>
> To find the height, you substitute 40 for t in the equation for x, which gives
>
> $$x = 50 \times 1600 + \tfrac{1}{4} \times 64\,000 = 96\,000.$$
>
> To find a formula for the velocity you must differentiate, to get
>
> $$v = \frac{\mathrm{d}x}{\mathrm{d}t} = 100t + \tfrac{3}{4}t^2.$$
>
> Substituting 40 for t in this equation gives
>
> $$v = 100 \times 40 + \tfrac{3}{4} \times 1600 = 4000 + 1200 = 5200.$$
>
> So at the end of the first stage the probe is at a height of 96 000 m and moving at 5200 m s⁻¹. This is more conveniently expressed in kilometre units: the height is then 96 km, and the velocity is 5.2 km s⁻¹.

Since velocity is the derivative of displacement, and acceleration is the derivative of velocity, it follows that acceleration is the second derivative of displacement. (See P1 Chapter 15.)

> **For an object moving in a straight line, if x denotes the displacement from a fixed point O of the line at time t, v denotes the velocity and a the acceleration, then**
>
> $$v = \frac{\mathrm{d}x}{\mathrm{d}t} \quad \text{and} \quad a = \frac{\mathrm{d}v}{\mathrm{d}t} = \frac{\mathrm{d}^2 x}{\mathrm{d}t^2}.$$
>
> **The velocity is represented by the gradient of the (t, x) graph.**
>
> **The acceleration is represented by the gradient of the (t, v) graph.**

Notice that there has been a small change of notation from Chapter 1, where the letter s was used for displacement. The reason is that s and x may stand for different quantities. In Chapter 1, s was the displacement from the position of the object when $t = 0$, so that $s = 0$ when $t = 0$. But it is sometimes more convenient to measure the displacement x

from some other point of the line. For example, to describe the complete motion of a spacecraft, it may be better to measure the displacement x from the centre of the Earth rather than from the launch point. Or, if someone throws a stone upwards from the top of a cliff and you are standing on the beach, you may prefer to measure the height of the stone above the beach rather than from the top of the cliff.

EXAMPLE 11.2.2

A remote-controlled toy racing car moves along a straight track laid on the floor. It starts at a point O and for the next 6 seconds its displacement x cm is modelled by the formula $x = t^3(t-4)(t-7)$, where t is the time in seconds. Describe the motion of the car in detail.

The displacement is 0 when $t = 0$ and when $t = 4$. The formula also gives $x = 0$ when $t = 7$, but this can be ignored, because the model only holds for values of t from 0 to 6. Also, x is positive when t is between 0 and 4, and negative when t is between 4 and 6. So the car starts out in the positive direction, comes back through O after 4 seconds and after that is on the negative side of O. This is shown in the displacement–time graph in Fig. 11.1.

To investigate this in more detail you need a formula for the velocity, so you have to differentiate. Multiplying out the expression for x gives

$$x = t^5 - 11t^4 + 28t^3,$$

so

$$v = 5t^4 - 44t^3 + 84t^2,$$

which you can factorise as

$$v = t^2(5t - 14)(t - 6).$$

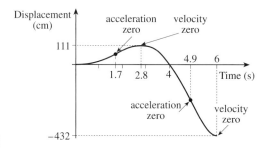

Fig. 11.1

This shows that other interesting values of t are 0, 2.8 and 6, when the velocity is zero. Also, v is positive when t is between 0 and 2.8, and negative when t is between 2.8 and 6. This is shown on the velocity–time graph in Fig. 11.2.

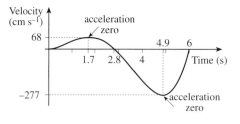

Fig. 11.2

The times at which the velocity is zero correspond to the stationary points on the displacement–time graph. (This is why such points are called 'stationary'.) By substituting $t = 2.8$ and $t = 6$ in the original formula for x, you can find the maximum distances from O in the positive and negative directions respectively. The values of x are $2.8^3 \times (-1.2) \times (-4.2) = 110.6\ldots$ and $6^3 \times 2 \times (-1) = -432$. These are marked on Fig. 11.1.

Fig. 11.2 suggests that it would also be interesting to find the maximum and minimum values of the velocity. These occur when $\dfrac{dv}{dt} = 0$, which is when the acceleration is zero. You already know the formula for v, so you can work out

$$a = \frac{dv}{dt} = 20t^3 - 132t^2 + 168t = 4t(5t^2 - 33t + 42).$$

This shows that $a = 0$ when $t = 0$ and when $t = \dfrac{33 \pm \sqrt{33^2 - 4 \times 5 \times 42}}{2 \times 5}$, which is when $t = 1.72\ldots$ and $t = 4.87\ldots$. Substituting these values of t into the formula for v gives $v = 68.3\ldots$ and $v = -277.3\ldots$. These are marked on Fig. 11.2.

You can now describe the motion of the car in detail. It starts off from O in the positive direction, and reaches a maximum velocity of about $68\,\mathrm{cm\,s^{-1}}$ after about 1.7 seconds. Then it decelerates, coming to rest after 2.8 seconds at a maximum displacement of about 111 centimetres from O. Its velocity then becomes negative, and the car moves back towards O, passing through O after 4 seconds and continuing onto the negative side of O. You can calculate, by substituting $t = 4$ in the formula for v, that it is then moving with a velocity of $(4^2 \times (5 \times 4 - 14) \times (4 - 6))\,\mathrm{cm\,s^{-1}}$, or $-192\,\mathrm{cm\,s^{-1}}$, which is a speed of $192\,\mathrm{cm\,s^{-1}}$ in the negative direction.

After about 4.9 seconds the car reaches its minimum velocity of about $-277\,\mathrm{cm\,s^{-1}}$, or $277\,\mathrm{cm\,s^{-1}}$ in the negative direction, and then starts to slow down. (But notice that this shows in Fig. 11.2 as a positive acceleration, not a deceleration! The velocity, which is negative, is increasing, but the speed is decreasing.) After 6 seconds, the largest value of t for which the formulae hold, the car has come to rest with a displacement of -432 centimetres; that is, at a distance of 432 centimetres from O in the negative direction.

The force applied on the car through the control mechanism must match the acceleration, which means that the controller has to anticipate the change of direction. So the force has to be switched from positive to negative when t is about 1.7 seconds, even though the car will not start to move backwards until $t = 2.8$. Similarly, to get the car to stop when $t = 6$, the force must be switched back to positive when t is about 4.9.

There is one last thing to notice. At the times when the velocity of the car is a maximum or minimum, after about 1.7 and 4.9 seconds, $\dfrac{\mathrm{d}v}{\mathrm{d}t} = 0$, so $\dfrac{\mathrm{d}^2x}{\mathrm{d}t^2} = 0$. These correspond to the points of inflexion marked on the displacement–time graph, which are the points where the displacement–time graph is steepest. Between $t = 0$ and $t = 1.7$, and between $t = 4.9$ and $t = 6$, where the acceleration is positive, the displacement–time graph bends upwards; between $t = 1.7$ and $t = 4.9$, where the acceleration is negative, the graph bends downwards.

Exercise 11A

In Questions 1 to 16, x metres is the displacement at time t seconds of a particle moving in a straight line, v is the velocity in $\mathrm{m\,s^{-1}}$ and a is the acceleration in $\mathrm{m\,s^{-2}}$. Only zero and positive values of t should be considered.

1 Given that $x = t^3 + 4t + 6$, find expressions for v and a in terms of t. Find the displacement, velocity and acceleration when $t = 2$.

2 Given that $x = 3 + 20t - t^4$, find expressions for v and a in terms of t. Find the displacement, velocity and acceleration when $t = 1$ and when $t = 3$.

3 Given that $x = t^3 + 5t$, find the displacement, velocity and acceleration when $t = 3$.

4 Given that $x = t(t - 2)(t - 5)$, find the displacement, velocity and acceleration when $t = 0$.

5 Given that $x = 36 - \dfrac{4}{t}$, find the velocity and acceleration when $t = 2$.

6 Given that $v = 3\sqrt{t}$, find the velocity and acceleration when $t = 4$.

7 Given that $x = 16 - 2t^3$, find the time when the displacement is zero. Find the velocity and acceleration at this instant.

8 Given that $x = 120 - 15t - 6t^2 + t^3$, find the time when the velocity is zero. Find the displacement at this instant.

9 Given that $x = 2 + 48t - t^3$, find the displacement when the velocity is zero.

10 Given that $v = t^2 - 12t + 40$, find the velocity when the acceleration is zero.

11 Given that $x = t^3 + 4t^2 + 3$, find the displacement and the velocity when the acceleration is $20\,\mathrm{m\,s^{-2}}$.

12 Given that $x = 10t - \dfrac{16}{\sqrt{t}}$, find the displacement and the acceleration when the velocity is $11\,\mathrm{m\,s^{-1}}$.

13 Given that $v = 32 - \dfrac{18}{t^2}$, find the acceleration when the velocity is $30\,\mathrm{m\,s^{-1}}$.

14 Given that $x = 2t^4 + 8t$, find the displacement and the acceleration when the velocity is $35\,\mathrm{m\,s^{-1}}$.

15 Given that $x = 4t^3 - 7t^2 + 10$, and that the particle has mass $5\,\mathrm{kg}$, find an expression for the resultant force acting on the particle in terms of t.

16 Given that $v = 4t(8 - t)$, and that the particle has mass $3\,\mathrm{kg}$,

  a find the maximum velocity,

  b sketch the (t, v) graph for $0 \leq t \leq 8$,

  c find the resultant force acting on the particle when $t = 2$.

17 A car is accelerating from rest. At time t seconds after starting, the velocity of the car is $v\,\mathrm{m\,s^{-1}}$, where $v = 6t - \frac{1}{2}t^2$, for $0 \leq t \leq 6$.

  a Find the velocity of the car 6 seconds after starting.

  b Find the acceleration of the car when its velocity is $10\,\mathrm{m\,s^{-1}}$.

18 A train leaves a station and travels in a straight line. After t seconds the train has travelled a distance x metres, where $x = (320t^3 - 2t^4) \times 10^{-5}$. This formula is valid until the train comes to rest at the next station.

  a Find when the train comes to rest, and hence find the distance between the two stations.

  b Find the acceleration of the train 40 seconds after the journey begins.

  c Find the deceleration of the train just before it stops.

  d Find when the acceleration is zero, and hence find the maximum velocity of the train.

19 An insect flies in a straight line from one flower to another. The two flowers are 270 cm apart and the flight takes 3 seconds. At time t seconds after the flight begins, the insect is x cm from the first flower. Two alternative models are proposed:

A $x = 60t^2 - 10t^3$,   **B** $x = 40t^3 - 10t^4$.

For each of these models,

a show that the model fits the given information about the flight,

b find the maximum velocity of the insect,

c sketch the (t,v) graph.

Comment on the differences between the two models. Which do you consider to be the better model?

20 A flare is launched from a hot-air balloon and moves in a vertical line. At time t seconds, the height of the flare is x metres, where $x = 1664 - 40t - \dfrac{2560}{t}$ for $t \geq 5$.

The flare is launched when $t = 5$.

a Find the height and the velocity of the flare immediately after it is launched.

b Find the acceleration of the flare immediately after it is launched, when its velocity is zero, and when $t = 25$.

c Find the terminal speed of the flare.

d Find when the flare reaches the ground.

e Sketch the (t,v) graph and the (t,x) graph for the motion of the flare.

11.3 The reverse problem

Section 11.2 shows how to find the acceleration, and therefore the force, if you know the displacement–time formula. But more often you want to work the other way round; that is, you know the force and want to find how fast an object is moving, and how far it has travelled, after a given time.

For this you need to use integration rather than differentiation. (See P1 Chapter 16.) The rules given in Section 11.2 can be turned round as follows.

> **For an object moving in a straight line, if a denotes the acceleration as a function of the time t,**
>
> $$v = \int a \, dt \quad \text{and} \quad x = \int v \, dt.$$

Remember that integration involves an arbitrary constant. You can usually find this by knowing the initial velocity, which was denoted by u in Chapter 1, and the initial displacement; these are the values of v and of x when $t = 0$.

EXAMPLE 11.3.1

A train of mass 500 tonnes is travelling on a straight track at $48 \, \text{m s}^{-1}$ when the driver sees an amber light ahead. He applies the brakes for a period of 30 seconds with a force given by the formula $4t(30 - t) \, \text{kN}$, where t is the time in seconds after the brakes are applied. Find how fast the train is moving after 30 seconds, and how far it has travelled in that time.

Begin by applying Newton's second law to find a formula for the acceleration of the train (which is in fact a deceleration, since the train is slowing down). To keep the numbers small, use units of tonnes for the mass and kilonewtons for the force. (Since 1 tonne = 1000 kg and 1 kN = 1000 N, the units are still consistent.) Then

$$-4t(30-t) = 500a, \qquad \text{so} \qquad a = -\tfrac{1}{125}t(30-t) = \tfrac{1}{125}t^2 - \tfrac{6}{25}t.$$

Integrating to find v,

$$v = \int\left(\tfrac{1}{125}t^2 - \tfrac{6}{25}t\right)\mathrm{d}t = \tfrac{1}{375}t^3 - \tfrac{3}{25}t^2 + k.$$

It is given that $v = 48$ when $t = 0$. Substituting these values gives

$$48 = 0 - 0 + k, \qquad \text{so} \qquad k = 48.$$

The formula for v is therefore

$$v = \tfrac{1}{375}t^3 - \tfrac{3}{25}t^2 + 48.$$

Integrating a second time to find x,

$$x = \int\left(\tfrac{1}{375}t^3 - \tfrac{3}{25}t^2 + 48\right)\mathrm{d}t = \tfrac{1}{1500}t^4 - \tfrac{1}{25}t^3 + 48t + c.$$

If x denotes the displacement from the instant when the brakes are first applied, then $x = 0$ when $t = 0$. Substituting these values gives

$$0 = 0 - 0 + 0 + c, \qquad \text{so} \qquad c = 0.$$

The formula for x is therefore

$$x = \tfrac{1}{1500}t^4 - \tfrac{1}{25}t^3 + 48t.$$

To find the final speed and the distance travelled, substitute $t = 30$ in the expressions for v and x. This gives

$$v = \tfrac{27000}{375} - \tfrac{3\times900}{25} + 48 = 72 - 108 + 48 = 12.$$

and

$$x = \tfrac{810000}{1500} - \tfrac{27000}{25} + 48 \times 30 = 540 - 1080 + 1440 = 900$$

The train slows down to a speed of $12\,\text{m s}^{-1}$, and travels 900 metres during the time that the brakes are on.

In this example, if you only want the distance the train travels while the brakes are on, and are not interested in the (t,x) formula, you could finish off the calculation by using a definite integral. The distance is

$$\int_0^{30}\left(\tfrac{1}{375}t^3 - \tfrac{3}{25}t^2 + 48\right)\mathrm{d}t = \left[\tfrac{1}{1500}t^4 - \tfrac{1}{25}t^3 + 48t\right]_0^{30}$$

$$= (540 - 1080 + 1440) - (0 - 0 + 0) - 900.$$

Since the definite integral gives the area under the velocity–time graph, this shows that the displacement is represented by this area.

For an object moving in a straight line, with the velocity v given as a function of the time t, the displacement between times t_1 and t_2 is given by

$$\int_{t_1}^{t_2} v \, \mathrm{d}t.$$

This displacement is represented by the area under the (t, v) graph for the interval $t_1 \leq t \leq t_2$.

EXAMPLE 11.3.2

For the car in Example 11.1.1, with velocity given by the formula $v = 14 + 0.45t^2 - 0.03t^3$, find the distance travelled while the car accelerates to its maximum velocity. Find also the average speed over this time.

It was shown that the car reaches its maximum velocity of $29 \, \mathrm{m\,s^{-1}}$ at time $t = 10$, so the displacement of the car over this time is

$$\int_0^{10} \left(14 + 0.45t^2 - 0.03t^3 \right) \mathrm{d}t = \left[14t + 0.15t^3 - 0.0075t^4 \right]_0^{10}$$
$$= (140 + 150 - 75) - (0 + 0 - 0) = 215.$$

The velocity is always positive during this time: the acceleration was found to be $0.09t(10 - t) \, \mathrm{m\,s^{-2}}$, which is positive for the first 10 seconds, so the velocity does not decrease. Therefore the distance travelled is equal to the displacement.

Hence the car travels 215 metres in the 10 seconds that it takes to reach its maximum velocity.

Recall from section 1.7 that $\text{average speed} = \dfrac{\text{distance travelled}}{\text{time taken}}$.

Its average speed is therefore $\dfrac{215 \, \mathrm{m}}{10 \, \mathrm{s}} = 21.5 \, \mathrm{m\,s^{-1}}$.

11.4 The constant acceleration formulae

Motion with constant acceleration is simply a special case of general motion in a straight line, so you can get the formulae in Chapter 1 by the integration method in Section 11.3.

First, since $\dfrac{\mathrm{d}v}{\mathrm{d}t} = a$, where a is now a constant number,

$$v = \int a \, \mathrm{d}t = at + k.$$

To find k, use the fact that the initial velocity is u, so that $v = u$ when $t = 0$. Therefore $u = a \times 0 + k$, which gives $k = u$. The velocity–time formula is therefore $v = at + u$, which is usually written as

$$v = u + at.$$

A second integration gives the displacement formula. Since u and a are both constant,

$$v = \int v \, \mathrm{d}t = \int (u + at) \mathrm{d}t = ut + \tfrac{1}{2}at^2 + c.$$

Now the quantity s in the constant acceleration equations is the displacement from the initial position at time $t = 0$, so that

s = displacement at time t − displacement at time 0

$$= \left(ut + \tfrac{1}{2}at^2 + c\right) - \left(u \times 0 + \tfrac{1}{2}a \times 0^2 + c\right)$$

$$= \left(ut + \tfrac{1}{2}at^2 + c\right) - (0 + 0 + c) = ut + \tfrac{1}{2}at^2.$$

Once you have the (t,v) and the (t,s) equations, you can find the other three equations in Section 1.5 algebraically, by eliminating a, t or u. This is Question 21 in Exercise 11B.

11.5 A shorthand notation

Expressions like $\dfrac{dx}{dt}$, $\dfrac{dv}{dt}$ and $\dfrac{d^2x}{dt^2}$ occur so often in mechanics that people often use a shorter notation when writing them. In this notation a dot is written over the top of a letter to denote the derivative with respect to time. Thus $\dfrac{dx}{dt}$ is written as $\dot{x}$ (pronounced 'x dot'), and $\dfrac{dv}{dt}$ as $\dot{v}$. A second derivative with respect to time is written with two dots, so that $\dfrac{d^2x}{dt^2}$ becomes $\ddot{x}$ (pronounced 'x double-dot').

In this notation the equation for Newton's second law becomes $F = m\ddot{x}$. For example, the first equation in Example 11.3.1 would be written

$$-4t(30 - t)500\ddot{x}$$

and the motion would be described by

$$\ddot{x} = \dot{v} = \tfrac{1}{125}t^2 - \tfrac{6}{25}t.$$

In fact, this notation did not begin life as a shorthand; it is very similar to the notation which Isaac Newton invented when he introduced his theory of 'fluxions'. The $\dfrac{dx}{dt}$ notation was invented by the German mathematician Gottfried Leibniz, who was working on the ideas of calculus at the same time as Newton but from a different point of view.

You do not need to use the dot notation yet, but if you intend to go on to more advanced mechanics you will find it very useful later. In that case, you may like to practise using it in the next exercise.

Exercise 11B

In Questions 1 to 20, x metres is the displacement at time t seconds of a particle moving in a straight line, v is the velocity in $m\,s^{-1}$ and a is the acceleration in $m\,s^{-2}$. Only zero and positive values of t should be considered.

1 Given that $v = 3t^2 + 8$ and that the displacement is $4\,m$ when $t = 0$, find an expression for x in terms of t. Find the displacement and the velocity when $t = 2$.

2 Given that $a = 10 - 6t^2$, and that the velocity is $4\,m\,s^{-1}$ and the displacement is $12\,m$ when $t = 1$, find expressions for v and x in terms of t. Find the displacement, velocity and acceleration when $t = 0$.

3 Given that $v = 6\sqrt{t}$ and that the displacement is $30\,\text{m}$ when $t = 4$, find the displacement, velocity and acceleration when $t = 1$.

4 Given that $a = 2 - \dfrac{6}{t^3}$, and that the velocity is $6\,\text{m}\,\text{s}^{-1}$ and the displacement is zero when $t = 1$, find the displacement, velocity and acceleration when $t = 3$.

5 Given that $v = 9 - t^2$ and that the displacement is $2\,\text{m}$ when $t = 0$, find the displacement when the velocity is zero.

6 Given that $a = 3t - 12$, and that the velocity is $30\,\text{m}\,\text{s}^{-1}$ and the displacement is $4\,\text{m}$ when $t = 0$, find the displacement when the acceleration is zero.

7 Given that $v = t^2 + 10t$ and that the displacement is $6\,\text{m}$ when $t = 0$, find the displacement when the acceleration is $16\,\text{m}\,\text{s}^{-2}$.

8 Given that $a = 4 - 2t$, and that the velocity is $5\,\text{m}\,\text{s}^{-1}$ when $t = 0$, find the acceleration when the velocity is zero.

9 Given that $v = 3t^2 + 4t + 3$, find the distance travelled between $t = 0$ and $t = 2$.

10 Given that $v = 12 - 8t^3$, find the distance travelled between $t = 0$ and $t = 1$.

11 Given that $v = 4 + 3\sqrt{t}$, find the distance travelled between $t = 1$ and $t = 4$.

12 Given that $v = \dfrac{3}{t^2}$, find the distance travelled between $t = 2$ and $t = 10$.

13 Given that $v = t^2 - 20$, find the distance travelled between $t = 0$ and $t = 4$.

14 Given that $v = \dfrac{1}{t^2} - 2$, find the distance travelled between $t = 1$ and $t = 5$.

15 Given that $a = 4t - 1$ and that the velocity is $5\,\text{m}\,\text{s}^{-1}$ when $t = 0$, find the distance travelled between $t = 0$ and $t = 3$.

16 Given that $a = 12 - 3\sqrt{t}$ and that the velocity is $15\,\text{m}\,\text{s}^{-1}$ when $t = 1$, find the distance travelled between $t = 1$ and $t = 25$.

17 Given that $v = 3(t - 3)(t - 5)$, find the distance travelled

   a between $t = 0$ and $t = 3$,

   b between $t = 3$ and $t = 5$,

   c between $t = 5$ and $t = 6$.

   Hence find the total distance travelled between $t = 0$ and $t = 6$.

   Sketch the (t, v) graph and the (t, x) graph (assume that the displacement is zero when $t = 0$).

   How far is the particle from its starting point when $t = 6$?

18 Given that $a = \dfrac{1}{t^2}$ and that the velocity is $4\,\text{m}\,\text{s}^{-1}$ when $t = 1$, find the velocity when $t = 100$. State the terminal speed of the particle.

19 Given that $a = -\dfrac{4}{t^3}$, and that the velocity is $2\,\text{m s}^{-1}$ and the displacement is zero when $t = 1$, find the displacement when $t = 4$. Show that the velocity is always positive but the displacement never exceeds $2\,\text{m}$.

20 Given that $v = 13 + 5t$, find the distance travelled as the velocity increases from $13\,\text{m s}^{-1}$ to $33\,\text{m s}^{-1}$. Show that the acceleration is constant, and verify that the formula $v^2 = u^2 + 2as$ gives the same result.

21 A particle moves in a straight line with constant acceleration a. In Section 11.4 integration was used to obtain the equations $v = u + at$ and $s = ut + \frac{1}{2}at^2$.

   a Eliminate a from these equations to show that $s = \frac{1}{2}(u + v)t$.

   b Obtain the equations $v^2 = u^2 + 2as$ and $s = vt - \frac{1}{2}at^2$.

22 A car starts from rest and for the first 4 seconds of its motion the acceleration $a\,\text{m s}^{-2}$ at time t seconds after starting is given by $a = 6 - 2t$.

   a Find the maximum velocity of the car.

   b Find the velocity of the car after 4 seconds, and the distance travelled up to this time.

23 A truck, with initial velocity $6\,\text{m s}^{-1}$, brakes and comes to rest. At time t seconds after the brakes are applied the acceleration is $a\,\text{m s}^{-2}$, where $a = -3t$. This formula applies until the truck stops.

   a Find the time taken for the truck to stop.

   b Find the distance travelled by the truck while it is decelerating.

   c Find the greatest deceleration of the truck.

24 A force of $(36 - t^2)$ newtons acts at time t seconds on a particle of mass $2\,\text{kg}$. When $t = 0$ the particle has velocity $2\,\text{m s}^{-1}$ in the direction of the force. Find the velocity of the particle when $t = 6$ and find the distance travelled between $t = 0$ and $t = 6$.

25 A trailer of mass $250\,\text{kg}$, initially at rest, is pushed along a horizontal straight line. After t seconds the forward force is $150(4 - t)$ newtons, for $0 \le t \le 4$, and there is a constant resistive force of $75\,\text{N}$ acting backwards. For $t > 4$ there is no forward force but the resistive force continues to act.

   a Find the maximum velocity of the trailer.

   b Find when the trailer comes to rest, and find the total distance travelled.

   c Sketch the (t,v) graph and the (t,x) graph for the motion of the trailer.

26 A train is travelling at $32\,\text{m s}^{-1}$. The driver brakes, producing a deceleration of $k\sqrt{16 - t}\,\text{m s}^{-2}$ after t seconds. The train comes to rest in 16 seconds. Find k, and how far the train travels before coming to rest.

27 A truck starts from rest. Its acceleration up to its maximum speed is given by $a = (p - qt)^n$, where p, q and n are constant. Express the maximum speed in terms of p, q and n.

28 A load is being lifted by a crane and moves in a vertical straight line. Initially the load is on the ground and after t seconds its velocity $v\,\text{m s}^{-1}$ (measured upwards) is given by $v = \frac{3}{5}t(t-3)(t-4)$ for $0 \leq t \leq 4$.

  a Sketch the (t,v) graph for the motion of the load.

  b State when the magnitude of the acceleration is greatest, and calculate this greatest acceleration.

  c State when the load is at its highest point, and find the acceleration at this instant.

  d Find the height of the load above the ground when $t = 3$ and when $t = 4$.

  e Sketch a graph showing the height of the load for $0 \leq t \leq 4$.

  f Find the total distance moved by the load.

Miscellaneous exercise 11

1 The diagram shows the velocity–time graph for the motion of a machine's cutting tool. The graph consists of five straight line segments. The tool moves forward for 8 s while cutting and then takes 3 s to return to its starting position. Find

  i the acceleration of the tool during the first 2 s of the motion,

  ii the distance the tool moves forward while cutting,

  iii the greatest speed of the tool during the return to its starting position.

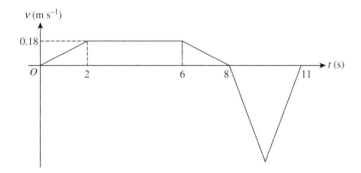

(Cambridge International AS and A level Mathematics 9709/41 Paper 4 Q2 June 2010)

2 A particle P starts at the point O and travels in a straight line. At time t seconds after leaving O the velocity of P is $v\,\text{m s}^{-1}$, where $v = 0.75t^2 - 0.0625t^3$. Find

  i the positive value of t for which the acceleration is zero,

  ii the distance travelled by P before it changes its direction of motion.

(Cambridge International AS and A level Mathematics 9709/41 Paper 4 Q4 June 2012)

3 A particle starts from rest. Its acceleration after t seconds is $\dfrac{1}{(1+2t)^3}\,\text{m s}^{-2}$. Find its speed and how far it has moved after 2 seconds.

4   An object P travels from A to B in a time of 80 s. The diagram shows the graph of v against t, where $v\,\mathrm{m\,s^{-1}}$ is the velocity of P at time t s after leaving A. The graph consists of straight line segments for the intervals $0 \le t \le 10$ and $30 \le t \le 80$, and a curved section whose equation is $v = -0.01t^2 + 0.5t - 1$ for $10 \le t \le 30$. Find

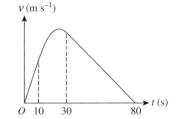

   i   the maximum velocity of P,

   ii   the distance AB.

(Cambridge International AS and A level Mathematics 9709/04 Paper 4 Q7 June 2008)

5   A particle P is held at rest at a fixed point O and then released. P falls freely under gravity until it reaches the point A which is 1.25 m below O.

   i   Find the speed of P at A and the time taken for P to reach A.

   The particle continues to fall, but now its downward acceleration t seconds after passing through A is $(10 - 0.3t)\,\mathrm{m\,s^{-2}}$.

   ii   Find the total distance P has fallen, 3 s after being released from O.

(Cambridge International AS and A level Mathematics 9709/04 Paper 4 Q7 November 2008)

6   A particle moving in a straight line has displacement x metres after t seconds for $0 \le t \le 5$, where $x = t^3 - 12t^2 + 21t + 18$.

   a   Find the displacement, velocity and acceleration when the time is zero.

   b   Find the time, velocity and acceleration when the displacement is zero.

   c   Find the time, displacement and acceleration when the velocity is zero.

   d   Find the time, displacement and velocity when the acceleration is zero.

7   A particle moving on the x-axis has displacement x metres from the origin O after t seconds for $0 \le t \le 5$, where $x = t^2(t-2)(t-5)$.

   a   For what values of t is the particle on the positive side of O?

   b   For what values of t is the particle moving towards O?

   c   For what values of t is the force on the particle directed towards O?

8   The displacement, x metres, of a particle moving on the x-axis at a time t seconds after it starts to move is given by $x = t^5$ for $0 \le t \le 1$, and by $x = \dfrac{4}{t} - \dfrac{3}{t^k}$ for $t \ge 1$.

   a   Verify that both formulae give the same value for x when $t = 1$.

   b   Find the value of k for which there is no sudden change of velocity when $t = 1$.

   For the rest of the question, take k to have the value you found in part b.

   c   Show that the particle stays on the same side of O throughout the motion.

   d   What is the greatest distance of the particle from O?

   e   For what values of t is the force on the particle acting in the positive direction?

180

9 A particle P starts from rest at the point A at time $t = 0$, where t is in seconds, and moves in a straight line with constant acceleration $a\,\mathrm{m\,s^{-2}}$ for 10 s. For $10 \leq t \leq 20$, P continues to move along the line with velocity $v\,\mathrm{m\,s^{-1}}$ where $v = \dfrac{800}{t^2} - 2$. Find

   i   the speed of P when $t = 10$, and the value of a,

   ii the value of t for which the acceleration of P is $-a\,\mathrm{m\,s^{-2}}$,

   iii the displacement of P from A when $t = 20$.

   (Cambridge International AS and A level Mathematics 9709/41 Paper 4
   Q7 November 2009)

10 A vehicle is moving in a straight line. The velocity $v\,\mathrm{m\,s^{-1}}$ at time $t\,\mathrm{s}$ after the vehicle starts is given by

$$v = A(t - 0.05t^2) \text{ for } 0 \leq t \leq 15,$$

$$v = \frac{B}{t^2} \text{ for } t \geq 15,$$

   where A and B are constants. The distance travelled by the vehicle between $t = 0$ and $t = 15$ is 225 m.

   i   Find the value of A and show that $B = 3375$.

   ii Find an expression in terms of t for the total distance travelled by the vehicle when $t \geq 15$.

   iii Find the speed of the vehicle when it has travelled a total distance of 315 m.

   (Cambridge International AS and A level Mathematics 9709/41 Paper 4
   Q7 June 2010)

Revision exercise 2

1   A man is sawing through a plank. He exerts a force of 80 newtons on each forward stroke, and 100 newtons on each backward stroke. The length of each stroke is 30 cm. If he completes 25 strokes a minute, what power is he exerting?

2   Find the resultant of forces of 2 N due north, 3 N on a bearing of 120° and 4 N on a bearing of 220°.

   Check your answer by showing that the sum of the resolved parts of the three forces perpendicular to the resultant is zero.

3   A water-skier of mass 60 kg holds a horizontal cable which trails behind a speedboat of mass 480 kg. The resistance of the water to the boat is 700 N, and the resistance to the skier is 90 N. If the engine produces a forward thrust of 1600 N, find the acceleration and the tension in the cable.

4   An object of weight 25 N is supported by two strings. The tensions in the strings are 20 N and X N. Find the angle between the strings when

   a $X = 20$,   **b** $X = 25$,   **c** $X = 30$.

5   A particle of mass 0.2 kg is at rest on a smooth surface. It is acted on by two constant forces, of magnitude 0.3 N and 0.5 N at an angle of 110° to each other. Find which direction it moves in, and how long it takes to move 10 m from its original position.

6   The power developed by a car's engine in top gear is 40 kW. When travelling at v m s^{-1} the car experiences air resistance of $0.32v^2$ newtons. Neglecting other resistances, calculate the top speed of the car.

   If the car has mass 1600 kg, calculate the acceleration of which it is capable when travelling at 40 m s^{-1}.

   When climbing a hill the driver finds that, with the engine at full power, the car will not go faster than 30 m s^{-1}. Find the angle that the road makes with the horizontal.

7   A long shelf has small light pulleys set into it at either end. A string passes over both pulleys, and loads of mass 0.6 kg and 0.9 kg are attached at the two ends.

   a Find the acceleration with which the heavier load descends.

   b It is desired to reduce the acceleration to 0.4 m s^{-2}. This is done by cutting the string in the middle and inserting a block between the two parts, as shown in the diagram. The block slides on the shelf. If friction is neglected in the calculation, calculate the mass of the block.

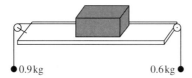

0.9 kg   0.6 kg

   c If friction is taken into account, calculate how large the coefficient of friction must be for the acceleration to be reduced to zero.

   d Explain why, however heavy the block is, the acceleration cannot be reduced to zero in this way if the surfaces are smooth.

8 A sphere of weight 50 N hangs by a light chain from a high ceiling. A person standing on the floor uses a pole pushed at $30°$ to the upward vertical to push the sphere sideways. The chain is then at an angle of $20°$ to the vertical. Find the force from the pole on the sphere, and the tension in the chain.

9 A particle is placed on a plane inclined at an angle α to the horizontal. It rests in equilibrium under the action of its weight W, the normal contact force N and a frictional force F. Express N and F in terms of W and α.

Each force is now split into components horizontally and parallel to the plane. Find the magnitude of the components in each direction. Check your answer by showing that the sum of the components of the three forces in each direction is zero.

10 A wire AB 10 metres long is bent into an arc of a circle. It is mounted in a vertical plane so that the tangent at B is horizontal and the tangent at A is at $40°$ to the horizontal, with the level of B below the level of A. A bead of mass 2 grams is threaded on the wire at A and released. Find its speed when it reaches B

    a if the wire is smooth,

    b if there is a resistance of constant magnitude 0.004 newtons.

11 A block of mass M is placed on a track inclined at $45°$ to the horizontal. A string attached to the block runs up parallel to the track, passes over a smooth rail at the top, and carries at its other end a counterweight of mass m which hangs vertically. The coefficient of friction between the block and the track is 0.6. Find an expression for the tension T in the string in terms of m, M and g, distinguishing the various situations that can occur for different values of m and M.

State the direction of the resultant force on the rail, and find an expression for its magnitude in terms of T.

12 A model railway engine of mass 2 kg runs on a straight horizontal track. Its displacement, x cm, from a point O on the track after t seconds is given, for $0 \leq t \leq 8$, by the formula

$$x = 3t^4 - 44t^3 + 144t^2 + 25.$$

Find an expression for the velocity of the engine in terms of t. Use this to sketch (t,v) and (t,x) graphs. Show that there is an integer value of t in the interval $0 < t < 8$ for which $x = 0$.

Describe the motion of the engine during the interval. Find an expression for the force needed to produce this motion, and describe how this force varies during the interval.

13 Ron, Sam and Tim are playing with a rope. Ron and Sam tie the rope round Tim's waist, and pull on the two ends with forces of 30 N and 40 N respectively at an angle of $50°$ to each other. Find the magnitude and direction of the force on Tim.

The weights of the boys are 250 N, 200 N and 350 N respectively. The boys are all wearing identical shoes. What is the least value of the coefficient of friction if none of their feet are to slip?

14 **a** If $x = p^2 t^2$, where p is a positive constant and $t > 0$, express the velocity v and the acceleration a in terms of t. Prove that $v = 2p\sqrt{x}$. Hence show that $a = v\dfrac{dv}{dx}$.

b If $x = \dfrac{p}{t}$, find expressions for v and a in terms of t, and for v in terms of x. Is it still true that $a = v\dfrac{dv}{dx}$?

15 An angler of mass 80 kg standing on a riverbank is slowly reeling in a 15 kg fish at the end of a line. The tip of the fishing rod is 8 m above the water level, and there are 17 m of line between the tip of the rod and the hook. As the fish comes in at constant speed there is a horizontal resistive force from the water of 105 N. Calculate the tension in the line.

Draw diagrams to show the forces on

a the fish, **b** the angler and rod (considered as a single object).

Find the magnitude of each force. The mass of the rod can be neglected.

16 A skip of mass 2 tonnes has to be dragged along a track. The coefficient of friction is 0.7. A cable attached to the skip runs horizontally to a winch powered by an electric motor. Using the controls on the motor, the tension in the cable is gradually increased, so that after t seconds its value is $400t$ newtons, until it reaches its maximum value of 16 000 newtons. This maximum tension is then maintained until the skip is moving at a speed of 3.5 m s^{-1}. The tension is then reduced instantaneously so that the skip continues to move at this speed.

a How long does it take before the skip starts to move?

b How fast is the skip moving when the tension in the cable reaches its greatest value?

c How long does it take after that for the skip to reach its greatest speed, and how far has it then moved altogether?

d What is the tension in the cable when the skip is moving at its greatest speed?

e Just before the skip reaches its destination the cable is disconnected. How much further after that will the skip move?

f Draw sketches of the (t,x), (t,v) and (t,a) graphs to illustrate the motion of the skip.

17 Forces of 7 N in the x-direction and 5 N in the y-direction, together with a third force of magnitude 6 N , have a resultant at an angle of 45° with the positive x-axis. If the third force makes an angle $\theta°$ with the positive x-axis, measured anticlockwise, show that $\sin\theta° - \cos\theta° = \frac{1}{3}$.

Show that the functions $\sin\theta° - \cos\theta°$ and $\sqrt{2}\,\sin(\theta - 45)°$ have the same graph. Hence find two possible values for θ.

Draw a polygon of forces to show why there are two possible directions for the third force.

18 A string passes over a rough cylindrical rail, and objects of mass 10 kg and m kg attached to the ends hang vertically on either side. Because of friction between the string and the rail, when the objects are in motion the tension in the string on the descending side is twice the tension on the ascending side. Find the acceleration of the system in the cases

a $m = 3$, **b** $m = 30$, **c** $m = 15$.

19 Four coplanar forces act at a point. The magnitudes of the forces are 5 N, 4 N, 3 N and 7 N, and the directions in which the forces act are shown in the diagram. Find the magnitude and direction of the resultant of the four forces.

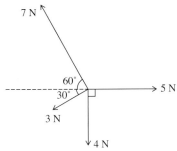

(Cambridge International AS and A level Mathematics 9709/41 Paper 4 Q3 June 2014)

20 Three strings *AB*, *BC* and *CD*, each of length 1 m, are knotted together at *B* and *C*. The ends *A* and *D* are pinned to a horizontal beam at a distance of 2 m apart, and weights of 20 N are hung at *B* and *C*. Use triangles of forces to calculate the tensions in each of the three strings.

The weight at *B* is now replaced by a heavier one, so that the figure is no longer symmetrical, and the string *AB* makes an angle of 70° with the horizontal. Use either scale drawing or trigonometry to find the new values of

a the distance of *B* from *D*,   **b** the angle *ABD*,

c the angle *CBD*.

Use a triangle of forces to calculate the tension in *BC*. Then use another triangle of forces to calculate the new value of the weight hung at *B*.

21 Two cyclists *P* and *Q* travel along a straight road *ABC*, starting simultaneously at *A* and arriving simultaneously at *C*. Both cyclists pass through *B* 400 s after leaving *A*. Cyclist *P* starts with speed 3 m s^{-1} and increases this speed with constant acceleration 0.005 m s^{-2} until he reaches *B*.

i Show that the distance *AB* is 1600 m and find *P*'s speed at *B*.

Cyclist *Q* travels from *A* to *B* with speed *v* m s^{-1} at time *t* seconds after leaving *A*, where

$$v = 0.04t - 0.0001t^2 + k,$$

and *k* is a constant.

ii Find the value of *k* and the maximum speed of *Q* before he has reached *B*.

Cyclist *P* travels from *B* to *C*, a distance of 1400 m, at the speed he had reached at *B*. Cyclist *Q* travels from *B* to *C* with constant acceleration *a* m s^{-2}.

iii Find the time taken for the cyclists to travel from *B* to *C* and find the value of *a*.

(Cambridge International AS and A level Mathematics 9709/41 Paper 4 Q7 June 2014)

22 A runner accelerates from 5 m s^{-1} to 6 m s^{-1} as she enters the final straight. Her speed *v* m s^{-1} after *t* seconds is given by $v = \sqrt{25 + 11t}$ for $0 \le t \le 1$. Find

a her acceleration at the beginning and end of the final straight,

b how far she runs while accelerating.

Practice exam-style paper 1

Time 1 hour 15 minutes

Answer all the questions.

The use of an electronic calculator is expected, where appropriate.

1

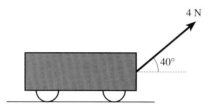

A toy truck is pulled along horizontal ground by means of a force of magnitude 4 N acting at 40° to the direction of motion (see diagram).

i Find the work done by the force in moving the truck a distance of 5 m. [3]

ii Given that the truck moves with constant speed, state the magnitude of the force resisting its motion. [1]

2 A child standing at the edge of a cliff 100 m high throws a stone vertically downwards. The stone hits the sea 4 s later. Ignoring air resistance, find

i the initial speed with which the stone is thrown, [2]

ii the speed with which the stone hits the sea. [2]

3

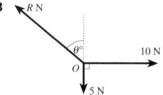

Three forces, with magnitudes 5 N, 10 N and R N, act at a point O in the directions shown in the diagram. Given that the three forces are in equilibrium, find the values of R and θ. [6]

4 An athlete of mass 60 kg runs a distance of 1 km up a hill inclined at 2° to the horizontal. The athlete's speed at the bottom of the hill is 5 m s⁻¹ and at the top of the hill is 4 m s⁻¹. Find, for this 1 km run,

i the athlete's increase in potential energy, [2]

ii the athlete's decrease in kinetic energy, [2]

iii the average power exerted by the athlete, assuming that he takes 4 minutes to cover the 1 km distance and that any resistance to motion can be neglected. [3]

5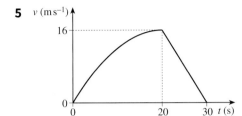

The diagram shows the velocity–time graph for the motion of a cyclist riding along a road. The cyclist starts from rest, reaches a speed of $16\,\mathrm{m\,s^{-1}}$ after $20\,\mathrm{s}$, and then decelerates uniformly to rest after a further $10\,\mathrm{s}$.

i For the final $10\,\mathrm{s}$ of the motion, find the deceleration and the distance travelled. [3]

ii For the first $20\,\mathrm{s}$ of the motion, state with a reason whether the cyclist's acceleration is increasing or decreasing. [2]

iii The equation connecting v and t, for $0 \le t \le 20$, is $v = \frac{1}{25}t(40 - t)$. Calculate the distance travelled by the cyclist during the first $20\,\mathrm{s}$. [4]

6 i A car of mass $1200\,\mathrm{kg}$ travelling along a horizontal road experiences a resistance to motion of magnitude $150\,\mathrm{N}$. The car is accelerating at $0.5\,\mathrm{m\,s^{-2}}$. Find the forward driving force acting on the car. [3]

ii A trailer of mass $800\,\mathrm{kg}$ is now attached to the car. When the car and trailer are travelling along the same road the resistance to motion on the trailer has magnitude $500\,\mathrm{N}$. The resistance on the car, and the forward driving force are the same as before the trailer was attached. Find the acceleration of the car and trailer, and find also the force in the towbar between the car and the trailer. [6]

7 i A suitcase of mass $16\,\mathrm{kg}$ is placed on a ramp inclined at $15°$ to the horizontal. The coefficient of friction between the suitcase and the ramp is 0.4. Determine whether the suitcase rests in equilibrium on the ramp, and state the magnitude of the frictional force acting on the suitcase. [4]

ii

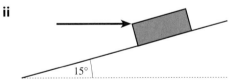

A person tries to push the suitcase up the ramp by applying a horizontal force (see diagram). Show that, for the suitcase to start moving, the magnitude of this force must be at least $120\,\mathrm{N}$, to the nearest newton. [7]

Practice exam-style paper 2

Time 1 hour 15 minutes

Answer all the questions.

The use of an electronic calculator is expected, where appropriate.

1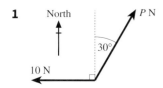

Two horizontal forces, of magnitudes 10 N and P N, act on a particle. The force of magnitude 10 N acts due west and the force of magnitude P N acts on a bearing of 030° (see diagram). The resultant of these two forces acts due north. Find the magnitude of this resultant. [4]

2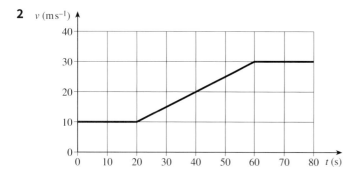

The diagram shows the velocity–time graph for a train during a part of its journey.

i Calculate the distance travelled by the train during the period of 80 s shown in the diagram. [3]

ii The train has mass 400 tonnes. Calculate the resultant forward force acting on the train while it is accelerating. [3]

3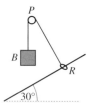

A small ring R of mass 0.2 kg is threaded onto a fixed rod which is inclined at an angle of 30° to the horizontal. The ring is attached to a block B of mass 0.5 kg by means of a light string which passes over a smooth pulley P. The part RP of the string is perpendicular to the rod, and the part PB of the string is vertical (see diagram). The system is in equilibrium.

i State the tension in the string. [1]

ii Calculate the magnitude of the normal component of the force acting on R due to the rod. [2]

iii Given that the equilibrium is limiting, calculate the coefficient of friction between R and the rod. [3]

4 The sloping part of a 'slide' in a children's playground is 8 m long and slopes at 40° to the horizontal. A child of mass 20 kg slides down, starting at rest at the top and reaching a speed of 6 m s⁻¹ at the bottom.

   i Calculate the total change in energy of the child during this motion, stating whether it is an increase or a decrease. [4]

   ii The child's motion is resisted by a force of constant magnitude F N. Find F. [2]

5 A particle moving in a straight line has velocity v m s⁻¹ at time t s, where $v = t(t - 6)^2$.

   i Calculate how far the particle moves between the two times when it is instantaneously at rest. [5]

   ii Find the set of values of t for which the acceleration is negative. [4]

6 The total mass of a cyclist and her bicycle is 120 kg. While pedalling she generates power of 640 W. Her motion is opposed by road resistance of magnitude 16 N, and by air resistance of magnitude $8v$ N, where v m s⁻¹ is her speed.

   i Find the cyclist's acceleration when she is riding along a horizontal road at a speed of 5 m s⁻¹. [3]

   ii Find the greatest speed that she can maintain on a horizontal road. [3]

   iii When cycling down a hill she finds that she can maintain a speed of 10 m s⁻¹. Find the angle of inclination of the hill to the horizontal, giving your answer correct to the nearest 0.1°. [3]

7

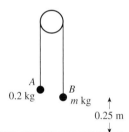

A
0.2 kg

B
m kg

0.25 m

The diagram shows particles A and B, of masses 0.2 kg and m kg respectively, connected by a light inextensible string which passes over a fixed smooth peg. The system is released from rest, with B at a height of 0.25 m above the floor. B descends, hitting the floor 0.5 s later. All resistances to motion may be ignored.

   i Find the acceleration of B as it descends. [2]

   ii Find the tension in the string while B is descending, and find also the value of m. [5]

   iii When B hits the floor it comes to rest immediately, and the string becomes slack. Find the length of time for which B remains at rest on the ground before being jerked into motion again. [3]

Answers

Most non-exact numerical answers are given correct to 3 significant figures.

1 Velocity and acceleration

Exercise 1A (page 4)

1 200 s

2 72 km south

3 21.2 hours

4 25.2 km south

5 About $5\frac{1}{2}$ minutes

6 8.2×10^{13} km

7 $33\frac{1}{3}$ m s^{-1}

Exercise 1B (page 8)

1 4 m s^{-2}, 125 m

2 $7\frac{1}{2}$ m s^{-1}

3 1.6 m s^{-2}, 60 m s^{-1}; 15.5 s

4 6 s, $1\frac{2}{3}$ m s^{-2}

5 30 s, 2 m s^{-2}

6 20 m s^{-1}, 1500 m

7 25 s, 175 m

Exercise 1C (page 10)

1 **a** 11   **b** 16   **c** $-\frac{3}{2}$
   d 45   **e** 102   **f** 1.2
   g 14   **h** $2\frac{1}{2}$ **i** 24
   j $\pm26\frac{2}{3}$ **k** 20   **l** 2
   m $1\frac{1}{3}$ **n** 25

2 40 s, $\frac{7}{8}$ m s^{-2}

3 $\sqrt{\frac{1}{5}}s$

4 0.06 m s^{-2}

5 1500 m

6 **a** 2.7 km   **b** 250 s

7 **a** $\sqrt{900-20s}$ **b** 10 m s^{-1} **c** 5 m

8 60 m

9 $(5+0.8t)$ m s^{-1}, $\left(5t+0.4t^2\right)$ m; 15 s, 17 m s^{-1}

10 $2\frac{1}{2}$ m s^{-2}, 2 m s^{-2}

11 1800 km h^{-2}; 40 km h^{-1}

12 $\left(\frac{1}{2}t^2-4t+10\right)$ m ; yes

Exercise 1D (page 15)

1 22 s

2 **a** 18 minutes   **b** 21 minutes

3 30 m s^{-1}, 675 m; $1\frac{1}{2}$ m s^{-2}; 20 s

4 20 m s^{-1}, 2 m s^{-2}

5 12 m s^{-1}, 44 s

6 **a** 22 s   **b** $53\frac{1}{3}$ m

7 **a** 7 m s^{-1} **b** $\frac{1}{2}$ **c** $\frac{11}{28}$

8 $\frac{1}{36}$ m s^{-2}

9 **a** 50 m s^{-1} **b** 5000 m

10 $5D$ metres

Miscellaneous exercise 1 (page 17)

1 **a** 0.4   **b** 2 km

2 **a** 2.5 m s^{-2} **b** 10 s

3 0.1 m s^{-2}; 0.65 m s^{-1}

4 **a**

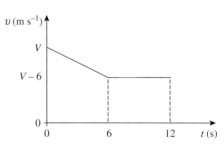

   b 19.5

5 $T=6.8$ $V=12.28$

6 **i** 3600 s   **ii** 46 500 m   **iii** 300 s, 3400 s

7 0.2 m s^{-2}; 0.34 m s^{-2}

8 10.8 m

9 0.08 m s^{-2}

10 **i** Graph must show:

   v is single valued, continuous and positive for $0<t<1000$; 1st segment has positive slope

   And two or more of:

   $v(0)=0$; $v(1000)=0$; 2nd segment has zero slope; 3rd segment has negative slope

   ii $V=25$

   iii 2920 m

2 Force and motion

Exercise 2A (page 23)

1 1.5 m s^{-2}

2 0.625 m s^{-2}

3 9240 N

4 65 kg

5 4 s

6 1.44 m s⁻², 0.576 N — $1.44\,\mathrm{m\,s^{-2}}, 0.576\,\mathrm{N}$

7 $0.96m\,\mathrm{N}$

8 850 kg

9 18.75 m

10 $45\,\mathrm{m\,s^{-1}}$

11 $6.4\,\mathrm{m\,s^{-2}}, 12.8\,\mathrm{N}$

12 2.47

13 $0.12\,\mathrm{m\,s^{-2}}, 22.4\,\mathrm{s}$

14 13.5 cm

15 40.5 kN

Exercise 2B (page 27)

1 115

2 4

3 2120 N

4 300 N, 400 N

5 165 N

6 a 16 N   **b** 25.6 N

7 $45\,\mathrm{N}, 2\,\mathrm{m\,s^{-2}}$

8 $7.91\,\mathrm{m\,s^{-1}}$

9 3125 N

10 $1.3 \times 10^4\,\mathrm{N}$

11 10.75 N, 2.81 m

12 2625 kg

13 52.2

14 780 N, 1 min 20 s

15 7.5 s

Miscellaneous exercise 2 (page 29)

1 $1.1\,\mathrm{m\,s^{-2}}$

2 11.0 s

3 1400 N

4 10

5 750 N, 938 N

6 20 kg

7 4500 N

8 Yes; a force of 92.6 N would be needed for the box to decelerate at the same rate as the car.

9 $0.25\,\mathrm{m\,s^{-2}}, 25\,\mathrm{N}$

10 4500 N

11 a $0.33\,\mathrm{m\,s^{-2}}$ **b** $1160\,\mathrm{N}, 0.04\,\mathrm{m\,s^{-2}}$

12 1720 N

13 12 s, $6\frac{2}{3}$

3 Vertical motion

Exercise 3A (page 36)

1 a 30 N   **b** 0.1 N   **c** 8000 N

2 17 kg

3 $2\,\mathrm{m\,s^{-2}}$

4 17 900 N

5 $13\,000\,\mathrm{N}; 0.4\,\mathrm{m\,s^{-2}}$

6 7.92 N

7 $72.4\,\mathrm{m\,s^{-2}}$

8 $1270\,\mathrm{N}; 1.5\,\mathrm{m\,s^{-2}}$

9 a 10 700 N   **b** 10 500 N
   c 10 300 N   **d** 10 700 N

10 1275 N

11 40 kg

12 $90\,\mathrm{kg}; 6.67\,\mathrm{m\,s^{-1}}$

13 1.6 N

14 40 N, 16 kg

15 $s = \dfrac{Mv^2}{2(T - Mg)}$

16 33, 900

17 8400 N

Exercise 3B (page 41)

1 2.8 kg

2 a 40 kN   **b** 38 kN

3 700 N, the drum leaves the ground.

4 a 380 N   **b** 448 N
   c 380 N

5 140 kg

6 67 200 N

7 $0.6\,\mathrm{m\,s^{-2}}$

8 The scales register the normal contact force between the man and the scales, not the 'weight'; decelerating at $0.444\,\mathrm{m\,s^{-2}}$.

9 $\frac{2}{3}mg$

10 $0.5\,\mathrm{m\,s^{-2}}$

11 80, 20

12 10.75, 1.63

Miscellaneous exercise 3 (page 42)

1 760 N

2 6.8 m

3 4800 N

4 6528 N   **a**   40 kg   **b**   7.5 s

6 $W(3-2k)$

7 $\frac{7}{3}mg$ **a**   20 m s^{-1} **b**   6 s

8 a   There are forces acting upwards: buoyancy and water resistance.

   b   8.5, 0.225 N

9 35 m

4 Resolving forces

Exercise 4A (page 49)

1 a   4 N, 6.93 N; −7.88 N, −1.39 N

   b   3.46 N, −2 N; −3 N, 5.20 N

   c   −4 N, 0 N; 2.05 N, −5.64 N

   d   2.5 N, 4.33 N; −2.5 N, 4.33 N

2 60, 8.66

3 2.89 m s^{-2}

4 35.1 N

5 166 N

6 350, 8350 N

7 5 m s^{-2}, 10 mN

8 8.05 kg, 85.7 N

9 6 kg

10 1.23 m s^{-2}

11 986 N, 127 N

12 $\left(50 - \frac{1}{2}T\right)$N

13 a   25.4   **b**   31.6 N

14 1.50 m s^{-2}, 415 N

15 1.41

16 11.7°, 511

17 21.9, 822 N

18 170 N, 339 N

Exercise 4B (page 55)

1 a $F\cos\theta°$, $F\cos(90-\theta)° = F\sin\theta°$

   b $F\cos(90+\theta)° = -F\sin\theta°$, $F\cos\theta°$

   c $F\cos\theta°$, $F\cos(\theta-90)° = F\sin\theta°$

   d $F\cos\theta°$, $F\cos(90+\theta)° = F\sin\theta°$

2 5 m s^{-2}, 5.48 m s^{-1}

3 2270 N

4 1.05 m s^{-2}

5 6.44 N

6 8.66

7 21.8 N, 63.9 N

8 35.2 N, 691 N

9 a   5.74 N   **b**   7.00 N   **c**   6.33 N

   In case **b** a component of the applied force will be added to 10 cos 35°; in **c** it is subtracted.

10 4.66 N, 28.0, 1.73 m s^{-2}

11 559 N, 26.6

12 41.0 N, 113 N

13 83.5, 74.9 N

14 a   To prevent the plank sliding down the slope

   b   176 N

   c   11.0 N

15 52.3

16 470, 4620

Miscellaneous exercise 4 (page 57)

1 i   2.5 m s^{-2} **ii**   14.5

2 $F = 28.3$ $G = 44.8$

3 A is 36 N B is 31.2 N

4 $\theta = 52.4°$ $F = 16.4$

5 i $F = 102.8$ **ii**   122.5 m

6 i $u = 1.4$, $a = 2$ **ii** $\theta = 11.5$

7 i $F = 3.80$ N, $\tan\theta = 0.5$

   ii   7.60 m s^{-2}, direction is 26.6° clockwise from positive x-axis

5 Friction

Exercise 5A (page 66)

1 a $(P-Q)$ N in the direction of the force of magnitude Q N

   b $(Q-P)$ N in the direction of the force of magnitude P N

2 $80 \le P \le 120$

3 6.93 N

4 0.4, 63 N

5 0.25

6 a   5900 N,   **b**   6000 N   **c**   6000 N

   a, **b** The boat remains at rest.

   c The boat accelerates at 0.125 m s^{-2}.

7 **a** $(P - 50\sin\alpha°)$ N acting down the plane

b $(50\sin\alpha° - P)$ N acting up the plane

8 $8.2 \le P \le 37.7$, to 1 d.p.

9 **a**, **b** 0 **c** 0.054 N

a, **b** The bowl remains at rest (with limiting equilibrium in **b**).

c The bowl slides down with acceleration $0.108\,\text{m s}^{-2}$.

10 28.1 cm

11 $\frac{3}{7}$

12 80

13 33.3 N

14 $4.8\,\text{m s}^{-2}$; 2.25 m

15 $4\,\text{m s}^{-2}$

16 $1\,\text{m s}^{-2}$

Exercise 5B (page 71)

1 In the direction of motion of the train; accelerating; 0.4

2 0.49

3 725 kg

4 9 m

5 3.96 N down the plane

6 0.024

7 0.2

8 0.806

9 **a** 1180 N, $2.44\,\text{m s}^{-1}$

b 1690 N, $2.44\,\text{m s}^{-1}$

10 4.10 m, 1.49 s

11 0.733

12 0.465 N; 1.55 N

13 0.525

14 0.374; $1.58\,\text{m s}^{-2}$

15 0.186; $3.34\,\text{m s}^{-2}$

Miscellaneous exercise 5 (page 73)

1 **i** $N = 3200 - (\frac{24}{25})X$

ii $X = 1875$

2 **i** 1.67 N **ii** 0.668

3 **ii** 1.62

4 **i** 4.632 N **ii** 0.824 N

iii 0.178

6 **i** Frictional component is 14.4 N, normal component is 75.2 N

ii 0.364

7 **i** 1.416 m **ii** 0.152 **iii** $6.58\,\text{m s}^{-1}$

8 **i** Decelerations of P and Q are $2\,\text{m s}^{-2}$ and $2.5\,\text{m s}^{-2}$

ii Speed of $P = 6.09\,\text{m s}^{-1}$, speed of $Q = 0.614\,\text{m s}^{-1}$

9 **i** $R = T\sin 60°$, $F = 40 + T\cos 60°$ **ii** 377

10 **i** Frictional component is 0.546 N, normal component is 5.71 N, coefficient is 0.096

ii 2.18

11 **ii** $\mu < \frac{9.6}{12.8} = \frac{3}{4}$

6 Motion due to gravity

Exercise 6A (page 78)

1 $30\,\text{m s}^{-1}$, 45 m

2 $14.1\,\text{m s}^{-1}$

3 9.8 m

4 14.7 m

5 $17.5\,\text{m s}^{-1}$

Exercise 6B (page 81)

1 $5\,\text{m s}^{-1}$ upwards, 30 m

2 1.8 m

3 $21.0\,\text{m s}^{-1}$

4 2.65 s

5 24.2 m

6 0.6 s

7 $10\,\text{m s}^{-1}$ downwards, 15 m

8 $16\,\text{m s}^{-1}$

9 3.6 s, $18\,\text{m s}^{-1}$ downwards

10 1.1 s

11 2.59 s, $13.9\,\text{m s}^{-1}$ downwards

12 64.8 m

13 u downwards

14 $9\,\text{m s}^{-1}$, 4.05 m

15 **a** 61.25 m **b** 6 s

Exercise 6C (page 87)

1 **a** $9\,\text{m s}^{-2}$, $1\,\text{m s}^{-2}$ **b** 8 m, $\frac{4}{3}$ s

c 4 s, $4\,\text{m s}^{-1}$

For no friction.

a 14.4 m, 2.4 s **c** 2.4 s, $12\,\text{m s}^{-1}$

2 48 m, 24 m s⁻¹, 8 s; 30 m, 12 m s⁻¹, 7.5 s

3 50 m s⁻¹, 7.5 m s⁻²

4 45 m, 30 m s⁻¹; both smaller; 0.5; 8 m s⁻²

5 1.4 s, 14 m s⁻¹; 10 m s⁻¹, $(10 - v)$ m s⁻²

   a Smaller with air resistance

   b Larger with air resistance

6 $\frac{1}{160}$ m; 20 m s⁻¹;

   a 8.4 m s⁻²   **b** 3.6 m s⁻²

7 3.7 m, 1.6 s;

   a 11.6 m s⁻² downwards

   b 10 m s⁻² downwards;

      i Less than 3.7 m   **ii** Less than 8 m s⁻¹

      iii Between 8.4 m s⁻² and 10 m s⁻²

   Not more than 50 m s⁻¹

Miscellaneous exercise 6 (page 88)

1 0.8 s, 8 m s⁻¹

2 **i** 20   **ii** 40 m s⁻¹   **iii** 80 m

3 **i** 30 m s⁻¹   **ii** 2 s   **iii** 35 m s⁻¹

4 3 s, 13 m s⁻¹

5 11.25 m, 2.1 s

6 **i** 13.5 N

   ii Graph consists of two line segments; the first starts at the origin and has a positive gradient. The second starts where first one ends and has positive but less steep gradient. $v_S = 10$ m⁻¹ at surface and $v_B = 12$ m s⁻¹ at bottom. $t_1 = 1$ s at surface and shown on sketch, $t_2 = 1.36$ s at bottom.

7 245 m

8 $5t^2$ m, $20(t - 1)$ m, $\left(500 - 5(t-2)^2\right)$ m, 0; 180 m

9 90; not more than 28.3 m s⁻¹, not more than 25.4 m s⁻²

10 0.36 m s⁻¹, 2.36 m s⁻¹, 6.4 m s⁻² deceleration, 4.53 m s⁻² acceleration; between 10 and 28 seconds

11 0.5 m, 0.25 m, $(10 - 0.5v)$ m s⁻², $\left(10 - 0.025v^2\right)$ m s⁻²; model 2

Revision exercise 1 (page 91)

1 0.161 m s⁻¹

2 **a** 0.5 m s⁻²   **b** 40 s

3 $\left(15t + 1.25t^2\right)$ m, $(1.5 + 2.5t)$ m s⁻¹; 8 s, 35 m s⁻¹

4 6 s, 4.5

5 300 kN; smaller

6 60 N

7 54 kN

8 24 s, 405 m

9 125 N; 130 N

10 14.5 m s⁻¹

11 $\frac{2}{3}$ m s⁻²; 408 m, 35 s

12 80 m, 4.90 s

13 2.56 s

14 7 N

15 **a** 18.2 N   **b** 345 N

16 8 m, 3.96 s

17 17.5 kN; no, the weight is negligible compared with the other forces.

18 10 kg; 60 m

19 40.5 s

20 $\frac{1}{3} \le \mu < 1$

22 8 m s⁻¹, 0.08; 2.03 m s⁻², 15.7 m

23 **a** 0.84 m s⁻²   **b** 0.48 m s⁻²

   c 6 m s⁻¹

24 0.4 s

25 $g \sin \alpha°$, $g \sin \beta°$

7 Newton's third law

Exercise 7A (page 100)

1 Weights of 80 N and 100 N respectively, and vertical contact forces 80 N upwards on the top crate, 80 N downwards and 180 N upwards on the bottom crate

2 **a** 200 N upwards

   b 200 N downwards

   c 1200 N upwards

4 720 N

5 **i** 375 N   **ii** 750 N

6 42

8 400 N, 500 N; 800 N forwards; it will appear that the car is being pushed from behind.

9 Weight 6000 N Contact from pile driver

   a 21 600 N   **b** 20 000 N;

   Force from Earth

   a 28 080 N   **b** 26 000 N

10 a 17 250 N   **b** 15 000 N

12 $P > \mu W$, middle box won't move; $P > 3\mu W$

13 a $W\cos\alpha°$ **b** $W\sin\alpha°$

    c $W\sin\alpha°$ **d** $2W\tan\alpha°$

    e $\dfrac{W\left(1+\sin^2\alpha°\right)}{\cos\alpha°}$

Exercise 7B (page 107)

1 a 10 N, 10 N

    b 10 N, 15 N (up the slope)

    c 20 N, 10 N; 10 N

    d 7.5 N, 7.5 N

    e 17.3 N, 2.32 N

    f 35.4 N, 55.4 N

2 10 kg

3 24, 2 m s^{-2}

4 a 1.67 m s^{-2} **b** 2.5 m s^{-2}

    c 0.769 m s^{-2} **d** 3 m s^{-2}

    e 0.464 m s^{-2} **f** 6.15 m s^{-2}

5 2.31 m s^{-2}; 30.8 N, 7.69 N

6 a 0.625 m s^{-2} **b** 1.25 m s^{-2}

7 3 : 1

8 $0.2m \le M \le m$; $\dfrac{(M-m)g}{M+m}$ if $M > m$, $\dfrac{(0.2m-M)g}{M+m}$ if $M < 0.2m$

Exercise 7C (page 111)

1 a 0.48 m s^{-2}, 170 N

    b 0.08 m s^{-2}, 170 N

2 250 N, 50 N

    a 0.05 m s^{-2} acceleration, 62.5 N

    b 0.05 m s^{-2} deceleration, 37.5 N

    c 0.156 m s^{-2} deceleration, 10.9 N

    d 0.175 m s^{-2}, 6.25 N tension

    e 0.2 m s^{-2}, zero

    f 0.25 m s^{-2}, 12.5 N thrust

3 $\dfrac{F-(P+Q)}{M+m}+g\sin\alpha°$

4 $4mg$, $3mg$, $2mg$, mg (uppermost to lowermost); $\dfrac{9}{10}g$

    a zero (all strings)

    b $\dfrac{1}{5}mg$, $\dfrac{3}{20}mg$, $\dfrac{1}{10}mg$, $\dfrac{1}{20}mg$ (uppermost to lowermost)

Miscellaneous exercise 7 (page 112)

1 Aceleration is 5 m s^{-2} and tension is 3 N

    ii Time taken is 0.6 s

2 i $\dfrac{2}{3}$ **ii** 2.8

3 i 0.4 kg   **ii** 0.5 kg   **iii** 4.5 N

4 i a 2.5 m s^{-2} **b** 3.75 N

    ii 0.3

5 i Acceleration is 4.9 m s^{-2}, tension is 2.754 N

    ii 0.392 m

6 i 1 m s^{-2}

    ii a P: 3 m, Q: 7 m   **b** 2 m s^{-1}

7 i 3.84 N, 1.6 m s^{-2} **ii** 1.5 s

8 i 4.2 N   **ii** 0.6 s

9 i 5 m s^{-2}, 0.9 m   **ii** $V = 3$, $T = 0.9$

    iii 1.35 m up, 2.45 m down, $h = 1.1$

10 2340, 5850

11 i

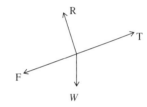

    iii 0.1 m s^{-2}

12 i 0.227

    ii Aceleration: 1.24 m s^{-2}, tension: 1.75 N

13 i Tension in AB is 6.4 N; tension in BC is 4.8 N

    ii 0.359

8 Work, energy and power

Exercise 8A (page 120)

1 a 1620 J   **b** 300 kJ

    c 5.21×10^6 J   **d** 1600 J   **e** 6.4×10^8 J

2 700 J, 0 J, 0 J, 700 J

3 4 N

4 50 N

5 240 J, 8 N

6 1008 J

7 1130 J

8 5440 J

9 4800 J

10 20 N

11 105 N

12 a 280 kJ   **b** 426 kJ   **c** 207 kJ

Anyone so irresponsible as to attempt to drive down such a steep gradient would need to apply the brakes to restrict the final speed to $30\,\text{m}\,\text{s}^{-1}$.

13 698 kJ

14 814 kJ

Exercise 8B (page 124)

1 33.3 kW

2 112.5 W

3 160 W

4 112.5 kW

5 600 N

6 16 kW

7 880 W

8 $2.5\,\text{m}\,\text{s}^{-2}$

9 30.7°

10 7.8 kW

11 $0.2\,\text{m}\,\text{s}^{-2}$, $2.55\,\text{m}\,\text{s}^{-1}$

12 2.43 s

13 $0.433\,\text{m}\,\text{s}^{-2}$

14 147 kW

16 3.01 kW, 6.02 kW

17 7.2 s; 96, 505 N

18 31.4 kW

Miscellaneous exercise 8 (page 126)

1 i 600 N   **ii** $0.25\,\text{m}\,\text{s}^{-1}$

2 $0.845\,\text{m}\,\text{s}^{-2}$

3 36.9

4 i 100 J   **ii** 5000 J   **iii** 50.4

5 i $1.12\,\text{m}\,\text{s}^{-2}$ **ii** $0.858\,\text{m}\,\text{s}^{-2}$

6 290 N

7 $1.25\,\text{m}\,\text{s}^{-1}$ **ii** 590 M

8 i 1000 J   **ii** 80 N

9 i $0.15\,\text{m}\,\text{s}^{-2}$

10 i $0.025\,\text{m}\,\text{s}^{-2}$ **ii** $50\,\text{m}\,\text{s}^{-1}$

11 i $7\,\text{m}\,\text{s}^{-1}$ **ii** 21.1°
   iii 2.8 J

12 i 7.5 m   **ii** $12\,\text{m}\,\text{s}^{-1}$ **iii** 2.11(2) J

13 i $0.4\,\text{m}\,\text{s}^{-2}$ **iii** 742.5 m

14 54.9 kW, mass must not exceed 1950 kg

15 $180\,\text{m}\,\text{s}^{-1}$; 6.51°

9 Potential energy

Exercise 9A (page 135)

1 400 J

2 40 J, 5 m

3 1.36×10^6 J, 68 kW, the kinetic energy of the rotor

4 $12.2\,\text{m}\,\text{s}^{-1}$

5 2.08×10^6 J

6 16.3°

7 9.8

8 8.75 m

9 $1.69\,\text{m}\,\text{s}^{-1}$, $1.54\,\text{m}\,\text{s}^{-1}$

10 26.0°

11 a $2.45\,\text{m}\,\text{s}^{-1}$ **b** $4.24\,\text{m}\,\text{s}^{-1}$

12 $u = 2\sqrt{ag}$

13 1.46 m

14 $40.7\,\text{m}\,\text{s}^{-1}$, $30.3\,\text{m}\,\text{s}^{-1}$

Exercise 9B (page 139)

1 $2.55\,\text{m}\,\text{s}^{-1}$

2 0.325 m

3 a 1.22 m   **b** $3.84\,\text{m}\,\text{s}^{-1}$

4 a $1.47\,\text{m}\,\text{s}^{-1}$ **b** 2.07 m

5 $2\,\text{m}\,\text{s}^{-1}$, 0.8 J, 1.33 N

6 2.45 m, 44.55 J, 18.2 N

7 3.83×10^9 J

8 $13.2\,\text{m}\,\text{s}^{-1}$

9 78.5 N, 132 N

Miscellaneous exercise 9 (page 141)

1 Work done is 3000 J, $F = 31.1$ N

2 i 25 000 J (25 kJ)   **ii** 20 s

3 i 32 000 J   **ii** 125 J
   iii 1250 W

4 $1.41\,\text{m}\,\text{s}^{-1}$, $2.5\,\text{m}\,\text{s}^{-2}$

5 i Gain in k.e. is 3240 J, loss in p.e. is 9070 J, work done is 5830 J
   ii 96.0   **iii** $0.771\,\text{m}\,\text{s}^{-2}$

6 $1.41\,\text{m}\,\text{s}^{-1}$, falling

7 i Acceleration $2.5\,\text{m}\,\text{s}^{-2}$, tension 15 N
   ii a 18 J   **b** 22.5 J   **c** 4.5 J
   iii 0.8 s

8 a $6.83\,\text{m}\,\text{s}^{-1}$ **b** (5.7, 5)

The bead retraces its motion back to A, with the same speed as before at each point of the wire.

9 b $\dfrac{m(Mg + F)}{M + m}$ **c** $\dfrac{M(mg - F)h}{M + n}$

10 b i $\sqrt{\frac{7}{5}gr}$ **ii** $\sqrt{\frac{3}{5}gr}$

 d The condition is satisfied.

10 Force as a vector quantity

Exercise 10A (page 149)

1 a Magnitude 22.8 N, bearing 044.7°

 b Magnitude 26.0 N, bearing 065.0°

 c Magnitude 10.9 N, bearing 095.9°

 d Magnitude 9.10 N, bearing 035.1°

2 543 N, making an angle 0.029° with the direction in which the car is facing

3 a Vertically upwards, magnitude 24 N

 b Vertically downwards, magnitude 8 N

 c 16.5 N at an angle 14.0° downwards from the horizontal

4 a 33.5 N **b** 27.6 N

 c 5.46 N **d** 32.0 N

5 i 1.83 N in a direction 14.9° backwards from the downward vertical

 ii 1.68 N in a direction 17.4° backwards from the downward vertical

 iii 1.46 N in a direction 18.1° backwards from the downward vertical

 a Immediately on leaving the bat

 b When descending at 18.2° to the horizontal

6 a 315 N **b** Horizontal to the left

 c 6.86 m s^{-2}

7 a 4.60 N **b** 7.51 m s^{-2}

8 6.90 m

9 a 34.1 N **b** 38.6 N

 c 18.3 N **d** 44.5 N

10 42.6°

11 a 13.1 N, 13.1 N **b** 47.0 N, 25 N

 c 42.4 N, 58.0 N **d** 17.8 N, 27.2 N

12 a 12.9 N south **b** 10 N north

13 a 8.68 N up the plane, 49.2 N perpendicular to the plane

 b 4.36 N to the left, 49.8 N upwards

 c 192 N up the plane, 190 N to the left

 d 51.6 N perpendicular to the plane, 8.99 N to the right

 e 4.51 N down the plane, 51.0 N upwards

 f 16.8 N perpendicular to the plane, 33.5 N upwards

14 At 90° to the banks, from south to north; 154 N

15 0.173 N

Exercise 10B (page 155)

1 a Magnitude 22.8 N, bearing 044.7°

 b Magnitude 26.0 N, bearing 065.0°

 c Magnitude 10.9 N, bearing 095.9°

 d Magnitude 9.10 N, bearing 035.1°

2 a Magnitude 22.8 N, bearing 044.7°

 b Magnitude 26.0 N, bearing 065.0°

 c Magnitude 10.9 N, bearing 095.9°

 d Magnitude 9.10 N, bearing 035.1°

3 543 N, making an angle 0.029° with the direction in which the car is facing

4 17 N, 151.9° anticlockwise from the positive x-axis

5 $\begin{pmatrix} 7.66 \\ 6.43 \end{pmatrix}$N, $\begin{pmatrix} -3.46 \\ 2 \end{pmatrix}$N, $\begin{pmatrix} -1.04 \\ -5.91 \end{pmatrix}$N; $\begin{pmatrix} 3.15 \\ 2.52 \end{pmatrix}$N;

 4.04 N, 38.6° anticlockwise from the x-axis

6 2.56 m s^{-2}, 20.6° above the horizontal

7 15.03, 4.65

8 0.5, −1.9

9 $\begin{pmatrix} -W\sin 15° + P\cos 20° \\ -W\cos 15° + P\sin 20° + C \end{pmatrix}$N;

 $W\cos 15° - P\sin 20°$, $P\cos 20° - W\sin 15°$

10 13 N, 67.4° anticlockwise from the x-direction

11 55 N; 36.9°, 106.3°

12 $\pm\frac{1}{3}$

Exercise 10C (page 161)

1 a 12.3 N, 11.3 N **b** 25.7 N, 37.6 N

2 4880 N, 8220 N

3 a Along the outward normal to the plane, 46.0 N

 b 46.0 N in the direction of the inward normal to the plane

 c 16.8

4 200

5 5.44 N, 6.05 N

6 12 300 N, 71 100 N

7 a 105.6°, 112.4° **b** 51.1°, 141.5°

8 a 23.9° **b** 86.7°

9 22.3°, 58.8°

10 Perpendicular to the thread, $mg \sin \alpha°$

11 a 38.2°, 21.8°

b The length of any one side of the triangle of forces cannot exceed the sum of the lengths of the other two sides (the case $m = 0.8$ is excluded because the pulleys are not in the same vertical line).

d K cannot be above the level of the pulleys.

12 a 7 **b** 90°

13 36.9° and 73.7° either side of the upward vertical; (−0.45, 0.6), (0.72, 0.21)

14 90°; 630 N, 160 N

Miscellaneous exercise 10 (page 163)

1 Magnitude is 5.09 N and direction is 9.4° anti-clockwise from force of magnitude 7 N

2 Tension in the string is 4.55 N, magnitude of resultant is 9.1 N

3 i $F = 8.06, \theta = 29.7°$

ii Magnitude 7 N, direction opposite to that of the force of magnitude 7 N

4 i a 10.8 N **b** 22.4 N

ii 64.2° anticlockwise from x-axis

5 $W_1 = 4.40$ and $W_2 = 3.26$

6 41.1°, 4.8

7 73.7°

8 20.0, 145.1°

9 5 N

10 150°

11 81.2°

12 i a 8.74 N **b** 11.5 N

ii Magnitude is 14.4 N, direction is 52.7° anticlockwise from the positive x-direction

13 i 3 N **ii** 2.4 N **iii** 1.4

14 231 N horizontally to the right, 115 N downwards parallel to the incline, zero

15 a 104 N, 72 N upwards **b** 104 N, 3 N upwards

c 176 N, 118 N downwards

16 i $P = 10$ and $R = 26.9$

ii $\alpha = 73.7$ **a** 24 N **b** 7 N

iii $\cos \theta = (24 - 2.8)26.9...$ or

$\sin \theta = (7 + 9.6)/26.9...$ or

$\tan \theta = (7 + 9.6)/(24 - 2.8)$

17 $R = 5.37, \theta = 33.9$

11 General motion in a straight line

Exercise 11A (page 171)

1 $v = 3t^2 + 4, a = 6t$; 22 m, 16 m s^{-1}, 12 m s^{-2}

2 $v = 20 - 4t^3, a = -12t^2$; 22 m, 16 m s^{-1}, −12 m s^{-2}; −18 m, −88 m s^{-1}, −108 m s^{-2}

3 42 m, 32 m s^{-1}, 18 m s^{-2}

4 0 m, 10 m s^{-1}, −14 m s^{-2}

5 1 m s^{-1}, −1 m s^{-2}

6 6 m s^{-1}, $\frac{3}{4}$ m s^{-2}

7 2 s; −24 m s^{-1}, −24 m s^{-2}

8 5 s; 20 m

9 130 m

10 4 m s^{-1}

11 27 m, 28 m s^{-1}

12 32 m, $-\frac{3}{8}$ m s^{-2}

13 $\frac{4}{3}$ m s^{-2}

14 $22\frac{1}{8}$ m, 54 m s^{-2}

15 $10(12t - 7)$ N

16 a 64 m s^{-1} **c** 48 N

17 a 18 m s^{-1} **b** 4 m s^{-2}

18 a 120 s, 1380 m **b** 0.384 m s^{-2}

c 1.15 m s^{-2} **d** 80 s, 20.5 m s^{-1}

19 b **A** 120 m s^{-1}, **B** 160 m s^{-1}

B, because $v = 0$ when $t = 3$.

20 a 952 m, 62.4 m s^{-1}

b −41.0 m s^{-2}, −10 m s^{-2}, −0.328 m s^{-2}

c 40 m s^{-1} **d** 40 s

Exercise 11B (page 176)

1 $x = t^3 + 8t + 4$; 28 m, 20 m s^{-1}

2 $v = 10t - 2t^3 - 4, x = \frac{1}{2}\left(23 - 8t + 10t^2 - t^4\right)$; $11\frac{1}{2}$ m, −4 m s^{-1}, 10 m s^{-2}

3 2 m, 6 m s^{-1}, 3 m s^{-2}

4 12 m, $7\frac{1}{3}$ m s^{-1}, $1\frac{7}{9}$ m s^{-2}

5 20 m

6 60 m

7 60 m

8 $-6\,\text{m s}^{-2}$

9 22 m

10 10 m

11 26 m

12 1.2 m

13 $58\frac{2}{3}$ m

14 7.2 m

15 28.5 m

16 1364.8 m

17 a 54 m   **b** 4 m

    c 4 m 62 m; 54 m

18 $4.99\,\text{m s}^{-1}$, $5\,\text{m s}^{-1}$

19 $1\frac{1}{2}$ m

20 90 m

22 a $9\,\text{m s}^{-1}$ **b** $8\,\text{m s}^{-1}$, $26\frac{2}{3}$ m

23 a 2 s   **b** 8 m

    c $6\,\text{m s}^{-2}$

24 $74\,\text{m s}^{-1}$, 282 m

25 a $3\frac{27}{40}\,\text{m s}^{-1}$ **b** 16 s, 32 m

26 $\frac{3}{4}$, 205 m

27 $\dfrac{p^{n+1}}{(n+1)q}$

28 b 0 s, $7.2\,\text{m s}^{-2}$ **c** 3 s, $-1.8\,\text{m s}^{-2}$

    d 6.75 m, 6.4 m   **f** 7.1 m

Miscellaneous exercise 11 (page 179)

1 i $0.09\,\text{m s}^{-2}$ **ii** 1.08 m   **iii** $0.72\,\text{m s}^{-1}$

2 i 8   **ii** 108 m

3 $0.24\,\text{m s}^{-1}$, 0.4 m

4 i $5.25\,\text{m s}^{-1}$ **ii** 233 m

5 i 0.5 s   **ii** 44.2 m

6 a 18 m, $21\,\text{m s}^{-1}$, $-24\,\text{m s}^{-2}$

    b 3 s, $-24\,\text{m s}^{-1}$, $-6\,\text{m s}^{-2}$

    c 1 s, 28 m, $-18\,\text{m s}^{-2}$

    d 4 s, -26 m, $-27\,\text{m s}^{-1}$

7 a $0 < t < 2$ **b** $1\frac{1}{4} < t < 2$ and $4 < t < 5$

    c $0.568... < t < 2$ and $2.931... < t < 5$

8 b 3   **d** $1\frac{7}{9}$ m

    e $0 < t < 1$ and $t > \frac{3}{2}\sqrt{2}$

9 i $6\,\text{m s}^{-1}$, 0.6   **ii** 13.9   **iii** 50 m

10 i $A = 4$ **ii** $\left(450 - \frac{3375}{t}\right)$ m

    iii $5.4\,\text{m s}^{-1}$

Revision exercise 2 (page 182)

1 22.5 W

2 2.56 N, bearing 179.4°

3 $1.5\,\text{m s}^{-2}$, 180 N

4 a 102.6°   **b** 113.6°   **c** 124.2°

5 At 74.6° to the 0.3 N force, 2.87 s

6 $50\,\text{m s}^{-1}$; $0.305\,\text{m s}^{-2}$; 3.75°

7 a $2\,\text{m s}^{-2}$ **b** 6 kg

    c 0.05

8 22.3 N, 32.6 N

9 $W\cos\alpha$, $W\sin\alpha$; $\dfrac{W}{\tan\alpha}$, $\dfrac{W\cos\alpha}{\sin\alpha}$, 0; $\dfrac{W}{\sin\alpha}$, $\dfrac{W\cos\alpha}{\tan\alpha}$, $W\sin\alpha$

10 a $8.19\,\text{m s}^{-1}$

    b $5.20\,\text{m s}^{-1}$

11 If $m < \frac{1}{5}\sqrt{2}M$, $\dfrac{Mmg}{M+m}\left(1+\frac{1}{5}\sqrt{2}\right)$; if $\frac{1}{5}\sqrt{2}M \le m \le \frac{4}{5}\sqrt{5}M$, mg; if $m > \frac{4}{5}\sqrt{2}M$, $\dfrac{Mmg}{M+m}\left(1+\frac{4}{5}\sqrt{2}\right)$; $22\frac{1}{2}°$ to the vertical, $2T\cos 22\frac{1}{2}°$

12 $12t(t-3)(t-8)\,\text{cm s}^{-1}$; $t = 5$; train goes forwards to 376, then backwards to -999; $0.24(3t-4)(t-6)$ N, positive for $0 < t < \frac{4}{3}$ and $6 < t < 8$ and negative for $\frac{4}{3} < t < 6$

13 63.6 N at 28.8° to Ron's rope; 0.2

14 a $2p^2 t$, $2p^2$

    b $-\dfrac{p}{t^2}$, $\dfrac{2p}{t^3}$, $-\dfrac{x^2}{p}$, still true

15 119 N

    a Weight 150 N, tension 119 N, resistance 105 N, buoyancy 94 N

    b Weight 800 N, tension 119 N, normal contact force 856 N, friction 105 N

16 a 35 s   **b** $2.5\,\text{m s}^{-1}$

    c 1 s, $7\frac{7}{6}$ m   **d** 14 000 N   **e** $\frac{7}{8}$ m

17 58.6, 211.4

18 a $2.5\,\text{m s}^{-2}$ **b** $2\,\text{m s}^{-2}$ **c** $0\,\text{m s}^{-2}$

19 1.23 N, direction is 152.9° from the positive x-axis

20 23.1 N, 11.5 N, 23.1 N;

    a 1.905... m   **b** 80.45...°

    c 17.65...°

    23.50... N, 68.0 N

21 i 5 m s^{-1} **ii** $k = \frac{4}{3}$, 5.33 m s^{-1}

    iii 280 s, $a = 0.0262$

22 a 1.1 m s^{-2}, 0.917 m s^{-2}

    b 5.52 m

Practice exam-style papers

Practice exam-style paper 1 (page 186)

1 i 15.3 J   **ii** 3.06 N

2 i 5 m s^{-1} **ii** 45 m s^{-1}

3 $R = 11.2$, $\theta = 63.4$

4 i 20 900 J   **ii** 270 J   **iii** 86.1 W

5 i 1.6 m s^{-2}, 80 m

    ii Decreasing, as the gradient of the curve is decreasing.

    iii $213\frac{1}{3}$ m (or 213 to the nearest metre)

6 i 750 N   **ii** 0.05 m s^{-2}, 540 N

7 i It does rest in equilibrium, 41.4 N.

Practice exam-style paper 2 (page 188)

1 17.3 N

2 i 1600 m   **ii** 200 000 N

3 i 5 N   **ii** 3.27 N

    iii 0.306

4 i Decrease of 668 J

    ii 83.6

5 i 108 m   **ii** $2 < t < 6$

6 i 0.6 m s^{-2} **ii** 8 m s^{-1}

    iii 1.5°

7 i 2 m s^{-2} **ii** 2.4 N, 0.3

    iii 0.2 s

Index

The page numbers refer to the first mention of each term, or the box if there is one.